Regarding Language

Regarding Language

Dwight Bolinger

 Harcourt Brace Jovanovich, Inc.
New York   Chicago   San Francisco   Atlanta   Dallas

DWIGHT BOLINGER is a distinguished linguist and a member of the faculty at Harvard University. This text is a rewriting of his college textbook, *Aspects of Language.*

ACKNOWLEDGMENTS: For permission to reprint copyrighted material, grateful acknowledgment is made to the following sources:

ALMQVIST & WIKSELL: Excerpt on p. 183 from *Regularized English* by Axel Wijk, Stockholm, Almqvist & Wiksell Förlag AB, 1958.

AMERICAN CIVIL LIBERTIES UNION: Excerpt on p. 101 from the *Forty-Third Annual Report* of the American Civil Liberties Union.

HARCOURT BRACE JOVANOVICH, INC.: Excerpts on p. 160 from *The Structure of English* by Charles C. Fries. Excerpt on p. 90 from *Problems in the Origin and Development of the English Language* by John Algeo and Thomas Pyles. Excerpts from *Working with Aspects of Language* by Mansoor Alyeshmerni and Paul Taubr, © 1970 by Harcourt Brace Jovanovich, Inc.

HARPER & ROW, PUBLISHERS, INCORPORATED: Excerpt on p. 20 from *Native Son* by Richard Wright. Excerpt on p. 267 abridged from "Cooper's Prose Style" from *Letters from the Earth* by Mark Twain, edited by Bernard DeVoto.

HARVARD UNIVERSITY PRESS: Excerpt on p. 200 from *Linguistic Science in the 19th Century* by Holger Pedersen, translated by John Webster Spargo.

HOLT, RINEHART AND WINSTON, INC.: Excerpt on pp. 20–21 from "A Friend of the Family" from *The Short Novels of Dostoevsky,* Introduction by Philip Rahv.

LINGUISTIC SOCIETY OF AMERICA: Excerpt on pp. 37–38 from "Mazateco Whistle Speech" by George Cowan from *Language,* Vol. 24.280–86.

Cover Design: An abstraction of a sound spectrogram of the word *unusual.*

To my son Bruce, in admiration and affection

Contents

Maps and Illustrations

Foreword

Linguists have long complained that the Wonder of Words approach to language has been almost their only contact with the outside world, but to date they have done very little about it. One looks in vain for the book that will maintain a proper balance of readability, informativeness, and fidelity to the interests, goals, and trials of linguists as linguists see them, to give the average reader an appreciation of what modern linguistics is about. Other sciences have been able to describe themselves to the general public and to the unspecialized student. The same should be possible for linguistics. At least it is time to try.

The reader of the typical book written in the Wonder of Words design sees in the spectacle no particular relevance to himself. Yet there is no science that is closer to the humanness of humanity than linguistics, for its field is the means by which our personalities are defined to others and by which our thoughts are formed and gain continuity and acceptance. Until linguists can bring their point of view clearly and palatably before the reader at large and the student in the language classroom, they will have only themselves to blame for what one linguist has called the towering failure of the schools to inform ordinary citizens about language. Of no other scientific field is so much fervently believed that isn't so. And not only believed but taught.

We do not need to travel abroad nor back in time to discover the facts of language. They lie all about us, in our handwriting and our own speech. Almost nothing of interest to the linguist goes on anywhere that does not go on in our communication here and now. This book is an invitation to the reader to see within him and around him the objects of a science, and to glimpse how the scientist interprets them. It is not intended to teach linguistics but to help ordinary people divine themselves as the creators and perpetuators of the most wonderful invention of all time.

There are no directions for reading this book beyond one mild word of caution. To follow the plays in a game one must first learn the rules. This demands a willingness to submit to certain initiatory rites. The beginning chapters, in particular

Chapters 2 and 3, carry the heaviest burden of terms and concepts. They ask a measure of patience from the reader. After that he should find the going fairly easy.

To recognize individually all those whose scholarship was drawn upon in this volume would be impossible, and to settle on a few is to risk unintentionally slighting others to whom the debt may be just as great. I can only thank my intellectual mentors and creditors in a general way and assure them that the gratitude is not less for not being more specific.

Nevertheless a few must indeed be singled out—those who have criticized the manuscript in whole or in part: John Algeo, Fred W. Householder, Jr., George Lakoff, William G. Moulton, Thomas Pyles, John R. Ross, and James Sledd. Without their help this book could not have kept true to its aim, and if even so it has fallen short, the author is all the more to be blamed.

chapter 1

Some Traits of Language

Language Acquisition

First steps

Thomas A. Edison is supposed to have parried the question of a skeptic who wanted to know what one of his inventions was good for by asking "What good is a baby?" Appearances suggest that a baby is good for very little, least of all to itself. Completely helpless, absolutely dependent on the adults around it, seemingly unable to do much more than kick and crawl for the greater part of nine or ten months, it would seem better off in the womb a little longer until ready to make a respectable debut and scratch for itself.

Yet if the premature birth of human young is an accident, it is a fortunate one. No other living form has so much to learn about the external world and so little chance of preparing for it in advance. An eaglet has the pattern of its life laid out before it hatches from the egg. Its long evolution has equipped it to contend with definite foes, search for definite foods, mate, and rear its young according to a definite pattern. The environment is predictable enough to make the responses predictable too, and they are built into the genetic design. With human beings this is impossible, and the main reason for its impossibility is language.

We know little about animal communication, but nowhere does it even approach the complexity of human language. By the time he is six or eight years old a child can watch a playmate carry out an intricate series of actions and give a running account of it afterward. A bee can do no more than perform a dance that is related analogously to the direction and distance of a find of nectar, much as we point out a direction to a stranger. The content of the message is slight and highly stereotyped. For the child, the playmate's actions can be totally unpredictable; he will verbalize them somehow.

Attaining this skill requires the mastery of a system that takes literally years to learn. An early start is essential, and it cannot be in the womb. Practice must go on in the open air where sounds are freely transmitted, for language is sound. And if language is to be socially effective, it cannot be acquired within a month or two of birth when the environment is limited to parents and crib, but must continue to grow as the child becomes stronger and widens his contacts. Human evolution has ensured that this will happen by providing for a brain in which the speech areas are the last to reach their full development. So we might answer Edison's question by saying that a baby is good for learning language.

A child is born with an instinct for language, but not for any particular language, just as he is born with an instinct for walking but not for walking in a given direction. This is another reason why an early beginning is necessary: languages differ and even the same language changes through time, so that an infant born with a pre-set language pattern would be at a disadvantage. One still hears the foolish claim that a child of German ancestry ought to be able to learn German more easily than some other language. Our experience discredits this. An infant of any nationality or culture learns whatever language it hears, one about as easily as another. Complete adaptability confers the gift of survival. Children do not depend on a particular culture but fit themselves to the one into which they are born, and that culture in turn is maintaining itself in a not always friendly universe. Whatever success it has is largely due to the understanding and cooperation that language makes possible.

Another reason for an early beginning and a gradual growth is *permeation*. The running account that a child is able to give of a series of actions that he performs or sees performed betokens an organized activity that is not enclosed within itself but relates at all times to something else. It would seem absurd to us to be told that every time we stood up, sat down, reached for a chocolate, turned on a light, pushed a baby carriage, or started the car we should, at the same time, be twitching in a particular way the big toe of our left foot. But just such an incessant accompaniment of everything else by our speech organs does not surprise us at all. Other activities are self-contained. That of language penetrates them and almost never stops. It must be developed not separately, like walking, but as part of whatever we do. So it must be on hand from the start.

The idea that there is an instinct for language has recently been revived by psychologists and linguists working in the field of child learning. For a long time language was thought to be a part of external culture and nothing more. Even the physiology of speech was seen as more or less accidental: our speech organs were really organs of digestion which happened to be utilized to satisfy a social need. A child in a languageless society, deprived of speech but permitted to chew and swallow, would not feel that he was missing anything. That view has been almost reversed. Now it is felt that the organs of speech in their present form were shaped as much for sound production as for nourishment. The human tongue is far more agile than it needs to be for purposes of eating. Furthermore, the sensitivity of the human ear has evolved to the point that we can detect a movement of the eardrum that does not exceed one tenth of the diameter of a hydrogen molecule.

So there are three ingredients in the acquisition of language:

1. an *instinct* in the shape of mental and physical capacities developed through countless centuries of natural selection;

2. a preexisting language *system,* any one of the many produced by the cultures of the world;

3. a *competence* that comes from applying the instinct to the system through the relatively long period during which the child learns both to manipulate the physical elements of the system, such as sounds and words and syntactic rules, and to permeate them with meaning.

The development of so finely graded a specialization of our organs of speech and hearing and of the nervous system to which they are attached is not surprising if we assume that society cannot survive without language and individual human beings cannot survive without society. Language is a uniquely human trait, shared by cultures so diverse and by individuals physically and mentally so unlike one another — from Watusi tribesmen to nanocephalic dwarfs — that the notion of its being purely a socially transmitted skill is not to be credited.

An instinct for language implies that a child does more than echo what he hears. The first months are a preparation for language in which babbling, a completely self-directed exercise, is the main activity. Imitation begins to play a part, of course, but it too is experimental and hence creative. We see how this must be if we imagine a child already motivated to imitate and being told by his mother to say *papa*. This sounds simple to us because we already know what features to heed and what ones to ignore, but the child must learn to tell them apart. Shall he imitate his mother's look, her gesture, the way she shapes her lips, the breathiness of the first consonant, the voice melody, the moving of the tongue? Even assuming that he can focus on certain things to the exclusion of others, he has no way of knowing which ones to select. He cannot then purely imitate. He must experiment and wait for approval.

Progress

We do not know the extent to which children are taught and the extent to which they learn on their own. If learning is instinctive, then children will learn whether or not adults appoint themselves to be their teachers. But if there is an instinct to learn, for all we know there may be an instinct to teach. It is possible that parents unconsciously adopt special methods of speaking to very young children to help them learn the important things first, impelled by the desire not so much to teach the child as to communicate with him.

One psychologist noted the following ways in which she simplified her own speech when talking to her child:

1. the use of a more striking variant of a speech sound when there is a choice, for example, using the /t/ of **table** when saying the word **butter** in place of the more usual flapped sound (almost like **budder**);

2. exaggerated intonation, with greater ups and downs of pitch;

3. slower rate;

4. simple sentence structure, as, for example, avoidance of the passive voice;

5. avoidance of substitute words like **it,** as, for example, **Where's your milk? Show me your milk** instead of **Where's your milk? Show it to me.**

Most parents would probably add *repetition* to this list.

Whatever the technique, the child does not seem to follow any particular sequence, learning first to pronounce all the sounds perfectly, then to manage words, then sentences, then "correct expression." A child of twelve to eighteen months with no sentences at all will be heard using sentence intonations on separate words in a perfectly normal way—**Doggie?** with rising pitch, meaning "Is that a doggie?" or **Doggie,** with falling pitch, to comment on the dog's presence. The child's program seems to call for a developing complexity rather than for mastering one process before taking up the next.

The first stage of communication, when parents feel that their children have really begun to speak, is reached when individual words are being pronounced intelligibly—that is, so that parents can match them with words in their own speech—and related to things and events. This is the *holophrastic* stage, when utterance and thing are related one to one. The thing named may be a single object called **mama** or a whole situation called *mapank.* The parents will interpret the latter as a sentence—*Mama spank*—but to the child it is a word. He has no basis for dividing it. A thing or situation has a proper name. There is no syntax.

The second stage is *analytic:* the child begins to divide his proper names into true sentences. Besides *mapank* the vocabulary probably includes additional words like *mama, papa,* and *baby.* The day comes when Papa spanks, and the uniqueness of *mapank* is broken up—the different elements in the situation are recognized for what they are and *ma* is properly attached to *mama.* Now *mapank* is a sentence and will probably be modified to *Mama pank.* Before long the child begins to *look* for parts within wholes and to play with them: *Baby spank.* Words become playthings. When a two-and-a-half-year-old runs to his parents and says *House eat baby*—the sort of expression that unimaginative adults brush aside as preposterous or even punish as "untrue"—he is only exulting over the discovery that he can play with his words as with his building blocks, putting them together in fascinating ways. Much of learning a language is a pattern-flexing game. Children's monologues sometimes sound like students practicing in a language lab.

The third stage, called the *syntactic* stage, requires the recognition of more subtle kinds of samenesses in the connections. When *mama* and *spank* are recognized as recurring sames, their presence in both *Mama spank* and *Spank mama* (the latter accompanying a playful situation in which the mother makes the baby hit her for some real or pretended misdemeanor) is recognized and the difference in the two situations is assigned to the reversal of the order. *Kiss mama, Come-to mama, See mama* then constitute a different kind of same—verb plus object noun—that recurs like all the others and that the child will invent or reinvent using old material to see how far he can go.

The product of the syntactic stage is a variety of sentence types, all simple but distinguished by the number and arrangement of their parts—*Get Daddy, Baby go-play, Mama eat cereal.* The component parts too are simple. There are no such complications as articles or verb inflections. But the syntactic stage also offers combinations like *that doggie, baby chair* ('Baby's chair'), *more cereal,* which are used as verbless sentences but are the raw material for the fourth stage in which arrangements are added to arrangements.

Daddy sit chair contains a simple arrangement; *Daddy sit baby chair* contains an arrangement within an arrangement. This can be called the *structural* stage. Parts are made up of other parts. When the child discovers this he is in a position to make up his own "words." If, as happened with one child, he lacks the verb *to cross,* he can say *I'm going to the other side of the whole lake,* using *go-to-the-other-side-of* as a substitute (an adult will interpret the sentence as a mistake for *I'm going all the way to the other side,* a more complex structure). As a culmination of the structural stage the child learns how to treat whole sentences as if they were elements, and to insert them in larger sentences. A statement like *I go* and a question like *Will you stay?* are combined: *If I go will you stay?*

The step-by-step increase in complexity is illustrated in the responses given by one child at various ages to the command, *Ask your daddy what he did at work today.* At two years and five months it was *What he did at work today,* which shows enough understanding to separate the inner question from the command as a whole (*Ask your daddy* is not repeated), but no more. At the age of three, the response was *What you did at work today?,* with the right change of intonation and with *you* for *he.* The child is now really asking a question but has "optimized" its form—that is, he has fitted a newly acquired expression into the mold of an old one that resembles it and is familiar and easy, in this case making the word order of statements serve also for questions. Finally, at three years and five months, he made the right transformation of the verb and produced *What did you do at work today?*

Optimizing occurs at all stages. It may replace a difficult sound with an easy one, as when children say *woof* for *roof.* It may result in a correct sentence or an incorrect one. *What you did at work today?* is incorrect. Correct optimizing occurs when the language offers two different constructions, both correct, but one more frequent or more in harmony with familiar constructions. When four-year-olds are given a sentence like *I gave the dog the bone* they will repeat it and understand it, but if they are asked to report the same event themselves they will say *I gave the bone to the dog.* The construction without *to* is less general (for instance, it seldom occurs in the question *Who(m) did you give the money?* — the more normal form is *Who(m) did you give the money to?*) and is not like the related constructions in which prepositions are required: *I got the money from Dad, I got the present for Dad and then I gave it to him,* etc.

The final stage is *stylistic*. The child now has a repertory of constructions among which he can choose. Choice makes for flexibility. He is no longer restricted to conveying just the primary information but is able to show the way in which the message is to be taken. *Give the bone to Dingo* and *Give Dingo the bone* "mean the same," but if there is also a cat named Tillie who gets raw liver and both pets are about to be fed, *Give Dingo the bone* is the choice to make when Dingo is about to be given Tillie's ration; it puts the emphasis in the right place.

Attainment

A favorite generalization of one school of linguists used to be that every child has complete control of his language by the age of five or six. Without disparaging the truly phenomenal control of an enormously complex system that six-year-olds do achieve, we must realize that no limit can be set and that learning by the same processes continues throughout life, though at a rate diminishing so rapidly that it seems almost to have come to a stop well before adolescence. The rate of learning might be described as a curve that starts by virtually touching infinity and ends by approaching zero (see table, page 11).

If learning never ceases, it follows that a language is never completely learned. There is always someone who knows a bit of it that we do not know. In part this is because the experimental and inventive way in which learning is accomplished ensures that no two people ever carry exactly the same network of shapes and patterns in their heads. A perfect command of language eludes us because as we catch up it moves off — "the" language exists only as imperfect copies, with original touches, in individual minds; it never stays exactly the same. All we can say is that interplay is so fast, frequent, and vital that great differences are not tolerated, networks are forced to acquire a similar pattern and all within cooperating distance are said to "speak the same language."

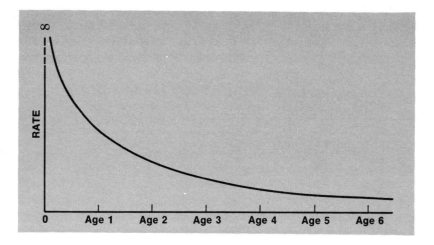

Rate of learning expressed as a proportion of new to old over equal intervals of time

Exercise 1

There are five stages in the child's acquisition of language. The first is the *holophrastic* stage, when each utterance is a word that has just one meaning. During the second stage, the *analytic* stage, the child discovers that what he considered a single word is in fact a combination of words. He notices in the third, or *syntactic*, stage that different classes of words occur in different places in a sentence, and that this variation affects meaning. The fourth stage is *structural*, when the child learns how to place utterances he has learned earlier within other utterances. The final stage is *stylistic*, when the child knows how to construct different sentences for the same meaning. Classify these sentences, taken from the unit you have just read, as characteristic of one or another of these five stages.

a. Mama eat cereal.
b. Mapank.
c. $\begin{cases} \text{I gave the dog the bone.} \\ \text{I gave the bone to the dog.} \end{cases}$ (The child knows that these are paraphrases.)
d. Daddy sit chair.

e. $\begin{cases} \text{Pank mama.} \\ \text{Mama pank.} \end{cases}$ (The child does not know that these are different in adult English.)

f. House eat baby.

g. Get daddy.

h. $\begin{cases} \text{Spank mama.} \\ \text{Mama spank.} \end{cases}$ (The child knows that these are different.)

i. Daddy sit baby chair.

j. Kiss mama.

k. Come-to mama.

l. I'm going to the other side of the whole lake.

Language Is Patterned Behavior

One estimate puts the number of languages in active use in the world today somewhere between three and four thousand; another makes it five thousand or more. The latter is probably closer to the truth, for many languages are spoken by only a few hundred persons, and many areas of the world are still not fully surveyed. In one subdistrict of New Guinea, for example, there are sixteen languages spoken by an average of fewer than a thousand persons each. However, it is impossible to make an exact count for no one knows just what constitutes "one language." Danish and Norwegian have similar structures and a high degree of mutual intelligibility; this makes them almost by definition dialects of a single language. Do we count them as two? Cantonese and Mandarin, in spite of being "Chinese," are about as dissimilar as Portuguese and Italian. Do we count mainland Chinese as one language? To be scientific we have to ignore politics and forget that Denmark and Norway have separate flags and mainland China one. Even then, we must decide which languages should be called distinct languages and which merely dialects of other languages.

Whatever distinctions one makes between language and dialect, the number of different languages is formidable, especially if we include the tongues once spoken but now dead. Languages are like people: for all their underlying similarities, great numbers mean great variety. The variety is so great that we may be led to ask this question: Do we know enough about languages to be able to describe language? Can we penetrate the differences to arrive at the samenesses underneath? The more languages we study—and previously unexplored ones give up their secrets each year by the score— the more the answer seems to be *yes*.

We see more and more that all languages share certain basic, observable traits which we will consider one by one to arrive at a broad understanding of what language is, and what it is not.

Our five-hundred-year romance with printer's ink tempts us to forget that a language can disappear without leaving a trace when its last speaker dies and that this is still true of the majority of the world's languages in spite of presses and tape recorders. Written records and tape recordings are embodiments of language, but language itself is more truly a way of acting. Language is skilled behavior which has to be learned.

Our habit of viewing language as a *thing* and not as behavior is probably unavoidable, even for the linguist, but in a sense it is false. It is the system that underlies language behavior that is somewhat thing-like, because it persists through time and from one speaker to the next. Probably as the child acquires the system it is engraved somehow on the brain, and if we had the means to make it visible we could "read" it. For the present all we can see is the way people act, and linguists are useful precisely because, not being able to look into the brain, we need specialists to study the behavior, discover the patterns, and infer the system.

Exercise 2

The linguist approaches language as a set of patterns or rules. In the phrase *the five young Canadian girls* he can show that the order of the words is not random but is determined by a pattern which any native speaker will follow instinctively. Unscramble each of the related noun phrases below and establish this pattern.

a. American / new / five / astronauts / the
b. latest / fashions / French / the / eight
c. Scottish / young / six / the / lasses

   d. two / senior / Spanish / the / professors
   e. recent / incidents / forty-two / the / Asian
   f. Italian / thirteen / the / violins / old

    Now describe this pattern by placing the five classes of words in their proper sequence.

   g. number / determiner / noun / age / nationality

Exercise 3

    The pattern of English noun phrases differs from the patterns found in other languages, but there are basic similarities, often surprising, from one language to the next. Examine the four columns of corresponding expressions below and try to make out the language pattern they embody. (In Persian the **æ** is pronounced somewhat like the *a* in *bat,* and the *x* like *ch* in German *Bach.* In Hebrew the *š* is pronounced like the *sh* in *shin.*

English	*German*	*Persian**	*Hebrew*
man	Mann	mærd	iš
a man	ein Mann	mærdi	iš
the man	der Mann	an mærd	haiš
the woman	die Frau	an zæn	haiša
a good man	ein guter Mann	mærdi xub	iš tov
the good man	der gute Mann	an mærde xub	haiš hatov
a good woman	eine gute Frau	zæni xub	iša tova
the good woman	die gute Frau	an zæne xub	haiša hatova

    Basing your conclusions on the limited data given, indicate the language or languages for which each of the following statements is true.

   a. There is an expression with the meaning of
      English *a.*   E/G/P/H
   b. The adjective follows the noun.   E/G/P/H
   c. The adjective changes according to the
      noun.   E/G/P/H
   d. The adjective ending may change according to the presence or absence of the
      definite article.   E/G/P/H

° *An* is translated as 'the' in this column. It is actually closer to *that* than to *the,* but it may be considered as *the* for the purposes of this exercise.

Exercise 4

There are patterns of pronunciation in English that tell the native speaker how to change the stress placed on a word as he changes the form or the function of the word. Indicate the stressed syllable of the repeated expressions in the following sentence pairs; state the pattern you have discovered.

> a. I combine them regularly.
> The combine is good for business.
> b. He won't permit it.
> Do you need a permit?
> c. Did the contract give you trouble?
> Did you contract the German measles?
> d. Why did you run away?
> That horse is a runaway.

Now indicate the stressed syllable in each word in the first column below. Study the second and third columns, indicate the shifted stress, and describe the pattern you have discovered.

provoke	provocative	provocation
repeat	repetitive	repetition
derive	derivative	derivation

The Medium of Language Is Sound

All languages use the same channel for sending and receiving: the vibrations of the atmosphere. All set the vibrations going in the same way, by the activity of the speech organs. And all organize the vibrations into small units of sound that can be combined and recombined in distinctive ways. Except for the last, human communication is the same as that of most other warm-blooded creatures that move on the earth's surface: the most effective way of reaching another member of one's kind seems to be through disturbances of the air that envelops us.

The capacity for intricate organization is what sets human language apart from animal languages and also sets it above dependence on any particular medium. It makes no difference to the human brain what bits of substance are used as the medium of language. Rather than on sounds, language could be based on pebbles graded for color or size, or, if we had a dog's olfactory sense, a scheme of discriminated smells. The choice of sound is part of our pre-human heritage, probably for good reason. We do not have to look at or touch the signaler to catch the signal, and we do not depend on wind direction as with smell.

Language is sound in the same sense that a given house is wood. We can conceive of other materials, but it is as if the only tools we had were woodworking ones. If we learn a language we must learn to produce sounds. We are unable to use any other medium except as an incidental help. So part of the description of language must read as if the sound that entered into the organization of language were as indispensable as the organization itself.

Exercise 5

Study the following diagram of the communication process. In human language, the device that transmits the message is the mouth, tongue, and other speech organs. The device that receives the message is the ear, which forwards the sound waves as electrical impulses to the brain. The medium, of course, is sound. The encoder and decoder is the brain.

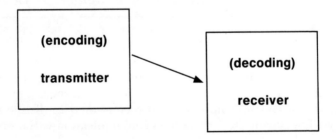

Try to imagine a language based on a medium other than sound. To describe this language you would have to specify the transmitter and the receiver as well as the medium. Do so. Now describe the way you would encode, transmit and decode the following message: *No! I won't go!*

Exercise 6

Bees communicate by dancing movements that indicate, among other things, the distance and direction of places where nectar or pollen can be found. The closer the food, the faster the dance. If the distance is more than 240 feet, the direction to follow is shown by a wriggling motion of the abdomen. The angle of deviation from a vertical line shows the direction in which the other bees must fly, using the sun as their point of reference. No other information can be communicated, and no conversation or correction is possible.

This technique actually works as a means of communication, but its effectiveness is restricted by the medium. The only bees who can receive the message are those in physical contact with the dancer's body.

Invent a technique for communicating a single message. Adapt your technique to any medium except sound. Then describe how you would send this message: *There is food five miles to the west.*

Sound Is Embedded in Gesture

If language is patterned behavior, we cannot say that it stops short at the boundaries of *speech* behavior, for human actions are not so easily compartmentalized. It is true that we can communicate over the telephone, which seems to prove that the essentials of language can be carried by electrical impulses. We can also communicate pretty efficiently in writing, and we know that writing leaves out a great deal—intonation, for example. But no communication is quite so effective as face-to-face communication, for some part of the communicative act is always contained in the expression and posture of the communicators. We call this element *gesture.*

Not all gestures are equally important to language. Of the three identifiable kinds of gestures the simplest are *instinctive* gestures—automatic reactions to a stimulus. They are not learned. Dodging a blow, widening the eyes in astonishment, leaning forward to catch a sound, smiling with pleasure, and others of the kind either are instincts or are based on instinct in such a way that, like the flight of a young bird, it takes no more than a slight parental or social push to set them going. Of course all such gestures give information to anyone observing them, and this is soon noted by the one performing the gesture, who may then control his instincts to give an intended message or produce an intended effect. He may smile to please rather than to show pleasure, bow when he would rather hurl insults, and weep when he feels no pain. In the long run all gestures acquire a social significance and take on local modifications, which is one reason why members of one culture behave awkwardly when transplanted to another.

Whereas instinctive gestures tell something—true or false—about the person making them, *semiotic* gestures are free to mean anything. They are not like distinctive sounds, because they do have their own meanings (semaphoric signs, which are simply ways of signaling the alphabet, are not included here); they are more like words or even whole sentences. Thus a waving hand may mean "good-bye," both hands held palm up and outstretched with shoulders raised may mean "I don't know," the thumb and forefinger held close together may mean "small." Being arbitrary, however, semiotic gestures are not the same everywhere. In some places the gesture for "come here" is to hold out the hand cupped palm up with the fingers beckoning; in other places it is the same except that the hand is cupped palm down, and to an outsider it may appear to be a greeting rather than a summons. Semiotic gestures are used independently of language. Correspondence between the two is only incidental: a "come-hither" gesture reinforces the words **come here,** in the same way that a red light at a railroad crossing reinforces the sign reading **Stop, look and listen.**

The third class, *paralinguistic* gestures, are closest to language proper. Paralinguistic gestures are a subclass of instinctive gestures, more or less systematized, much as intonation was perhaps systematized out of a set of instinctive cries. They cooperate with sound as part of a larger communicative act. Consider the following utterance:

You
    don't
        mean it.

If everything else remains the same, and one's head is held slightly forward, eyes widened, and mouth left open after the last word, the result is a question ('You surely don't mean it, do you?'). With the head erect, eyes not widened, and mouth closed afterward, it is a confident statement ('I'm sure you don't mean it'). Similar paralinguistic gestures are sometimes the only way to tell a question from a statement. Other paralinguistic gestures include the use of the hands and head to reinforce the syllables on which an accent falls. A person too far away to hear a speaker can often tell what syllables he is emphasizing by the way he hammers with his fist or jabs downward with his jaw. How closely the sound and gesture are related can be shown by a simple test. Take a sentence like **I wíll nót dó it** and reverse the movement of the head, going up instead of down on each accent. The gesture is so unusual that it is hard to manage on the first attempt.

Exercise 7

Read the following sentence aloud, with the intonation shown.

fa

Don't push him too r.

Now repeat the sentence, varying your gestures as indicated.

- *a.* head tilted, looking out the corner of one eye
- *b.* eyes lowered, leaning back in chair, shaking head slowly
- *c.* chin raised, head tilted to the side, eyes on the listener, waggling an index finger, smiling
- *d.* fists clenched, leaning forward, eyes narrowed
- *e.* arms extended toward listener, hands open, palms out, eyes widened, eyebrows raised.

Describe the changes in the situation and emotions of the speaker and an imaginary listener. Identify the semiotic gestures and the paralinguistic gestures and explain your selection.

Syntax is no less arbitrary than words. Take the order of elements. *Ground parched corn* has *first* been parched and *then* ground—the syntactic rule calls for reversing the order in which the events occur. Often the same meanings can be conveyed by quite different sequences of elements which may themselves be the same or different: *nonsensical,* which contains a prefix and a suffix, means the same as *senseless,* which has only a suffix; *more handsome* and *handsomer* are mere variants. Here and there one detects a hint of kinship between form and function—in *He came in and sat down* the phrases are in the same sequence as the actions; but other syntactic devices quickly override it: *He sat down after he came in.*

The most rigidly arbitrary level of language is that of the distinctive units of sound by which we can distinguish between *skin* and *skim* or *spare* and *scare* the moment we hear the words. We said earlier that the very choice of sound itself for this purpose was, while practical, not at all necessary to the system built up from it. And once it was determined that sound was to be the medium, the particular sounds did not matter so long as they could be told apart. What distinguishes *skin* from *skim* is the sound of [n] versus the sound of [m], but could just as well be [b] versus [g]—there is nothing in the nature of skin that decrees it shall be called *skin* and not *skib.* The only "natural" fact is that human beings are limited by their speech organs to certain dimensions of sound—we do not, for example, normally make the sound that would result from turning the tip of the tongue all the way back to the soft palate at the rear of the mouth; it is too hard to reach. But given the sets of sounds we *can* make (not identical, of course, from one language to another, but highly similar), arbitrariness frees us to combine them at will—the combinations do not have to match anything in nature, and their number is therefore unlimited.

Arbitrariness is the rule throughout the central part of language, the part that codes sounds into words, words into phrases, and phrases into sentences. To use computer terminology, language is *digital,* not *analog:* its units function by being either present or absent, not by being present in varying degrees. If a man is asked how many feet tall a friend is and answers *six,* he gives a digital answer; for a lower height he will no longer say *six.* If words were coded analogically he might, to express "six," take half of the word *twelve,* say *twe.* We actually do communicate analogically in situations like this, not using words but holding up our hand in a paralinguistic gesture to the desired height. The height of the hand is now "analogous" to the height of the person.

Farther out and away from the center, language is suffused with nonarbitrary, analog characteristics. For example, the feebleness of the voice will show how tired one is; the loudness of the voice will tell how angry one is. And wrapped around everything that is spoken is a layer of intonation which in many languages comprises an analog system that is highly formalized; for example, varying degrees of finality can be expressed by deeper and deeper lowering of the pitch at the end of an utterance.

There also seems to be a connection, transcending individual languages, between the sounds of the vowels produced with the tongue high in the mouth and to the front, especially [i] (the vowel sound in *wee, teeny*), and the meaning of "smallness," while those with tongue low suggest "largeness." The size of the mouth cavity—[i] has the smallest opening of all—is matched with the meaning. We *chip* a small piece but *chop* a large one; a *slip* is smaller than a *slab* and a *nib* is smaller than a *knob.* We tend to do this spontaneously. "A *freep* is a baby *frope,*" said a popular entertainer in a game of Scrabble. And people say *"leetle"* when they mean something smaller than *little.*

Exercise 10

Physics considers the color spectrum as a continuous scale of light waves ranging from 40 to 72 hundred-thousandths of a millimeter in length. Languages mark off different parts of this scale into discrete units, usually without precise boundaries.

English

purple	blue	green	yellow	orange	red

Shona (a language of Rhodesia)

cips^wuKa	citema	cicena	cips^wuka

Shona (a language of Rhodesia)

$cips^wuKa$	citema	cicena	$cips^wuka$

Bassa (a language of Liberia)

hui	ziza

On the basis of the information presented in the three diagrams, answer each of these questions.

a. Using only the English color-names on page 23, how could you describe the color of a turquoise? Of the sea? How might a Bassa speaker describe, using only Bassa color-names, the color of chartreuse liqueur? The meat of an avocado?

b. Provide slots for the following English color-terms and insert them in their appropriate positions:

violet, apricot, lemon yellow
turquoise, gold, amber
Chinese red, Swedish blonde, Prussian blue

What is the source for each group of names? How might a Bassa speaker use the same sources to extend his list of color words?

c. Describe one color shown on the cover of this book, using the color names shown in the diagrams, first as a native speaker of English, then as a speaker of Shona. Explain how the Shona speaker might find additional terms to make distinctions not covered by his three color categories.

d. What evidence, if any, do you note for the thesis that language is largely arbitrary?

e. What evidence, if any, do you see of basic differences in human vision?

f. How would you explain the difference in color classification between English and Shona or Bassa? Does the number of discrete units suggest anything about the importance of color in a given language?

Exercise 11

Although natural languages are mainly digital or arbitrary rather than analog or symbolic, it is not hard to imagine a language based largely on analogical principles.

a. English and many other languages include pairs of contrasting terms (such as **good — bad**) which are unrelated in sound or structure. Certain Eskimo dialects, on the other hand, create one term by making a negative of its opposite (**good — ungood** would be the English equivalent). This device is clearly analogical.

Show how an analogical code might handle the following pairs of contrasting terms. Remember to show the link between sound (or shape) and sense in terms of the physical structures of the words. One analogical code might simply represent **bad** as **doog** where the contrast in meaning is suggested by reversed structure.

1. good — bad
2. beautiful — ugly
3. large — small
4. wet — dry
5. fat — thin

b. Imagine two characters called Ick and Ock. Pronounce their names, paying attention to the position of your lips and the position of your tongue as it moves away from or toward the roof of your mouth. Which character is the smaller? List five word-pairs in which a similar correspondence exists.

c. We think of families of words that are related in meaning as being less arbitrary if the relationship shows somehow in the form of the words. So the metric terms (*meter, millimeter, centimeter, kilometer*) seem less arbitrary than in English measurements of length (*inch, foot, yard, rod, mile*). Which of the following word groups are less arbitrary in the sense described above? Arrange your answers in two groups—those that seem arbitrary and those in which relationships in form are clear.

1. Whole numbers from 1 to 12
2. Whole numbers from 12 to infinity
3. American monetary terms
4. English monetary terms
5. Common terms for plants and flowers
6. Botanical terms for plants and flowers
7. Decimal numbers
8. Russian first names (Ivan, Natasha)
9. Russian patronyms (Ivan *Ivanovitch*, Natasha *Ivanovna*)
10. The notes of the scale (do-re-mi-fa-sol-la-ti)
11. Acronyms (NATO, SMERSH)
12. Abbreviations (Inc., St.)

Exercise 12

Some words seem to have a fairly close relationship between their sound and their meaning, even though there is no necessary connection beyond the agreement of those who use the words. Speakers of Urdu, a language of Pakistan, agree that the words in the column on the left all imitate certain natural sounds. Try to guess what each word imitates without looking at the column on the right. Then match each imitative word with the object or animal it refers to. What is the English equivalent for each imitative word? Do speakers of English and Urdu agree on any of the "natural" relationships between sound and meaning?

a. vow vow	*1.* a cat
b. myow	*2.* a horse
c. ba	*3.* a slamming door
d. sahee	*4.* a bell
e. cuck-roo-coo	*5.* a cock

f. bwack	6. a dog
g. guwru guwrun	7. a sheep
h. dhun	8. a clock
i. tik	9. a pig
j. ting-ting	10. a duck

Languages Are Similarly Structured

The average learner of a foreign language is surprised and annoyed when the new language does not express things in the same way as the old. The average linguist, after years of struggling with differences between languages, is more surprised at similarities. But at bottom the naive learner is right: there are differences in detail, but in broad outline languages are put together in similar ways.

A study on universals in language reached these conclusions about syntax:

1. All languages use nominal phrases and verbal phrases, corresponding to the two major classes of noun and verb, and in all of them the number of nouns far exceeds the number of verbs. One can be fairly sure that a noun in one language translates a noun in another.

2. All languages have modifiers of these two classes, corresponding to adjectives and adverbs.

3. All languages have ways of turning verb phrases into noun phrases (*He went* — I know *that he went*).

4. All languages have ways of making adjective-like phrases out of other kinds of phrases (*The man went* — The man *who went*).

5. All languages have ways of turning sentences into interrogatives, negatives, and commands.

6. All languages show at least two forms of interaction between verbal and nominal, typically "intransitive" (the verbal is involved with only one nominal, as in *Boys play*) and "transitive" (the verbal is involved with two nominals, as in *Boys play marbles*).

Perhaps nouns make up the one category of syntax that can be assumed for all languages, with the other elements being defined (differently, from language to language) by how they combine with nouns. One of the promising developments of transformational-generative grammar (a contemporary linguistic theory) is the hypothesis that all languages are fundamentally alike in their "deep structure," an underlying domain of universal grammatical relationships and universal semantic features, and different only on the surface, in the more or less accidental paths along which inner forms link themselves and make their way to the top. One is reminded of what is so often said about sexual behavior — that it can be modified by social restrictions but never seriously changed. If the hypothesis is true then our bent for language is as much a part of us as our mating instincts and our hunger drives.

Learning a new language is always in some measure repeating an old experience. Variety may be enormous, but we have seen that similarities abound, so we can now attempt a definition, perhaps something like: "Human language is a system of vocal-auditory communication using conventional signs composed of arbitrary, patterned sound units and assembled according to set rules, interacting with the experiences of its users." Obviously no one-sentence definition will ever be adequate, but we can at least derive from it a sense of a basic minimum that all languages share. Languages are alike because people are alike in their capacities for communicating in a uniquely human way.

Exercise 13

Which of the language universals outlined on page 27 are shown by the following examples?

a. A man should hitch his wagon to a star.
   Hitch your wagon to a star.
   Should you hitch your wagon to a star?
   Don't hitch your wagon to a star.
b. Food is put before him.
   He eats the food that is put before him.

c. Scientists work.
   Scientists work miracles.
d. Caesar was assassinated.
   Brutus knew that Caesar was assassinated.

chapter 2

The Phonetic Elements

Articulations

Language comes in a kind of envelope of speech sounds; it is wrapped in other disturbances of the air that convey such information as whether the speaker has a cold or has been eating or feels angry or is a long way off or is a man rather than a child. Only part of the sound wave corresponds to the central organization — a narrow and precisely limited set of contrasts between various combinations of pitches, durations, loudnesses, and voice and whisper, which are the audible results of the ways we exercise our speech organs. Though no two languages are identical, these ways are similar enough to generalize about them.

All languages use certain articulations that shut off or constrict the breath stream and others that let it flow freely through the mouth cavity. The first are the consonants, the second the vowels. This alternate checking and releasing is essential for getting the variety of sounds that we need to produce a large set of signaling units. The two kinds of articulations depend on each other; the consonants separate the vowels and the vowels allow the speech organs to get from one consonant position to the next. It is possible to have vowels side by side, but such combinations tend to be unstable, resulting in some kind of loss or change, as when **pro-te-in** with three vowels was reduced to **pro-tein** with two. Certain consonants can also stand side by side, but again separation is the rule. Furthermore, we are partly dependent on the vowels to hear the consonants — it is largely the effect of a given consonant on the vowel or vowels next to it that makes the consonant audible, for the vowels, produced with the breath stream unimpeded, are the sounds that carry best. Each consonant distorts the portion of a vowel that lies next to it in its own way.

In making a consonant we either shut off the air completely or narrow the passage at some point so that it comes through noisily. The first kind is called a *stop*, the second a *fricative*. The stopping or narrowing can be at any point that our speech organs permit, and this of course makes for a good deal of variety in the particular consonants that different languages create. In English we use the following:

1. The lips. The [p] and [b] in *pane* and *bane* are stops: the lips are closed completely and then abruptly parted. The [f] and [v] in *feign* and *vane* are fricatives: the air keeps coming through, but with friction. We call [p b] *bilabials*, because both lips are involved; [f v] are *labiodentals*, involving the lower lip and the upper teeth. English has no bilabial fricatives (unless the exclamation variously spelled *whew!* and *phew!* is counted as a word), but many languages do.

2. The tongue tip on the upper front teeth. English makes no stops this way, but it has two fricatives for which the symbols [θ] and [ð] are used — the initial sounds in *thin* and *that* respectively. Since the tongue is involved in all consonants made in the interior of the mouth, we name the sound just by the position that the tongue touches or approaches. Accordingly, these two sounds are *dentals* (or *interdentals*).

3. The tongue tip on the ridge back of the upper front teeth. The [t] and [d] of *to* and *do* are stops. The [s z] of *seal* and *zeal* are fricatives. As the ridge in question is known as the alveolar ridge, these sounds are called *alveolar* (or *apicoalveolar*).

4. The whole fore part of the tongue on the roof of the mouth, or palate. English has no stops made with this contact, but has other sounds including the two fricatives symbolized [š ž], which occur at the ends of the words *ash* and *rouge.* Sounds made on the palate are called *palatal* (or *frontopalatal*).

5. The rear of the tongue backed against the velum or soft palate, the fleshy part of the roof of the mouth at the rear. English has two stops, [k g]; examples, *caw* and *go.* These sounds are *velar* (or *dorsovelar*). Scottish dialect has a velar fricative, for example in *loch,* and many other languages, including German, use this sound.

Of course, other positions and tongue contacts are possible. There is a stop sound that is used freely in many languages but is not generally counted among our distinctive sounds in English, although we use it in two peculiar ways. This is the glottal stop, symbolized [ʔ], which many people put between *the* and a following word that begins with a vowel. Most of us use it in the warning *oh-oh!* (meaning 'Look out, you're about to make a mistake') and in the negative *hunh-uh.* Some languages, of which a number in Africa are typical, produce certain of their stops by an intake of air such as one hears in the smack of a kiss or in the sound spelled *tsk! tsk!* which to us is a sign of disapproval.

The stops and fricatives are the two chief "manners" of manipulating the air at the various contact points. But there are others, one of which is simply a combination of a stop and a fricative. If instead of breaking the contact crisply and cleanly at the end of a [t] the tongue is withdrawn gradually, the result is the initial sound in the foreign borrowings *Tsar* and *tsetse.* Such sounds are called *affricates.* English has two palatal affricates in its native stock of words, the initial sounds in *chump* and *jump,* symbolized [č] and [ǰ] respectively.

Another manner consists in the direction in which the air is allowed to escape. If it is diverted through the nose, the result is a *nasal* sound, of which English has three: the labial [m] in *ram,* the alveolar [n] in *ran,* and the velar [ŋ] in *rang.* If it is diverted around the sides of the tongue instead of along the median line, the result is a lateral sound, typified in English by [l], as in *Lee.*

The most fundamental difference of all is that of voice and voicelessness. If the vocal cords are vibrating the result is a *voiced* sound, as in [v] (if we prolong a [v] and hold a finger on our Adam's apple, we can feel the vibration); if the air moves past the vocal cords without causing them to vibrate, the result is a *voiceless* sound, as in [f]. Voiced and voiceless consonants generally come in pairs for each position and manner: [b-p v-f ð-θ d-t z-s ž-š ǰ-č g-k]. Vowels are typically voiced, but English has a consonant that is simply a vowel without a voice: in the words *heat, hope, hail, hoot,* and so on the [h] is made by starting the sound of the vowel without voice.

The descriptions that have been given apply to English. It does not follow that other languages, even when they have closely similar sounds, necessarily make them in exactly the same way. This should cause no surprise, since English speakers themselves have different ways sometimes of producing the "same" sound. Take the sound of [s]. Many people do not make it with the tip of the tongue but get the tip out of the way by curling it slightly downward so that it is more or less directly behind the lower front teeth, and instead use the blade or flat part of the tongue by bunching it up against the alveolar ridge. In French a stop such as [p] is followed so quickly by the vowel that it sounds almost like [b] to a speaker of English (English does the same with a [p] after an [s], so that it is hard to hear any difference between *Monk Spread* and *Monk's Bread*); in English the vowel is delayed somewhat after a voiceless stop at the beginning of a word and we hear a puff of voiceless air in between, called an aspiration. It is enough to blow out a match held close to the lips when we say a word like *pin.*

The ways of making [r] are so different that if it were not for the common origin of many words containing it we would not consider it to be the same at all from one language to another. To show how widely it can vary even in one language it is enough to mention the Bostonian's **paahk** and the Mid-westerner's **parrk**, for **park.**

With the vowels it might seem that since the air comes through unimpeded they should all sound alike. But as it happens more things can be done with the breath stream, especially when it is voiced, than merely obstructing it. The *shape* of the mouth cavity makes a difference: for example, whether it is narrow, wide, or elongated as when we purse our lips for the word **coo.** It is mostly the tongue and lips that produce these shapes. Notice how the tongue is pushed well forward in the mouth for the word **key** but drawn back for the word **coo.** English vowels can be described thus by noting whether the tongue is *front* as in **key**, *back* as in **coo**, or *central* as in **cut**, and by whether it is *high* (close to the palate) as in **key** and **coo**, *low* (lowered away from the palate by dropping the jaw) as in **bat** and **tot**, or *mid* as in **bet** and **tote.** (In making these comparisons the vowels must be abstracted from the neighboring consonants, which of course have their own positions.) In addition we have to note whether the lips are *spread* as in **key** or *rounded* as in **coo.** Ordinarily it is assumed that they are spread unless rounding is mentioned.

The "vowel quadrilateral," opposite, shows positions of the tongue for the English full vowels. Except for [a], rounding does not need to be mentioned because all the vowels on the right-hand side, that is, all the back vowels, are automatically accompanied by rounding of the lips. The vowel [a] usually has little or no rounding. (In French, rounding would have to be indicated in such a diagram, for there are front vowels with rounding and front vowels without.)

Diphthongs — two vowels or vowel-like sounds in combination — are treated by some phoneticians as two separable elements, by others as indivisible units. The simplest way of transcribing them is with double symbols, as if they were divisible. The tongue glides in producing a diphthong, usually toward either a high front position or a high back position, symbolized [y] and [w] respectively: **Roy** is [rɔy] and **now** is [naw]. Or the glide may be in the opposite direction, from rather than to the high front or high back position: **yore** [yɔr], **wan** [wan] — in fact, if **Roy** and **now** are played backward on a tape recorder they will sound like **yore** and

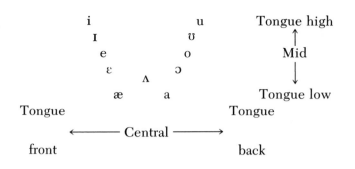

[i] as in *beat*	[a] as in *pot*
[ɪ] as in *bit*	[ɔ] as in *bought*
[e] as in *bait*	[o] as in *boat*
[ɛ] as in *bet*	[ʊ] as in *put*
[æ] as in *bat*	[u] as in *boot*
[ʌ] as in *butt*	

wan. For reasons that are not very important here, the [y] or [w] element is generally called a *semivowel* when it comes after the main vowel and a *semiconsonant* when it comes before. The sound [r] may also be regarded as a semivowel (or semiconsonant). There may of course be additional consonants bordering the diphthong on either side: *coin* [kɔyn], *proud* [prawd], *fiord* [fyɔrd], *swan* [swan].

To complete the picture of the vowels we should include three others, called *reduced* to distinguish them from the *full* ones just diagrammed. They are the vowels in the last syllables of the words *hairy, Harrah,* and *harrow,* and can be symbolized ⌊ɨ ə ɵ⌋. The second of these — ⌊ə⌋ — is often called *schwa* and is the most frequent vowel in English; for example, it occupies all but the first syllable of the word *formidableness* [fɔrmədəbəlnəs]. The contrast between full and reduced vowels is what produces the choppy rhythm that speakers of many other languages find so characteristic of English. Where syllables with full vowels succeed one another, as in *Irene Carstairs' pet chimpanzee Nimrod dotes on fresh horehound drops,* the syllables are spaced out with a fairly even beat; but where syllables with reduced vowels intervene, the reduced vowels borrow their time from the preceding full vowels, producing an irregular beat: *Minnie Abbott's little kitten Missie's fond of liverwurst.* The vowel [ɨ] has a tongue height anywhere from about that of [e] to about that of [i], but the tongue is not pushed forward as far. Similarly, [ə] has a range close to that of [ʌ] but the mouth is less open, and [ɵ] ranges close to [o] and [ɔ] but the tongue is less drawn back. Because of the less extreme positions of the tongue, reduced vowels are often called *centralized.*

The vowels show more clearly than the consonants how readily one may find differences within a single language. The fact that the tongue moves smoothly backward and forward and up and down enables it to take not only the positions shown in the vowels of the quadrilateral but also any position between. A consonant is an easy target as a rule — the teeth, for example, occupy a discontinuous part of the mouth and the tongue knows exactly what to aim for; but with the continuum of the mouth cavity as a whole there are no definite targets and it is not so easy to aim true. So we find many speakers whose vowels would disagree here and there with those of the chart, in their position and even sometimes in how many of them there are. In some dialects of American English no distinction is made between [a] and [ɔ] — the pairs *bot-bought, cot-caught, tot-taught,* and others like them are pronounced the same. Other speakers may make a distinction sometimes, for example between [ɪ] and [ɛ] in *bit* and *bet,* but disregard it at other times, as in *pin* and *pen.* This is apt to happen in a language, like English or French, that crowds a large number of vowels into the mouth-cavity continuum — they tend to interfere with one another. In a language with few vowels — as few as three is possible and five is commonplace — this is not so apt to happen.

All languages make their vowels in much the same way by carving up the continuum, but the number of slices varies, as does the position of each slice. Some languages multiply their vowels by adding another dimension. The potentiality for adding dimensions is universal, though not all languages make use of the same ones. We can note three:

The first is *rounding.* As was mentioned earlier, this does not really count in English because it automatically accompanies all the back vowels, but French uses it for front vowels as well so that there is a rounded series and an un-rounded series. The word pairs *fée* 'fairy' and *feu* 'fire,' *père* 'father' and *peur* 'fear' differ only in that the first member has the lips spread and the second has them rounded.

The second is *nasalization*. English disregards this as a feature of vowels. In saying **Did he go?** the nasal passage can be left loosely open for all three vowels without affecting the meaning. But—to use French again—the word pairs **beauté** 'beauty' and **bonté** 'goodness,' **seau** 'pail' and **son** 'sound' differ in that the pronunciation of the second member of each pair is nasalized.

The third is *length*. The Classical Latin **mēto,** with its *e* lengthened and approximating the quality of [e], meant 'to measure'; **meto** [mɛto], without the extra length, meant 'to reap.' (Consonants are sometimes lengthened too—Italian has this feature. It is often hard to decide whether a lengthened sound ought to be regarded as a single sound with extra length, or as two identical sounds side by side.)

A possible fourth dimension is *tone*. In many languages a higher or lower pitch on a vowel can make each one count for more than one. In Ticuna, a language of the upper Amazon, five steps of pitch are observed; the "word" *čanamu* is actually four words depending on the combination of tones that go with it: numbering 1 for highest tone and 5 for lowest, *ča₃na₃mu₃* means 'I weave it,' *ča₃na₃mu₄* means 'I send it,' *ča₃na₃mu₅* means 'I eat it,' and *ča₃na₃mu₃₋₅* means 'I spear it.'[1] In situations where the words and meanings apt to be appropriate are fairly familiar and predictable, it is sometimes possible just to transmit the series of tones and be understood—the hearer can guess at the rest. This in stylized form is the basis of African drum signaling as well as of the "whistle speech" of Mazatec in Oaxaca, Mexico. Following is Dr. George M. Cowan's description of a whistled conversation:

Eusebio Martínez was observed one day standing in front of his hut, whistling to a man a considerable distance away. The man was passing on the trail below, going to market to sell a load of corn leaves which he was carrying. The man answered Eusebio's whistle with a whistle. The interchange was repeated several times with different whistles. Finally the man turned around, retraced his steps a short way and came up the footpath to Eusebio's hut. Without saying a word he dumped his load on the ground. Eusebio looked the load over, went into his hut, returned with some money, and paid the man his price. The man turned and left. Not a word had been spoken. . . .[2]

Exercise 1

The chart below shows the organs of speech that regulate the flow of air from the lungs to create the sounds of speech. (Speech almost always takes place during exhalation only.) As the air leaves the lungs, it is modified by muscular actions of the *vocal cords,* the *uvula,* the *tongue,* the *jaw,* and the *lips.*

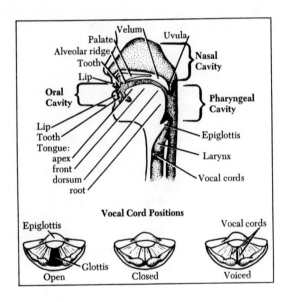

PRINCIPAL ORGANS OF SPEECH

a. The first modification of the air stream is the vibration of the muscles of the vocal cords. When these muscles are set in vibration, the sounds produced are called *voiced.* Compare the voiced sound *z* with the *voiceless s.* If you place your hands on your ears and pronounce *z* and then *s,* you will hear the vibrations which accompany the *z* but are missing in *s*. Another test is to place your hand on your throat and repeat the sounds. All sounds in English may be distinguished as voiced or voiceless in this manner. Make a list of the following letters and then place V beside a voiced sound and VL beside a voiceless sound.

b	o (*oh*)	r
p	t	l
f	d	m
v	th (*thin*)	a (*ah*)
y (*your*)	th (*then*)	

Try other vowels. What happens? What are the sounds *n, y,* and *w*?

b. The second possible modification takes place at the *velum*. If the velum is lowered, the sound produced by the other organs is characteristically nasal. Which of the following are nasal sounds?

b	n	ng (*sing*)
m	t	f

c. For which of these sounds are the lips rounded?

ow (*know*)	y (*yes*)	oo (*boots*)
a (*Kate*)	s (*sing*)	l (*like*)

d. Most of the contrasts in the sounds of speech are made by modifying the relation of the *lower jaw* and the *tongue* to the *upper jaw*. The generally stationary organs of the upper jaw are called *points of articulation*. They are the upper lip and *teeth*, the *alveolar ridge*, the (hard) *palate*, the *velum* (or soft palate), and the *uvula*. The uvula and the upper lip are the only organs in the upper jaw that move. The organs along the lower jaw are called *articulators*. They are the *lower lip* and *teeth*, and the *apex*, *front*, and *dorsum* of the tongue. (See diagram, page 38.) There are six major positions of articulation made by the relation of the articulator to the point of articulation. They are defined as follows:

Articulator	Point of Articulation	Position of Articulation	Examples
lower lip	upper lip	bilabial	[m b]
lower lip	upper teeth	labiodental	[f]
apex of the tongue and lower teeth	upper teeth	interdental	[θ]
apex of the tongue	alveolar ridge	apicoalveolar	[n t s l r]
front of the tongue	palate	frontopalatal	[š]
dorsum of the tongue	velum	dorsovelar	[k]

Add another example of a sound for each position.

e. Further modifications of sound are determined by the distance between the articulator and the point of articulation. The two may touch and stop the air stream for a moment; these sounds are called *stops* [p t k b d g]. Nonstop sounds are called *continuants*. The continuants may be divided into *fricatives*, already discussed, in which the air is constricted at the position of articulation [fvθðszšž], and other sounds collectively called *resonants*. The resonants [m n ŋ l r y w] and all vowels are either *nasal* (the first three) or *oral* (the remaining). In the articulation of the oral resonants, the air stream may leave from the side of the mouth as in [l] which is called a *lateral*, or it may leave through the more common *central* position. The central oral resonants are the *semivowels* [r y w] and the *vowels*. The jaw is lowest in the production of vowels. It is lower for some vowels than others.

Arrange the following three sets of consonants, vowels, and semivowels in the order of increasing jaw opening, using 1 for the sound in which the jaw is the lowest compared to the other sounds in the set. (Do not lower the jaw more than necessary to produce the sound clearly.)

t	k	a (*father*)
ɪ (*bit*)	a (*father*)	ɪ (*sit*)
æ (*bat*)	o (*note*)	ɛ (*set*)
	ʊ (*good*)	

f. Most popular given names, especially when not abbreviated, have one or more resonant sounds other than vowels. Some names such as **Mary** and **Wayne** are composed of only resonant sounds, whereas the names **Joseph** and **Edith** have no resonant sounds other than vowels. Names of the latter type are rare. Make a list of names and analyze it with regard to resonant and non-resonant sounds and meaning. What can you infer about the sounds of names? About names for males and females?

g. Do you hear a *glide*—a kind of sliding change in the quality of the sound—at the end of [i e o u] that is lacking in the other vowels? Try saying **beet, bait, boat, boot** and contrast them with **bit, bet, bat,** and **but,** to detect this difference. (Some phoneticians prefer to think of such words as **beet, bait, boat,** and **boot** as containing diphthongs and transcribe them [biyt], [beyt], [bowt], and [buwt].) Can you find a reason for the fact that the glided sounds and the unglided sounds alternate with each other on the right and left sides of the quadrilateral on page 35?

Exercise 2

a. Write the phonetic symbols of sounds defined as follows:

   1. low back vowel   [a]
   2. apicoalveolar semivowel
   3. voiceless apicoalveolar stop
   4. lower high front vowel
   5. voiceless dorsovelar stop
   6. frontopalatal semivowel
   7. mid central reduced vowel
   8. apicoalveolar lateral
   9. mid back vowel
  10. voiceless palatal afficate

b. Give a phonetic description, such as those in the preceding exercise, for each of the sounds below. Descriptions differ for consonants and vowels. For consonants the order is (1) voicing (indicated only when there is a voicing contrast), (2) position of articulation, and (3) manner of articulation. Vowels are described by (1) tongue height, (2) degree of frontness, (3) "reduced" (not indicated if vowel is not reduced), and (4) "vowel" (always included).

1. [f]	*3.* [n]	*5.* [t]	*7.* [k]
2. [ə]	*4.* [ɛ]	*6.* [ɨ]	*8.* [s]

c. Write the phonetic symbol for the first consonant of the following words. Consult the list of phonemes and phonetic symbols on page 291.

physics [f]	cycle	ship
Thor	compute	check
there	knee	chauffeur
khaki	gnome	Zhivago
ghoul	psyche	
rheumatism	who	

d. Transcribe these words into conventional English spelling.

1. [kæt] *cat*	*6.* [hayt]	*11.* [batl]
2. [trɪk]	*7.* [hol]	*12.* [yuθ]
3. [trit]	*8.* [čip]	*13.* [klæŋ]
4. [tem]	*9.* [bʌtn]	*14.* [bɛt]
5. [taym]	*10.* [pæč]	

Distinctive Features

Adding "dimensions" like rounding, nasalization, and tone suggests the possibility of describing not just certain characteristics of vowels but all speech sounds in terms of them. We have already noted that all sounds divide according to whether they are voiced or voiceless, and of course they also divide according to whether they are consonants or vowels. Are there other equally general dimensions, or "distinctive features" as those who work with this kind of description call them, that would enable us to analyze each sound into its components, to "split the atom of phonology," as one writer puts it? If we could find them we not only would reduce the number of units but also could make more scientific comparisons; for example, between one sound and another: "Sound A differs from Sound B by x number of features" or "Sound A does not occur next to Sound B because both contain y feature, which in that language cannot be repeated"; or between one language and another: "Language A has a series of consonants like a similar series in Language B, but differing by one particular feature." Keeping the number of features small would call for the ability to see an underlying sameness in two or more superficially different manifestations of sound.

Sameness in language is not strictly in the way sounds are *made*, though this is a factor. Rather there is sameness in *sound*. Usually a similar articulation produces a similar sound, and classifying the features by articulations is easier to grasp. Otherwise, to see the kinships in exact acoustic terms would call for a certain amount of acoustic analysis. But certain of the kinships in sound are quite easy to see. The quality of *nasal* is obvious and ties together the sounds [n m ŋ] in **bun, bum,** and **bung.** Another that is slightly less obvious but easy to hear is *stridency,* which is simply the harsh noise by which we associate the eight consonants [f v s z č ǰ š ž], for example in **laugh, love, loss, buzz, rich, pledge, plush, rouge.** Thus [f] has the feature of stridency and in addition that of *diffuseness* (a quality of sound produced by a rather tight narrowing at the front of the mouth) and that of *continuation* (the sound can be emitted steadily as long as the breath holds out), plus a few others. Grouping sounds by features is useful in describing various things that happen when sounds occur together. The feature of *stridency,* for instance, helps to explain how English forms the plural of nouns: it is always pronounced -[əz] following a strident sound other than [f v]. If we try to state this rule without referring to distinctive features we have to list all six sounds.

By eliminating redundancies in this way, feature analysts have arrived at a set of about fifteen features (including opposites) with which all sounds of all languages can theoretically be defined. Viewed in this light the differences between one language and another sink to the same unimportance as that of the two ways of saying English [s] or the difference between French and English [p] — all languages draw from the same pool of features but do not use exactly the same number or the same combinations.

A "consonant" for feature analysis means a sound that is both *consonantal* and *nonvocalic,* as defined on the following page. That is why the sounds [r l h] are missing from the chart.

The features are made to do double service by interpreting their *absence* to signify the *presence* of an opposite fea-

DISTINCTIVE-FEATURE REPRESENTATION OF THE CONSONANTS OF ENGLISH

	p	b	m	f	v	k	g	t	d	θ	ð	n	s	z	č	ǰ	š	ž
VOCALIC	−	−	−	−	−	−	−	−	−	−	−	−	−	−	−	−	−	−
CONSONANTAL	+	+	+	+	+	+	+	+	+	+	+	+	+	+	+	+	+	+
GRAVE	+	+	+	+	+	+	+	−	−	−	−	−	−	−	−	−	−	−
DIFFUSE	+	+	+	+	+	−	−	+	+	+	+	+	+	+	−	−	−	−
STRIDENT	−	−	−	+	+	−	−	−	−	−	−	−	+	+	+	+	+	+
NASAL	−	−	+	−	−	−	−	−	−	−	−	+	−	−	−	−	−	−
CONTINUANT	−	−	−	+	+	−	−	−	−	+	+	−	+	+	−	−	+	+
VOICED	−	+	+	−	+	−	+	−	+	−	+	+	−	+	−	+	−	+

FROM Morris Halle, "On the Bases of Phonology," in Jerry A. Fodor and Jerrold J. Katz (eds.), *The Structure of Language: Readings in the Philosophy of Language* (Englewood Cliffs, N.J.: Prentice-Hall, Inc., 1964), pp. 324–33.

ture. For that reason both the feature proper and its "non-" or opposite have to be described:

Vocalic: The sound has a distinctive pitch or set of pitches (such as all vowels have, whether voiced or whispered) and the mouth is relatively open — there is no narrowing anywhere greater than approximately that suitable for the sound of [i]. *Nonvocalic* means either that there is a greater narrowing of the oral cavity or that the sound does not have a clearly defined pitch or pitches.

Consonantal: There is a tight enough narrowing at some point in the mouth cavity either to stop the flow of air completely or to let it through with friction. *Nonconsonantal* sounds have lesser degrees of narrowing.

Grave: There is a narrowing at the extreme front (lips) or extreme back of the mouth cavity; *nongrave* sounds are narrowed at the middle of the cavity—for example, at the teeth or palate.

Diffuse: There is a narrowing at least as tight as that of the sound of [i], at the front of the mouth. *Nondiffuse* sounds are located in the back part of the mouth cavity.

Strident: The air stream has enough of an obstacle in its path to create a noisy turbulence but not enough to check the flow of air completely. *Nonstrident* sounds lack this turbulence.

Continuant: The air passes through without being completely shut off. Noncontinuant or *interrupted* means the same as *stop.*

Nasal-nonnasal and voiced-voiceless have already been defined.

Exercise 3

a. Among the dimensions in the distinctive-feature system the one called *stridency* refers to a marked amount of noise in pronouncing consonants as against little or none. Which English consonants have the feature of stridency?

b. One of the values of distinctive-feature analysis is its recognition that there is no sharp distinction between consonants and vowels. A sound that is *plus consonantal* and *minus vocalic* has no characteristics of vowels. One that is *plus consonantal* and *plus vocalic* is consonantlike and vowellike at the same time. Is this true of [r] and [l]? Consider the words **bottle** and **butter.** What is the vowel element in the second syllable of these two words?

Exercise 4

Find all sounds that are defined by the combination of the following sets of features.

1. [− vocalic, + consonantal, + grave, + nasal] [m] , [ŋ]

2. [− vocalic, + consonantal, + nasal] ? , ? , [ŋ]

3. [− vocalic, + consonantal, + grave, + strident] ___?___,
   ___?___

4. [− vocalic, + consonantal, + strident] ___?___, ___?___, ___?___,
   ___?___, ___?___, ___?___, ___?___, ___?___

Compare the number of sounds defined in 1 and 2 and in 3 and 4. Note that 1 and 3 have one feature more than 2 and 4. Does the addition of a feature increase or decrease the number of sounds defined?

Intonation

Language resembles music in making use of both the musical and the unmusical qualities of sound. The unmusical qualities — noises — we have seen as components of certain consonants, for example, the hissing stridency of an [s] or the sudden explosion of a [p]; in music, noise is characteristic of the percussion section of an orchestra. But the musical qualities — pitches or tones — are equally important. Just as in music, two kinds of musical quality are used: the singing or tune-carrying quality and the quality of timbre or depth. In music if we think of the "message" as being carried by the tune (the succession of sounds that are written as notes on a musical score), and the "mood" as contributed by the richness or depth of the particular instrument on which the notes are played, we see the two-dimensional nature of musical communication. The organ makes a good example because it is like many instruments combined in one.

The organist can play the tune and in addition can vary the mood by manipulating the stops, which imitate various musical instruments. Putting this acoustically, the tune is a succession of *fundamental* pitches and the depth is the *overtones* which are controlled by the stops. (Another kind of "depth," of course, is harmony, achieved by playing two or more notes at the same time; but the depth referred to here is the richness of a single tone, which varies according to the stops.) Most instruments, including the organ (but not the tuning fork, which is made intentionally to get "pure" tones), when played at a given pitch, produce not only that pitch — known as the fundamental — but an infinite series of higher pitches, each an even multiple of the number of vibrations in the fundamental. If the organ is emitting a middle A at 440 vibrations per second, it also gives out a pitch exactly an octave higher at 880, another three times as high at 1320, and so on up. The higher pitches are the overtones and the depth they contribute depends on how well we hear them. This is determined by the stops. A given stop may make the overtone at 880 practically inaudible while building up the one at 1320, with the fundamental or singing pitch going on unabated all the while. In a violin it is mainly the combination of the size and the shape of the body of the instrument that cuts out certain overtones and reinforces others, giving the quality of sound that we associate with violins.

The human vocal cords when they are set vibrating are just another musical instrument and are so used when we sing. Depth is controlled when we vary the shape of the mouth cavity. Each shape checks certain overtones and reinforces others.

Here the resemblance to music ends. For if in music the fundamental gives the message and the overtones the mood, in language the overtones are crucial to the message and the fundamental is mostly used for mood and punctuating effects. Varying the shape of the mouth cavity affects the overtones, and that is precisely what we do to make the difference between the [u] of *fool* and the [i] of *feel.* Whether we say the words at a low or a high singing pitch makes no difference to their meaning.

The overtones, not the fundamental, are the chief musical ingredients of language. Only in tone languages is the fundamental used to a limited extent as an ingredient of distinctive sound. As we have seen, Ticuna — like Chinese and a number of other languages from all parts of the world — adds fundamental pitch at varying heights as an extra dimension to vowels.

But all languages, including tone languages, use the fundamental for mood and punctuating effects over longer stretches of speech. We call these *intonations* — speech melody — as distinguished from the *tones* of tone languages.

They have several characteristics. The main ones are *range, direction, height, abruptness,* and *pattern.*

Probably all languages use the *range* of intonation to show emotion. When we are excited our voice extends its pitch upward; when we are depressed we speak almost in a monotone. Displaying emotion in this way is probably instinctive.

Probably all languages use the *direction* of intonation to show where major divisions of utterances start and stop. One effect that is found everywhere is a running down, a tendency to drift toward a low pitch when the speaker nears the point where he intends to stop. He starts full of energy but deflates at the end like a bagpipe running out of wind. But if he is unsatisfied—as he normally would be in asking a question—his pitch goes up. As with excitement and depression these tensions and relaxations may be instinctive, but we seem to have learned how to use them intentionally. The following is a typical intentional use:

$$\text{If you're } \text{read}^{\text{y}} \text{ let's} \\ \qquad\qquad\qquad\qquad \text{g} \\ \qquad\qquad\qquad\qquad\quad \text{o}.$$

The pitch follows a generally upward movement in **If you're ready** and switches to a downward movement in **let's go.** The separation between the clauses is marked by the change in direction.

Probably all languages use relative *height* as a sign of importance. If in an example like the one just given there happen to be two separations instead of one, it may be necessary to show which is major and which is minor:

$$\text{If you're } ^{\text{ready}} \text{ when I } ^{\text{get } \text{there}} \text{ we'll} \\ \qquad\qquad\qquad\qquad\qquad\qquad\qquad\qquad\qquad \text{g}_{\text{o}}.$$

$$\text{If you're } \text{read}^{\text{y}} \text{ when I } ^{\text{get there}} \text{ we'll} \\ \qquad\qquad\qquad\qquad\qquad\qquad\qquad\qquad\qquad \text{g}_{\text{o}}.$$

The first says 'If you're ready when I get there'—the extra-high rise in pitch puts the major break between *there* and *we'll.* The second says 'when I get there we'll go' — the extra-high pitch puts the major break between *ready* and *when.*

Many languages use abrupt jumps in pitch to make certain elements stand out. This is *accent.* Usually it is combined with a slight lengthening and a certain extra loudness, but the main element is the sudden change in pitch. Usually it involves highlighting one word as more important than the words that surround it. Children learning to speak catch the important words in this way and reproduce them first: *Mama spank* culls the words that really count from the sentence *Mama is going to spank you.* It makes little difference whether the jump in pitch is up or down. In the sentence *His brother was the one who cheated him, brother* can be emphasized by raising it,

His brother was the one who cheated him.

or by lowering it,

His brother was the one who cheated him?

But in either case the stressed syllable of the important word is pushed out of the intonational line. (In these examples accent is marked by the jump; question versus statement by the direction.)

Probably all languages use *patterns* of successive pitches to distinguish different kinds of utterances. In English one can usually tell a command regardless of the syntactic form of the sentence:

On your feet.

makes a good command, but would be unusual as a statement, while

$$\text{On your}\ {}^{\text{fe}}\ {}_{\text{et.}}$$

makes a good answer to **How am I supposed to get there?** but not a good command (though it might do for a repetition of a command). Since patterns involve directions with their punctuating functions, the two cannot be clearly distinguished. The ambiguity of the word **finality** itself—with which the falling pitch at the end is associated—tells us this: there is a finality or decisiveness about a command and a finality or conclusiveness about the end of a statement.

Exercise 5

a. When written, a sentence like **Was he more or less courteous?** is ambiguous. Is it ambiguous in speech? If not, why not?

b. Explain how the following sentences differ.

$$\text{When did he }\text{rea}^{\text{lize it?}}$$

$$\text{When did he }{}^{\text{re}}\ _{\text{alize it?}}$$

c. See if you can make an important change by saying the **don't you** in **You want to marry her, don't you?** in two different ways. Explain why you think intonation is or is not helpful in distinguishing one kind of question from another.

Exercise 6

The major characteristics of intonation are *range, direction, height, abruptness,* and *pattern*. Apply these terms to the following examples:

a. How would a cheerleader's emotional expression of the results of a game differ in intonation if she were to report the following?

1. We won 48 to 13.
2. We lost 13 to 12.

b. Write the following sentences showing pitch direction.

1. He is hungry. Aren't you?
2. Where did you find it? In my room?
3. Q. Where did you find it? A. In my room.

c. Which characteristics are used to distinguish these two sentences in speech?

1. If you are happy when you see me, smile!
2. If you are happy, when you see me, smile!

d. In the sentence *I won't play chess with you,* which characteristic of intonation is used to express the desire

1. not to play chess, but another game.
2. not to play with you, but with anyone else.

e. Show the intonation pattern of *On the bus*

1. as a command.
2. as a reply to the question *Where did you hear that?*

is that of the roles of players in a baseball game. Each role is a "particle" — pitcher, catcher, outfielder, third baseman. The ways in which the roles interact in a game are its "strings": the catcher at a given moment interacts with the pitcher, and he regularly interacts more with the pitcher than with any other player. The abstract relationships among the players are the "field": a treatise on baseball might compare the function of shortstop with that of catcher on the one hand and second baseman on the other, explaining how the three roles are alike and how they differ.

Similarly with the three levels in language. At the level of *sound* we find first the sound particles themselves, such as /a f t m/.* Next are the strings — syllables and parts of syllables — within which the particles combine in characteristic ways. One trait of the particle /s/, for example, is that it can join with a following /l/ but not with a following /r/ to form the beginning of a syllable. Last are the contrastive field relationships among the particles; one such relationship is displayed in the vowel diagram in Chapter 2 on page 35.

At the level of *words* there are first the words themselves. Then there are the compatibility relationships among words which permit us to say **The man swallows the peanut** or **The peanut is swallowed by the man** but not ***The man is swallowed by the peanut.**† Finally there are the semantic fields that envelop "color words," "kinship words," "food-and-digestion words," and so on.

At the level of *syntax* we find words again, but now we find them as representatives of word classes (noun, verb, adjective, and so on) rather than of meanings. Then come syntactic strings, in which classes are allowed to occur in particular positions (noun-as-subject plus verb plus noun-as-object, for instance, gives a simple declarative string like **Monkeys love bananas**). Lastly, there is the syntactic field, in which syntactic elements are ranged according to similar functions — for example, **with gratitude** alongside **gratefully** (that is, prepositional phrase = adverb).

---

* Slant lines are used to mark *phonemes*. Thus, in the words **top** and **pot** there are two varieties of the phoneme /t/, an aspirated sound [tʰ] in the first and an unaspirated [t] in the second. Normally, speakers of English do not notice the difference; their intuitive reaction confirms the linguist in grouping both sounds together in the same phoneme /t/.

† We use the asterisk to mark expressions that cannot occur grammatically in English.

We will now take a look at each level and on the way, in this chapter and the next, will look more narrowly at such loose terms as *sound, word,* and *sentence.*

Exercise 1

Take baseball or another sport as an example of particle, string, and field, but consider the plays as the particles. Identify some of the particles, then describe some of the strings (definite sequences of plays) and some of the field relationships (for example, "all the ways to be put out").

Distinctiveness in Sound — The Phoneme

The earlier discussion of sound was concerned with how sounds are produced and how languages make use of different parts of the sound wave to carry a message. We saw that sound is not important in itself; it is only one kind of raw material for creating distinctive shapes that can be used to convey meaning. The distinctiveness of the shapes is no more dependent on sound than the distinctiveness of letters is dependent on ink, pencil, or chalk. Therefore "distinctive sound" must now be said with the emphasis on "distinctive." We are no longer interested in it as sound except to note here and there some trivial problem created by the fact that sound is sound—*East meets West* is hard to say because of interference among the consonants, just as the words *myself* and *Egypt* are hard to write because of interferences among the successive longhand loops.

The particles at the level of distinctive sound are called *phonemes.* Ideally, each phoneme is a set combination of distinctive features such as voicing, stoppage, nasalization, and friction. A phoneme is like a chord in music. A distinctive feature is like one of the notes that make up the chord. The notes in the chord, and the distinctive features in the phoneme, are sounded simultaneously; hearers react to the complex sound as a unit. The chords themselves—the phonemes— occur in succession. It is these successive bits of complex sound that constitute the apparatus for making syllables and words. The linguist's first job is to catalog them.

This is carried out by comparing utterances that are partly alike and finding out what it is that makes them different. If the analyst is working with his own language he has a head start since all speakers have a feel for the system of sounds they use, even though it may not be scientific. The person who makes a pun like *The undertaker said he was going to buy his little boy a rocking hearse* is aware—and expects his hearer to be aware—of a minimal or near-minimal contrast between *hearse* and *horse.* To speak pig Latin—*Arymay antsway ouyay otay aitway orfay erhay* for *Mary wants you to wait for her*—children have to sense the consonant-plus-vowel structure of the syllable. This makes it fairly easy for the native speaker to hit upon *minimal pairs*: items that differ from each other by only one element and that reveal phonemes when several of the items are compared. In English one can quickly list a riming set like *bay-day-Fay-gay-hay-jay-Kay-lay-may-nay-pay-ray-say-shay-way* which gives a strong hint of distinctive consonants /b d f g h ǰ k l m n p r s š w/, and it takes only a moment more to confirm them by other sets like *robe-rode-rogue-roam-roan-rope-roar.*

The analyst confronting a new language has a rougher time, for he lacks both a feel and a folklore to fall back on. Or rather he has a folklore—that of his native language—which misleads him. If he were a foreigner analyzing English he might, for instance, hear the words *vial* and *phial* and be told that they mean the same, and conclude, erroneously, that the difference between the sounds [v] and [f] is only accidental—that English has a labiodental consonant phoneme (which might be represented by some such symbol as /f̵/) that is indifferently voiced or voiceless. But eventually he would discover that the feature of voice is significant, in pairs like *vary-fairy, leave-leaf, shelve-shelf,* and hence /v/ and /f/ are phonemes, independent of each other.

Nor is it all smooth sailing even in one's native language. Since a phoneme consumes a certain length of time, however short, there is always the question of where the borders are and of whether a given span of time should be assigned to just one phoneme or split down the middle and assigned to two; this is the problem of *unit phoneme* versus *cluster.* The analogy with music is appropriate again. While it is true that the notes in a chord are heard simultaneously, sometimes chords appear as arpeggios, in which the notes are played one after the other and are both simultaneous and successive. Just as the succession CEGCE on a piano might be thought of either as a single arpeggio or as one arpeggio consisting of CEG followed by another consisting of CE, so with the phonemic "chord" in a language: one can often choose between regarding the clustered sound as one unit or two.

In words like *play-spay-sway-stay-splay-spray-clay-cray-flay-fray-gray-dray,* are the consonant sounds preceding the vowels units or clusters? If they are unit phonemes, then *sway* differs from *way* in that one starts with /sw/, and the other with /w/; if they are clusters, then the difference is that *sway* has one more phoneme than *way,* the initial /s/. The advantage to counting two phonemes is that by splitting /s/ from /w/ the total number of phonemes can be reduced— instead of three phonemes, /s/, /w/, and /sw/, to account for *say, way* and *sway,* only two are needed. By splitting /r/ from /d/ one can account not only for *dray* in addition to *day* and *ray* but also, by recognizing /dr/ as distinct from /rd/, for part of the contrast between *dry* and *yard.*

Such technical problems put a fringe of uncertainty around the catalog of phonemes, but it is not a wide fringe. Linguists agree on the main points.

Exercise 2

a. Tongue twisters are examples of difficult articulations. The phrase *critical flicker fusion frequency* is used in psychology. Try saying it fast. What makes it difficult?

b. What phonemic contrasts do the following minimal pairs point to? *gristly-grisly, confusion-Confucian, spite-spied, crutch-crush, luff-love, rode-roan, mutt-much, lean-dean.* Are the two members of each pair widely different from each other? If you could measure the difference in terms of the number of distinctive features that separate one phoneme from another, how many points of difference would you say there are in /f/ − /v/? In /m/ − /p/? (You may want to consult the discussion of distinctive features in consonants on pages 42–45.)

c. See if you have a contrast in the following: *fawned-fond, caught-cot, wrought-rot, cawed-cod.* If you do, does it carry over into *hornet-horrible, Laurie-sorry?* You almost certainly have a contrast in *mat-met, bat-bet, sad-said, shall-shell, sand-send;* see if this contrast carries over to *marry-merry, Barry-berry, arrow-error.* Do you observe anything here that suggests a blurring influence from a nearby /r/? Compare *met-mate* with *ferry-fairy.* Does something similar happen?

d. Compare the sound represented by the *s* of *pleasure* with the sound represented by the *dg* of *pledger.* Some phoneticians regard the latter as a cluster of two consonant sounds of which the sound represented by *s* in *pleasure* is the second. What would the other one be? Compare the words *shoes* and *choose.* Is there a similar possibility of regarding the second of these two compared sounds, [š] and [č], as a cluster of two consonant sounds?

Allophones

What happens to phonemes when they stand next to other phonemes or when they occur at different locations in an utterance? Do they keep their identities intact like a row of bullets laid end to end? If not, do traits of one somehow get mixed with others, and do given positions — say, at the beginning or end of the utterance — have some strengthening or weakening effect?

Phonemes are indeed affected by the company they keep, much as letters are affected in ordinary handwriting. When a letter that normally ends with a stroke above the bottom of the line, like a *b* or a *v*, is followed by one that normally starts at the bottom, such as an *i* or an *r*, the latter starts instead where the former leaves off: *bi, vi, br.* This is called *assimilation* of one shape to the other. Assimilation of one sound to another is equally common. Between vowels an English /n/ is generally alveolar, but in the word *tenth,* where it stands before an interdental /θ/, it too becomes interdental. English /r/ is normally fully voiced, but in a cluster after a voiceless /t/, as in *tree,* it is partially unvoiced.

Different positions in a word bring different influences to bear. The pairs *intent-indent, satin-sadden,* and *sat-sad* illustrate what happens to /t/ and /d/. We have no trouble hearing the difference between the two sounds. They are produced with the same position of the tongue in all three pairs, and we seem to "hear" voicelessness as the feature of the /t/, but it is actually manifested in three different ways. In *intent* it appears as a strong puff of breath, or aspiration. In *satin* it appears as a brief interval of silence right after the tongue makes contact—with *sadden* the sound flows on. In *sat* it appears as a sharp cut-off of sound, and the burden of the difference shifts to what happens to the vowel: it is drawled in *sad* but not in *sat*. In point of actual sound, *sad* is longer. But our ear interprets both words as having about the same length, and this means adding a little bit of nothing—silence—at the end of *sat*, the same silence that was manifested in *satin*. All these phenomena are read back into our minds as the voicelessness characteristic of /t/.

Noting these modifications and classifying the environments that cause them make it possible to define the materialization of a phoneme in sound. Each such different physical manifestation of a phoneme is called an *allophone*. The allophones of /t/ thus include one that is aspirated (any /t/ standing before a full vowel), one that is combined with an interval of silence (a /t/ before most consonants), and one that is *un*like the /d/ that has a lengthened vowel before it (a /t/ in final position). The allophones of /n/ include one that is interdental (*tenth*), one that is palatal (*inch*), and one that is alveolar (*tint*), among others.

Notice, too, that in words like *butter, totter, matter, pewter, bitter, atom, opulum, mollo, grotto, pity,* and *duty,* for most speakers of American English, the /t/ is reduced to a bare tap which picks up the voicing of the surrounding sounds and becomes almost if not completely indistinguishable from /d/. The result is that *bitter* sounds like *bidder, latter* like *ladder, He hit'er* like *He hid'er, let'em* like *led'em,* and so on.

Exercise 3

a. The neighbors that a phoneme is permitted to have are its distribution in the string sense. There are also questions of distribution in the field sense. One is frequency: how widely a given phoneme is used by comparison with other phonemes. Some phonemic contrasts are not much exploited — for example, the contrast between /u/ and /ʊ/ as in *cooed-could, pool-pull, gooed-good, hood(lum)-hood, fool-full, Luke-look.* Can you find other pairs with these two phonemes? The extent to which a contrast is exploited is called its *functional load*: /u/ versus /ʊ/ obviously has a light functional load. Can you guess why? What is apt to happen eventually to this contrast?

b. In the word *lapboard* there is little or no accommodation between the /p/ and the /b/ — both are articulated in almost the normal way. But the combination is a difficult one, and in the word ***cupboard*** it is possible to see what may some day happen to ***lapboard.*** Describe the steps that may bring it about.

c. Describe the allophones of /t/ in the following words: ***cat, shanties, Cervantes, mutton, pity, set.*** Describe the allophones of /n/ in the following words: ***pawnshop, naughty, neat, wince, panther;*** explain the effect of the environment that causes these changes in /n/.

d. The merging of /t/ and /d/ is not necessarily uniform even for speakers who merge them fairly generally. If you have it in the pairs ***latter-ladder, metal-meddle, pouter-powder,*** see if you also have it in the pairs ***traitor-trader, seater-cedar, (hoity-)toity-toidy.*** If not, can you account for the difference?

Exercise 4

For the following sets of phonemes of English, find pairs of words that are similar in all features but the sounds noted here. Find two pairs of words; one pair should contrast the initial position, another the final. Write them phonetically. The contrasting word pairs will be in the order of decreasing occurrence in English. If you cannot find examples, go on to the next pair. The pair /t r/ is illustrated here.

Pairs	Initial	Final	Pairs	Initial	Final
1. /t r/	[tʌn], [rʌn]	[tut], [tur]	16. /ŋ g/	(no example)	
2. /r n/			17. /g š/		
3. /n s/			18. /š č/		
4. /s l/			19. /č θ/		
5. /l d/			20. /θ ǰ/		
6. /d h/		(no example)	21. /ǰ ž/	(no example)	
7. /h m/		(no example)	22. /i ɪ/		
8. /m k/			23. /ɪ e/		
9. /k ð/			24. /e ɛ/		
10. /ð z/			25. /ɛ æ/		
11. /z v/			26. /æ ʌ/		
12. /v f/			27. /ʌ a/		
13. /f b/			28. /a ɔ/		
14. /b p/			29. /ɔ o/		
15. /p ŋ/	(no example)		30. /o ʊ/		

Exercise 5

The phoneme /k/ has the two allophones [c] and [k] in **keep** and **cool** respectively. Let us consider the major articulatory variations of the phoneme /k/. Take the following words: **cat, keep, cool, stack, scat!, act,** and **tack.** In order to show the similarities and differences among the allophones more clearly, a feature grid will be used. The symbols used in the grid will denote the following:

+ the feature in the column is *present* in that row
− the feature in the column is *absent* in that row

Check your pronunciation of the words with the phonetic transcription in the chart on page 62. Most of the features are apparent. A few minutes of concentration on the variations in pronunciation will aid you in mastering the notation of allophones.

MAJOR ALLOPHONES OF / k /

Word	Phonetic representation of /k/	Aspirated°	Released†	Fronto-palatal [c]	Dorso-velar [k]
cat	[cʰæt]	+	+	+	−
keep	[cʰip]	+	+	+	−
cool	[kʰul]	+	+	−	+
stack	[stæk ˺]	−	−	−	+
scat!	[sc ˻ æt]	−	+	+	−
act	[æk ˺t]	−	−	−	+
tack	[tæk ˺]	−	−	−	+

a. On the chart above, are all cases of initial /k/ aspirated? Final /k/? Would the [k] in *clip* be aspirated?

b. Are all aspirated sounds released? Are all released sounds aspirated?

c. Is the frontopalatal allophone [c] used before a front or before a back vowel?

d. When is the dorsovelar allophone [k] used?

e. Are there any cases of final [c]? Would the final sound in *meek* be a [c]? Would it more likely be released than the final sound in *tack*?

f. Examine the aspiration of the initial /k/ in these words:

I	II
cáncel	canál
cátalogue	catástrophe
call	collíde
cóntract	contráct
cóllege	collégiate
córporate	coóperative
kiln	kinétic

° *Aspirated* means that the sound is released with an outrush of air. If you hold a lighted match a couple of inches in front of your mouth, it will be blown out when you pronounce *pin*. The aspirated /p/ in pin is symbolized [pʰ].

† In *released* sounds, the articulator is sharply withdrawn from the point of articulation. In this case the dorsum of the tongue is withdrawn from the velum. Compare the release of /k/ in *scat* and its lack of release in *act*. The released sound is symbolized by [˻], the unreleased by [˺]. Aspirated sounds, for example, are always released.

The /k/'s in column II are followed by reduced vowels. Are they aspirated? Under what conditions do you find initial unaspirated stops?

g. Just as no initial /k/ before a full vowel (column I in **f.**) is unaspirated, no /k/ following /s/ is aspirated. Each position, initial and medial, has its own characteristics. These two positions are said to be in *complementary distribution*. When two allophones can fill the same position, they are said to be in *free variation*. Allophones are either in complementary distribution or in free variation. Find the distribution of the two allophones of the phoneme /l/ given below by examining the sets of words in which they occur.

[l]	[ɫ]
lip	bulk
loot	full
link	milk
lie	cool

What is the distribution?

The Syllable

If puns and pig Latin prove a dim awareness of phonemes, verse proves a full awareness of syllables: syllable-counting is as old as poets and poetry. Young children are aware of syllables too; they exploit the effect of spaced-out syllables in their jeering chants (**Fred-die-is-a-fraid-y-cat**) and emphatic warnings like this one from a four-year-old, with each syllable separately accented: **You-bet-ter-not-say-that-to-mo-ther!** But syllables have fuzzy borders. One can distinguish **Ben Tover** from **bent over** by the aspirated /t/ in the first which shows that the division is /bɛn-tovər/ rather than /bɛnt-ovər/; but often the separation is impossible to locate precisely. In ordinary speech **one's own** sounds like **one zone, an ungodly** like **a nun godly, palisades** like **palace aides,** and so on. Linguists have preferred to work with units that have sharper edges.

Syllables have a typical internal structure consisting of a *nucleus,* which is a vowel or a vowellike consonant (/r/ or /l/, for example), plus one or more *satellites* in the form of consonants before or after the nucleus.

Probably the most striking thing about any language, in the impression it makes on listeners who do not understand it and notice sounds rather than meanings, is the way its syllables are built. The main difference is between harmonic and inharmonic sounds, between music and noise. A language in which the satellites are few sounds musical; one with numerous satellites, especially voiceless ones, is noisy. English stands about midway. It has syllables consisting of a nucleus alone, as in the words *oh* and *ah,* and syllables in which the nucleus is flanked by two or more satellites on each side, as in *splashed* and *sprints.*

The syllable exists mainly because language is speech. If speakers did not have to *say* their phonemes we might be able to dispense with the syllable; but the sounds of most phonemes cannot be uttered effectively by themselves. One can barely produce the sound of /g/ without a vowel before it or after it—that is, without putting it in a syllable. One can manage the sound of a /t/ by itself but too faintly for it to be heard very far away. To describe the syllable we have to tell how phonemes make it up, and an essential part of the description of phonemes is how they arrange themselves in syllables.

Not all arrangements are possible. The permitted combinations can be seen by building consonants one by one around a nucleus. Starting with *oh,* for example, and adding successively to the left, one may get *row, crow,* and *scrow;* with *a* (that is, the sound /e/) might come *lay, play,* and *splay;* or with *ill* the words *will* and *twill.* Studying many such examples would reveal something about the possible arrangements of consonants to the left of the nucleus. If there is only one it can be any consonant in the language except /ŋ/. If there are two, /l/ and /r/ occur pretty freely as the second and the stops and voiceless fricatives as the first: *truce, pry, plea, sly, free.* If there are three the first will be /s/: *splurge, stray.* But there are restrictions: no /tl/-, no /sb/-, no /sfl/-, and so on. A similar build-up will reveal the situation at the end of the syllable—for example, *oh-own-owned, bur-Bearse-burst-*

bursts. The entire structure of English syllables can be stated in a rather complex set of rules embodying classes of consonants and positions relative to the nucleus and to one another.

Not all the combinations of sounds that speakers fail to use are avoided because they are hard to say or confusing to hear, given the speech habits of the language in question. Some have just never happened to develop. No language uses all the combinations that would be possible with its phonemes. English speakers have no trouble with initial clusters like /vl/- and /šp/- —we can easily say **Vladimir,** and **He shpilled his drink** is not unknown when one has had too much of it; but they are not put to any use worth mentioning. Some day they may be. We could easily grow accustomed to /vl/- if we adopted a few more words like **Vladimir** and **Vladivostok,** as we have grown accustomed to /šl šn šm/ by borrowing words from German and Yiddish: **schlemiel, schnook, schmo,** and so forth.

The inner structure of the syllable is only half its story. The other half is the role it plays in the phonetic description of words. No word can contain fewer than one syllable—it is the smallest unit that is normally pronounced by itself. And the syllable is the field of action for the three most important ways in which the sound of words is intentionally modified. The first of these is *accent:* when we say "The word **reverberate** is accented in this sentence" we mean, as far as physical sound is concerned, that just the syllable *-ver-* is accented. The second is *expressive length:* to make the word **awful** more emphatic we drawl just the first syllable, the accented one. The third is the rise and fall of *pitch:* normally, a marked change in the direction of the pitch curve coincides with the beginning of a syllable—**Do you have to spend your money so carelessly?** shows pitch rises on **have, mon-, care-,** and **-ly.**

Units of distinctive sound do not stop with the syllable, but they do become progressively vaguer so that it gets less and less profitable to try to single them out. Above the level of the syllable is the breath group—a series of syllables spoken with one expiration of breath. It generally coincides with a particular intonation shape. After the breath group comes the phonological sentence, which some linguists like to point out, marked by a pause. From there on it is next to impossible to decide on higher phonological divisions, though they must exist in a hazy kind of way—one can usually tell, for example, when someone reading a speech has come to the end of a paragraph because he makes an extra-long pause. One reason for ending the build-up of sound at the level of the syllable is that anything higher is almost necessarily related in some way to meaning. Meaningless syllables (syllables that are not already words by themselves) are common. Breath groups are almost always arranged by speakers to fit divisions of sense, and phonological sentences even more so.

For all their importance, units of sound are fundamentally meaningless. Meaningful units are on the higher levels of language.

Exercise 6

This exercise concerns the monosyllable, a frequent form in English. Give two English words in phonemic transcription that exemplify each of the following monosyllable types.

C = consonants (/p t k b d g č ǰ f v s š z ž m n ŋ l h/)
S = semivowels = semiconsonants (/y r w/)
V = all vowels

VC	VS	SVSC
CVC	SVS	VSS
CV	SV	VSC
CVS	SVCC	CVSC
SVC	V	CSVC

chapter 4

Structure in Language:

the higher levels

The Level of Morphemes and Words

When the laboratory is supplied with subatomic particles in the form of distinctive features, atoms in the form of phonemes, and molecules in the form of syllables, what is to be done with them? One might say that the next step is to go from physics to biology, to find the cells that perform their specialized functions in the collection of muscular and other structures that make up the body.

The organic function of language is to carry meaning. Meaning must therefore have something to do with the workings of the linguistic cell. Up to now we have spoken of words as if *they* were the cells of meaning. To be precisely that, the simplest meaning would have to stand in a one-to-one relationship with a word; but this is not always true. We would like to say that *roadblock* is "a word," yet it is made up of elements that are themselves words. And certainly **un-American** is a word, yet it is made up of an independent word, **America,** plus a prefix **un-** and a suffix **-an,** for each of which we seem to discern a kind of meaning—as is quickly confirmed by listing other places where they occur: **unhealthy, unwise, unsteady; Hawaiian, Alaskan, Russian.** It hardly seems that in our dissection of cells we can stop with the word.

The apparently meaningful bits that are smaller than words are termed *morphemes*. A sentence like **Every/one / admire/s / Bill/'s / man/li/ness** breaks up into nine morphemes bunched into four words: **everyone** is a compound containing the morphemes **every** and **one** (which also happen to be words when used separately), **admires** is a verb containing the stem **admire-** and the suffix **-s** meaning 'third person singular,' and so on. The word **morpheme** itself contains **morph-** and the suffix **-eme,** which also appears in **phoneme.**

If morphemes are the minimal units of meaning, one begins to wonder what words are good for—or even what words are. Is popular thinking about words an illusion? Do we only imagine that **roadblock** is one word but **road machinery** is two?

If it is only imagination, people are strangely consistent, for nearly everyone would make this distinction between these two examples. There is pretty general agreement on whether to regard a particular segment of speech as one word, two, or more. What is it that makes us feel that certain units are somehow distinct and separable?

Linguists sometimes answer this question by defining the word as 'the smallest unit of language that can be used by itself,' that is, used to form an utterance: **Henry** (in answer to **Who was it?**), **Tomorrow** (in answer to **When are you going?**), and **Nice** (in answer to **What do you think of it?**) qualify as words under this definition. But a good many forms that we like to regard as words don't qualify: one can't make an utterance with just **the** or **from** or **and.** Either they are not words, or the separateness of words does not always go so far as potentially complete independence.

Nevertheless, there is a mark of a lower degree of independence that does correlate very closely with our notion of what constitutes a word. This is our freedom to insert, be-tween one word and the next, a vocalized hesitation — typi-cally, the sound *uh: The — uh — workman — uh — who — uh — put up — uh — that — uh — roadblock — uh — didn't — uh — leave — uh any — uh — warning-light.* The gaps agree remarkably well with our feel for separations between words. No pause can be inserted between the morphemes in *workman, roadblock, didn't,* or *warning-light.* A pause can be inserted between *the* and *workman.* The one apparent disagreement, the un-likelihood of a pause between *put* and *up,* coincides with our uncertainty about whether to regard such forms as one word or two — grammarians often call *put up, leave out, take off,* and so on "two-word verbs."

The possibility of hesitating most likely reflects the free-dom we have to insert other words at the same point. Instead of separating the words of the example with repeated *uh's* we could separate them with other words: *The careless workman there who supposedly put up just that one roadblock surely didn't dutifully leave in view any red warning-light.*

A word is evidently "something that is not to be broken up." Words are *prefabricated units.* Language in action is a process of fabrication that takes two forms: the fabrication of larger segments using words and the fabrication of the words themselves. The first we call *syntax.* It goes on whenever a speaker says anything: *I got Mary some buttered popcorn at the movies last night* is a sentence that the speaker may never have said before in his life; he throws it together out of the prefabricated units he has at hand, to fit a situation. Once said, that sentence may never again be repeated and it may well be forgotten, as if the parts were disassembled and returned to the stockroom. But the parts themselves, the prefabricated units, are not forgotten and will be used again.

But what about the fabrication of words? Obviously, this is not something that happens every time we speak. If it were, the *Oxford English Dictionary* could not tell us that *frontage* appeared for the first time in English in the seventeenth century while the words *slippage* and *roughage* appeared in the latter part of the nineteenth century. It may be hard to decide sometimes who first used a word, or where and when it was first used, and many words are doubtless created inde-pendently by more than one speaker. But that is nothing new in the history of invention. The fact remains that a word is tied to its moment in history. If something is prefabricated there must have been a time when the job was done.

Words are not the only prefabricated units, of course. There are also idioms, platitudes, and proverbs. But words are the prefabricated units of syntax. The larger prefabs do not typically become parts of larger structures but are the complete structures themselves. They tend to be sentences, not parts of sentences.

The morpheme is now a bit easier to define. It is the semi-finished material from which words are made. Semi-finished means second-hand. The times when speakers set about constructing words out of the pure raw material of phonemes and syllables are few and far between—an occasional trade name such as *Kodak* or an acronym (word made up of initial letters) like *UNESCO*—and these are almost always of one part of speech, nouns. Practically all words that are not imported bodily from some other language (this too is an abundant source) are made up of old words or their parts. Sometimes those parts are pretty well standardized, like the suffix *-ness* or the prefix *un-*. Other times they are only broken pieces that some inventive speaker manages to re-fit, like the *bumber-*, altered from *umbr-* in *umbrella,* and the *-shoot,* based on the *-chute* of *parachute,* that go to make up the word *bumbershoot.* In between are fragments of all degrees of standardized efficiency and junkyard irregularity. *Hamburger* yields *-burger,* which is reattached in *nutburger, Gaines-burger,* and *cheeseburger. Cafeteria* yields *-teria,* which is reattached in *valeteria, groceteria,* and *washateria.* Trade names make easy use of almost any fragment, like the *-roni* of *macaroni* that is reattached in *Rice-a-Roni* and *Noodle-Roni.* The fabrication may re-use elements that have been re-used many times, or it may be a one-shot affair such as the punning reference to being a member of the *lowerarchy,* with *-archy* extracted from *hierarchy.* The principle is the same. Scientists and scholars may give themselves airs with high-bred affixes borrowed from classical languages, but they are linguistically no more sophisticated than the common speakers who are satisfied with leftovers from the vernacular. The only thing a morpheme is good for is to be melted down and recast in a word.

Word-making, for all its irregularity, has two fairly well defined processes. One process uses words themselves as raw material for new words. It is called *compounding*. The other attaches a lesser morpheme — an affix — to a major morpheme — a stem, frequently a word. It is called *derivation*. **Roadblock** and **warning-light** are compounds. **Worker** is a derivative (so, probably, is **workman**, since **-man**, pronounced **m'n**, has been reduced to an affix in English). **Troubleshooter** embodies both processes, derivation in **shoot** + **-er** and compounding in **trouble** + **shooter**. An affix that is rather freely used to make new derivatives is termed *active*. When one man referred to the occupants of flying saucers as **saucerians**, he was using the active suffix **-ian**. An affix that is not freely used is *inactive*, though one can never pronounce any element completely dead. The suffix **-ate** is a Latinism that can hardly be used to make new words — until some wag comes forward with **discombobulate** and makes it stick. If a word fragment like **-burger** can be used as if it were an affix, nothing prevents any piece of a word, inactive or not, from being reused.

There are other processes. A fairly common one is *reduplication*, where the same morpheme is repeated in the same or slightly altered form: **hushhush, mishmash, helter-skelter, fiddle-faddle.**

The meanings of morphemes can vary as widely as their forms. This is to be expected of second-hand materials. When an old dress is cut down to a skirt its former function may be partly remembered, but when a remnant of it becomes a dust-cloth the old function is forgotten. Almost no morpheme is perfectly stable in meaning. The morpheme **-er** forms agentive nouns — a **builder** is one who builds, a **talker** one who talks, a **wrecker** one who wrecks; but an **undertaker** is no longer one who undertakes — the morpheme has been swallowed up in the word. The suffix **-able** suggests something on the order of 'facilitation,' but this would be hard to pin down in words as various as **charitable, likable, tangible, terrible, reputable,** and **sensible.** Language is not like arithmetic; numerical composites are strictly additive: the number 126 is an entity but it is also the exact sum of $100 + 20 + 6$. When morphemes are put together to form new words, the meanings are almost never simply additive. This is because a word is coined *after* the speaker has the meaning before him. If he can lay hold of parts whose meanings suggest the one he had in mind, so much the better, but that is not essential. The speaker who first put together the word *escapee* was not bothered by the fact that he should have said *escaper*, since *-ee* is etymologically for persons acted upon, not for persons acting. He wanted something to suggest the same "set category of persons" idea that is carried by words like *employee* and *draftee*, and he twisted *-ee* to his purpose.

The high informality of word-making in English, the clutching at almost anything to nail up a new prefab, reflects the vast expansion of our culture. A supermarket that in 1966 stocked eight thousand items and in 1971 stocks twelve thousand is one ripple in a tide of growth that carries our vocabulary along with it. We have to have names for those new items. All cultures exhibit this to some extent: the list of content-carrying words — nouns, verbs, adjectives, and most adverbs — is the one list in the catalog that has no limit. Phonemes, syllable types, rules of syntax, and certain little "function words" that will be discussed later are "closed classes" — they are almost never added to; but the major lexicon is open-ended. The relationship of morphemes to words is therefore the hardest thing in language to analyze. Asking what morphemes a word contains and what they mean is asking what the coiner of the word had in mind when he coined it and possibly what unforeseen associations it may have built up since. It is less an analytical question than a question about history.

The morpheme at best continues to live a parasitic life within the word. It remains half-alive for one speaker and dies for the next; or it may be revived by education. A child who calls a tricycle a *three-wheeled bike* and later discovers other words with the prefix *bi-* may reanalyze *bicycle* into two morphemes instead of one. Hundreds of morphemes lie half-buried in the junkheaps of the etymological past. A corner of the Latin *pre-* sticks out in words like *predict, prearrange, predetermine,* and maybe *prepare* — we sense that *pre-* here has something to do with 'before'; but in the verb *present* it is almost hidden and in *preserve, pregnant,* and *prelate* it is lost from sight. No one but an etymologist remembers what the *luke-* of *lukewarm* means (it originally signified 'luke-warm' by itself — *lukewarm* = 'lukewarmly warm').

Still, in spite of the difficulties, looking for morphemes is a necessary part of linguistic analysis. This is true partly because not all languages are quite so unsystematic (or so burdened with conflicting systems, which comes to the same thing) as English; some of them have more regular habits of word formation. It is also true because even in English there is one class of morphemes that are more orderly in their behavior.

Exercise 1

a. Test the following for the possibility of inserting hesitation sounds: *We told him to put out the lights but he didn't want to.* (It is better to repeat the whole sentence and insert only one pause at a time; otherwise the impression is distorted.) Besides *put out* is there another pair of words that is difficult, if not impossible, to break up?

b. Cite some examples of acronyms or other words that appear to have been made up directly from sounds.

c. Would you regard *mother-in-law* as a single word? What is its plural? What does this tell you about elements that can be inserted in such compound words? Is it significant that many speakers resist the correct plural and say *mother-in-laws?* Comment on the following, which is from a letter by one college professor to another: *Three potent bourbon and sodas are worth more than these few words.* Comment also on this, from a magazine: *seven Assistant Attorney Generals.*

d. List the separate meanings of the components in *short-coming, plaything, upper-case* (letter), *motorcycle, nevertheless, sleight-of-hand,* and *man-of-war.* Are we as a rule consciously aware of these meanings?

e. English makes adjectives meaning 'having the quality of' by adding *-ly* to nouns. Pick out the ones from the following list that seem abnormal to you and comment on the discrepancies: *princely, kingly, presidently, husbandly, wifely, manly, childly, womanly, soldierly, sailorly, Christianly, Mohammedanly, sonly, unclely, fatherly, brotherly, auntly, daughterly.*

Exercise 2

a. Copy the following words and place a slash between the morphemes of each. Some are composed of only one morpheme.

aw/ful   knockabout
breakfast   lovely
crystallization miraculous
deformity   nowhere
evangelical   obstinate
forgetfulness periodical
honesty   query
insincere   restaurant
jargon   satisfied
gyroscope   trimmings

If you divided **obstinate,** for example, is it clear that it really ought to be divided?

b. The word **apparently** may be divided morphemically as **apparent/ly** or as **appar/ent/ly.** What is the rationale for dividing it the second way? Can you find other words that change in the same way as do **appear** and **appar-?** Are there examples to establish **-ent-** as a morpheme?

c. In the word **their,** one might say that **thei** is a morpheme (as in **they**) and **-r** is a morpheme (as in **your**). Comment on this justification of **their** as two morphemes.

Source morphemes and system morphemes

Most morphemes are like the ones already described: bits of form and meaning that provide the stuff for an expanding lexicon. These can be called *source morphemes.* At the first moment one of them is pressed into service, we say that a new word has been created. As with other creative acts, we cannot be sure which way it is going to go. The person who first invented the expression **stir-crazy** might have said **jail-happy, cell-silly, pen-potty,** or anything else that came handy and was colorful. But once **stir-crazy** had made its bow, anyone wishing to compare two individuals in terms of this affliction was almost certain to do it in just one way: "Abe is **more stir-crazy** than Leo." The use of *more,* or of the suffix *-er* in *crazier,* is seen not as a way of making new words but as a way of doing something to the words we already have. It is manipulative, not creative. In the early part of World War II, someone might have said *The news is that Hitler threatens to blitz London* and someone else might have replied *I don't know what "blitz" means but if he ever blitzed that place he'd get blitzed right back.* The second speaker added *-ed* automatically to something he had never heard before. He did not "create" a new word but used the same word in a different form.

Morphemes such as *more, -er,* and *-ed* are of the highest importance to the language as a system and may accordingly be called *system morphemes.* By and large they do two things: they signal relationships within language, and they signal certain meanings that are so vital in communication that they have to be expressed over and over. An example of the first function is the morpheme *than* (which also happens to be a word), which simply relates the terms of a comparison: *John is older than Mary.* An example of the second function is the morpheme that pluralizes nouns. We can say, without committing ourselves as to how many dogs there were, *John suffered several dog bites.* But if we mention *dog* in the usual way we are forced to reveal whether there was one or more than one: *John was bitten by his neighbor's dog(s).* English feels that "number" is important enough to be automatically tagged to the word. Languages do not always agree on the particular kinds of meanings that are given this sort of preferential treatment but certain ones are typical: number, tense, definiteness, animateness, possession—even, in certain languages, such things as size and shape.

The two uses of system morphemes just mentioned—to signal relationships within language and to signal certain favored meanings—are usually separated by linguists but are really impossible to keep apart. *Henry's book* uses the possessive morpheme *-'s* to describe ownership, a fact of the real world. *Henry's smoking* does not use it to say that Henry owns smoking but to show that *Henry* is the grammatical subject of the verb *smoke.* The word *that* in *That's the man!,* with a pointing gesture, singles out an object in the real world. In *I didn't mean that* it refers to something just said, something in language.

The last example with *that* and the earlier one with *than* reveal that system morphemes, like source morphemes, may be whole words as well as parts of words. Both the suffix *-ed* and the word *that* are system morphemes. When we attach them, system morphemes are called *inflections*. When we leave them outside they are called *function words*. The suffixes *-s*, *-ed*, *-'s*, and *-ing* are inflections (English likes to inflect by using suffixes, but other languages may incorporate their inflections at the beginning or in the middle of words). *That, the, my, he, and, when, than,* and numerous similar forms are function words.

The difference between inflections and function words is not in what they do with meanings and relationships. They are so similar in this respect that one occasionally finds an inflection and a function word both playing the same role or even alternating with each other, like *-er* and *more* in *quicker* and *more rapidly.* The difference between them lies in their behavior as physical entities. Function words share the freedom of words. Other words may be inserted between them and the items to which they belong. Thus *the man* can be split to give *the big man, the great big man, the wonderful great big man,* and so on; *more beautiful* can have additional *more's* inserted, giving *more and more beautiful* (we cannot say *prettier and -er*); *who* can be separated fore and aft by pauses: *the man—uh—who—uh—had to leave.* Function words may be contrastively accented, which is hardly possible with inflections: we can say *Mary is happier now,* but if someone asserts that she is less happy we cannot contradict him by saying **She is happiér*—we have to say *She is móre happy.*

As mere appendages, inflections are more exposed than function words to influences from their environment. Their resistance to phonetic and analogical changes is lowered, with the result that they have many more irregularities than function words. The nature of these irregularities is the subject of the next section.

System morphemes are more stable in meaning than source morphemes. Almost always their meanings are simply additive: *dog* + *-s* gives the plural of *dog,* no more. As we have seen, this is not true of source morphemes. Take one as comparatively stable as the adverbial *-ly.* We can generally predict that when a word can be used as an adjective its adverbial counterpart in **-ly** will have only the meaning 'adverbiality' added: *an enveloping affection, She is so envelopingly affectionate.* But this is not true of *presently.* It is true of *hopefully* in *He looked at me hopefully* but not in *Hopefully there will be no more complaints.*

The distinctions among the various kinds of morphemes are summarized in the following chart.

SUMMARY CHART OF MORPHEMES

TWO KINDS OF MORPHEMES	TWO DEGREES OF INDEPENDENCE	
	Words	**Affixes**
Source morphemes	Words incorporatable in new words by COMPOUNDING (*clam + bake → clambake*) Words incorporatable in new words by DERIVATION (*push + -y → pushy*) (mis- + *fire → misfire*)	More or less active prefixes (*un-* in *un*denatured) Inactive prefixes (*di* in *di*gest) More or less active suffixes (*-able* in orbit*able*) Inactive suffixes (*-ose* in verb*ose*) Word fragments (*-burger* in cheese*burger*)
System morphemes	Function words (*the, of, which, my, when, and, if . . .*)	Inflectional suffixes (*-s, -ed, -ing . . .*)

Exercise 3

Write a passage of about thirty words. Omit the function words and give it to someone else to fill in the blanks. Rewrite it, this time omitting the content words, and give it to someone else to fill in words that make sense. Which task is more difficult?

Exercise 4

Separate the source morphemes from the system morphemes in the following sentences taken from the previous discussion. List each morpheme only once.

   a. What are words?
   b. A word is evidently something that is not broken up.
   c. Semi-finished means second-hand.
   d. The only thing a morpheme is good for is to be melted down and recast in a word.
   e. The meanings of morphemes can vary as widely as their forms.

Which group is more numerous? Which group occurs more frequently? Would you expect a different result if the corpus were much larger? Did you encounter a special problem with **is**? (Compare **works** and **has**.)

Allomorphs

System morphemes might be said to lack phonetic bulk. As a class, they are usually insignificant in terms of their small number of phonemes and their lack of stress. This leads to changes that resemble the ones already discussed in the section on allophones. We noted that the interdental [n] of **tenth** is an allophone of /n/ induced by the following interdental /θ/. Now we note that the voiceless -/s/ of **cats** and the voiced -/z/ of **dogs** are similarly induced by the preceding voiceless /t/ and voiced /g/. To state these changes calls for recognizing a new unit, the *allomorph,* which is to the morpheme what the allophone is to the phoneme. Obviously, there are disadvantages in identifying morphemes by their spellings, as we have done in a few instances. A linguistic description is better done in terms of sounds, and it happens that with system morphemes this can often be quite precise.

The 'plural' morpheme has three allomorphs:

1. After the strident consonants /s z š ž č ǰ/ it is -/əz/: *losses, roses, dishes, rouges, riches, edges, axes, adzes.*

2. After any other voiceless consonant it is -/s/: *rocks, rats, hips, cliffs, harps, runts, gulps, fists, parks.*

3. After any other voiced consonant and after any vowel it is -/z/: *tubs, rugs, heads, stoves, lathes, fools, rooms, tons, tongues, cars, elves, birds, barns, elms, toys, cows, shoes, bras.*

The allomorphs of the 'past' morpheme are also three:

1. After /t/ or /d/ it is -/əd/: *tooted, added, insisted, parted, funded, tilted, welded.*

2. After any other voiceless consonant it is -/t/: *raced, roughed, pitched, rushed, rapped, clicked, axed, rasped, parked, milked, helped, pumped, risked.*

3. After any other voiced consonant and after any vowel it is -/d/: *hummed, planed, edged, rouged, felled, banged, purred, rubbed, rigged, loved, blazed, charmed, turned, delved, filmed, curbed, sowed, defied, plowed, weighed, booed, sawed, rah-rahed.*

Statements like these take care of system morphemes as living elements of speech. The first person who made *goofed* from *goof* knew exactly what to do: the 'past' morpheme had to be pronounced -/t/. However, what sets system morphemes apart as a class—their importance to grammar—also makes it necessary to recognize forms that are no longer productive. The grammar of English has to include the past tense of all verbs in the language, not just of the ones that carry the active allomorphs -/əd t d/. How can forms like *took* from *take, sold* from *sell, blew* from *blow,* and *went* from *go* be included? Or, with the plural of nouns, how can *geese* from *goose, oxen* from *ox, insignia* from *insigne, umbones* from *umbo, sheep* from *sheep,* and *jinn* from *jinnee* be included? Many of these oddities result from a language dragging its past into its present—*oxen* is an older plural that is matched by just one other word in everyday use, **children.** Others result from foreign borrowings—for example, **data,** which is the Latin plural of **datum, stigmata,** the Greek plural of **stigma,** and **cherubim,** the Hebrew plural of **cherub.** No matter what the source, the grammar cannot overlook any form the inflections may take.

This naturally complicates the listing of allomorphs. Along with -/əz s z/, the plural morpheme must now include -/ən/ to account for **oxen,** -/ə/ to account for **insignia** (the singular is **insigne** /Insignɨ/), -/ɨm/ to account for **cherubim.** In cases like **jinn** and **data,** the plural represents a phonemic loss, which can be shown by representing the dropped element as "going to zero": /ɨ/ → /Ø/, /m/ → /Ø/. With **geese** the change to plural is internal: /u/ → /i/. With **sheep** it is nothing: /Ø/. Along with each irregularity must go a list of the forms that take it, for there is no way to predict them; they are not conditioned by their neighboring sounds.

So the level of morphemes and words is different from that of distinctive sound. The dissimilarity among allomorphs having the same function is not found among allophones: phonetic similarity is essential. How can it be said that a minus quality /m/ → /Ø/ for the plural **data** is the "same morpheme" as -/s/, -/z/, and -/əz/, which do resemble each other? Only the tight organization of the grammar permits it, the need to make inclusive statements about all the noun plurals in the language. It would seem unnecessary to go to such extremes anywhere else.

The one other area requiring similar measures is with some irregular forms to which the system morphemes themselves are attached. With very few exceptions (such as **wife** with its plural **wives** or **goose** with its **geese**), these irregularities are found in English only with verbs: **write-wrote, dig-dug, see-saw-seen, read-read** /rɛd/, **do-does-did-done,** and so forth.

Every language has a few such maverick stems and endings among its regular forms. As a rule, they are relics of older kinds of inflection which through extremely frequent use have managed to maintain themselves against the tendency of speakers to make things easy by leveling and regularizing everything. Thus, if the older form **fon** was regularized to its modern form **foes,** fewer people would notice the "mistake" than would notice it with a more frequently used word such as *oxen.* So one is regularized, just as children today regularize the past tense *did* to *doed,* and the other is kept in its old irregular form.

There are two ways of handling irregularities. One can simply view them as divisible semantically but not physically, saying that *dug* is *dig* + past and *children* is *child* + plural, or one can try to identify their parts, saying that *d-g* represents the stem and that /ɪ/ → /ʌ/, the change of /ɪ/ to /ʌ/, is an allomorph of the past morpheme. Such morpheme-chopping was once a popular pastime among linguists but is no longer in vogue. After all, if the word *decade* includes the meanings 'period,' 'ten,' and 'year' without making us feel compelled to identify each meaning with a physical segment of the word, it should be possible to regard *wrote* as a unit including 'to write' and 'past' without having to decide which part corresponds to which meaning.

What about the other set of system morphemes, the function words? They suffer from fewer irregularities, because they are less exposed to influences from their environment. What variations they undergo are mostly phonetic — predictable if we know the nature of the nearby sounds. Consider the allomorphs of the articles, definite and indefinite, outlined in the chart on page 82.

In *the man, the* is /ðə/; in *the ether* it is also sometimes /ðə/; in *the ox* it is /ðɨ/; in *I don't want just any man, I want thé man for the job,* it is /ði/. There are thus three allomorphs, two of which are unaccented, with one, /ðə/, used before consonants and sometimes before the vowel /i/, and the other, /ðɨ/, before vowels; the third, /ði/, is accented and used without regard for the following sound. (Some speakers have only two, /ðə/ and /ði/, unaccented and accented respectively; they then, as a rule, add a glottal stop after *the* whenever it appears before a vowel: *the otter* /ðəʔatər/, *the ax* /ðəʔæks/.)

The indefinite article has four allomorphs: /ə ən e æn/. The first two are unaccented, the second two accented; the first and third are used before consonants, the second and fourth before vowels: *He lives in a* /ə/ *big house; Give me an* /ən/ *orange; I don't want just á* /e/ *lawyer, I want the bést lawyer; I don't want just án* /æn/ *editor, I want the bést editor.*

ALLOMORPHS OF THE ARTICLES

the		
Unaccented	Before consonants and /i/	ðə
	Before other vowels	ðɨ
Accented		ði

a, an		
Unaccented	Before consonants	ə
	Before vowels	ən
Accented	Before consonants	e
	Before vowels	æn

Most other function words have only two allomorphs, usually depending on whether they are accented. The normal thing is for the vowel — whatever it is — in the accented form to become schwa /ə/ in the unaccented form: *He works só-o-o* /so/ *hard!* versus *Don't work so* /sə/ *hard; It's all right, bút . . . !* /bʌt/ versus *Nobody went but* /bət/ *me; I don't know the place he went to* /tu/ versus *He went to* /tə/ *Chicago.* A few function words have somewhat more drastically altered allomorphs. The negative word *not* sometimes loses its vowel completely and becomes a consonant cluster attached to an auxiliary verb; the accented *I have nót* thus turns into *I haven't* /nt/. Some of the auxiliary verbs themselves, in combination with the /nt/ allomorph of *not,* take on a different allomorph even when accented: the /du/ of *do not* becomes the /do/ of *don't;* the /wɪl/ of *will not* becomes the /wo/ of *won't.* The pronouns *he, him, his,* and *her* lose their /h/ — for example, *he* has the allomorph /hi/ in *I'll bet hé never takes no for an answer* and the allomorph /ɨ/ in *I think he did.*

Allomorphs with reduced vowels reflect the subordinate role of all system morphemes. Their job is to serve the main carriers of meaning, the "content words": to relate them, refer back to them, combine them or separate them, augment them or diminish them, substitute for them, and so on. (It is the content words that are everlastingly being added to, and they are the ones that draw on the source morphemes.) System morphemes, including function words, hover about the content words or groups of words, attaching themselves in front or behind and sometimes in the middle; they get less attention, are less clearly articulated and less frequently accented, and the reductions and losses of sounds are the consequence of their second-class citizenry.

Not that it is always easy to draw a line between content words and function words. We ordinarily think of the word *man* as a content word — certainly it is one in *Do you see that man over there?* But if in answer to *Why is he on trial?* someone says *Because he killed a man*, de-accenting *man*, then *man* is little more than 'somebody' — it is a function word filling an otherwise empty grammatical slot, and the whole idea could just as well have been expressed with *Because he did a killing.* This is the process by which the word *body* became incorporated in *everybody, somebody,* and *nobody* and by which *-man* became an unstressed suffix in *workman.*

If /ə ən e æn/ are just different ways of pronouncing the "same morpheme," then what about things like *either* pronounced /iðər/ or /ayðər/ and the word for 'dry spell' pronounced /drawθ/ and spelled *drouth* by some people but /drawt/ spelled *drought* by others? Should these variants be regarded as allomorphs too?

The answer is a matter of definition. If in describing a language a linguist wants to include more than one variety of it, he can organize the variations in terms of dialectal allomorphs (He would recognize dialectal allophones too — the ways of pronouncing or not pronouncing /r/ at the end of a syllable are a striking example.) The question of how much to include in a linguistic description calls for a bit of reflection. Every speaker has a few peculiarities of his own. These characterize his "idiolect." Every region has something that is not shared by other regions. And every age and mood has its style — a speaker may be old or young, emphatic, indifferent, domineering, subservient. Most languages have forms that differ from other forms in terms of these variables. The ideal language is a language spoken by just one person, in one frame of mind, at one time, in one place. But such a language could never be described, because some of the circumstances would change before the description was finished. Every description must be at a certain level of generality, and this is reflected in the number of variants that it embraces, whether or not they are explicitly acknowledged in the form of allo-this or allo-that. The "scale of delicacy," as British linguists term it, is infinite.

Downgrading

A language achieves near-immortality by wasting nothing, renewing and enriching itself constantly by re-using all its old material. The levels below are continually being fed by those above, somewhat like the process of decay whereby older, simpler organisms are fragmented and returned to serve as material for newer, more complex ones.

It was doubtless in this way, in some millennium long past, that a handful of once-meaningful sounds, embodying the limited repertory of ideas of a race on the threshold of multiplying its ideas and needing far more shapes of sounds to express them, were rendered meaningless in order to serve as distinctive units out of which more numerous complexes could be built: the birth first of syllables, perhaps, then of phonemes, with no sense of their own.

This reclaiming process, which can be called *downgrading*, may have happened just once in the creation of phonemes, but it goes on constantly in the sphere of source morphemes and content words. The resources for making new content words are unlimited because words themselves can be downgraded to serve as source morphemes.

Sometimes it happens accidentally. In producing sentences a speaker is not always fully conscious of the units that count as words for him. And even if he were capable of holding each one in the full glare of awareness, the same might not be true of his hearer—especially his hearer who represents the next generation of speakers. An adult offers a child some *little bits of* candies. For him, *little bits of* is analytically clear. For the child, who sees merely some small candies, it is a unit, and soon the adjective *little-bitty*, or *itty-bitty* or *itsy-bitsy* is on its way in as a synonym of *tiny*. The words have unconsciously been downgraded to source morphemes. Goods are sold *as they are* or an article is sold *as it is,* meaning 'without guarantee,' but the practice and the name for it tend to become set — *as is* enters as a new adverb, a single word that no longer changes for singular and plural. It is unlikely that many speakers nowadays when they say *old maid* think either of *old* or of *maid.* The two words that make it up have sunk below the level of words; we no longer pause between them unless we are deliberately being humorous: **She's an old — uh — maid.*[1]

Often it happens intentionally. Old words are downgraded to make new ones in a process that we have already identified as *compounding.* It has a fairly well defined set of rules. One rule prescribes how verbs and adverbs are joined, with a shift of stress, to make nouns: *flareup, countdown, teach-in.* Another prescribes compounds of verb and noun, like *killjoy, breakwater, scarecrow.* English is rich in devices for compounding. Here are some examples of compound adjectives made up in various ways:

1. Noun plus adjective: *letter-perfect, garden-fresh, kissing-sweet.*
2. Adjective plus adjective: *icy-cold, red-hot, greenish-blue.*
3. Adjective or adverb plus participle: *low-slung, quick-frozen, easy-going, slow-running.*
4. Adjective plus noun plus *-ed: half-witted, one-eyed, old-fashioned.*
5. Adjective plus noun (related to 3 and 4 but without *-ing* and *-ed*): *bonehead(ed), high-class(ed), low-budget(ed), low-cost(ing), whole-grain(ed).*
6. Noun plus verb with *-ing: man-eating, truth-telling, heart-warming.*
7. Noun plus past participle of verb: *store-bought, heaven-sent, company-built.*
8. Noun plus noun plus *-ed: fish-faced, bull-headed, bow-legged.*

This does not exhaust the ways of making adjectives, and the resources for building other compounds are just as rich.

Exercise 5

For each of the following words transcribe phonemically the singular and plural allomorphs that occur in your own speech. Consult the list of phonemes on page 291.

Word	Singular Allomorph	Plural Allomorph
life	/layf/	/layv/-(example)
thief		
path		
knife		
booth		
wolf		
leaf		
sheaf		
loaf		
sheath		

Exercise 6

a. Which form of the negative prefix (*ir-, il-, im-, in-*) is used with each of the following words (as in *ir*-redeemable)?

relevant	adequate	possible
logical	movable	admissible
modest	legal	reversible
equitable	regular	literate

b. With which sound or position of articulation is each form of the prefix used?

c. Make a rule for the allomorphs of the possessive morpheme in English, as in *Pat's, the man's, Sis's, Butch's, Madge's, the boys'*. Express your rule in terms of the phoneme that belongs in each allomorph. Then write each word in phonemic transcription.

d. List the allomorphs of the plural morpheme for each of these words (remember that what counts is sound, not spelling): *trail, ditch, mouse, antenna, man, workman, ox,* *face, desk, alga, analysis.* Do some of the words have different plurals depending on the sense?

Exercise 7

a. Explain partial downgrading in **Leave me alone** 'Don't bother me' and **Never fear** 'Don't worry.' Find other examples of such idioms — complete sentences with a meaning that deviates from the sum of the meanings of the parts.

b. Make a rule for the formation of noun compounds like **man-eater, housebreaker, storyteller, bookmaker, letter carrier.** How does the way we write these compounds sometimes suggest how far the downgrading of the component words has gone?

Exercise 8

a. Determine the morphemes in the following list of Hebrew words. Proceed by isolating the one that means 'wrote.'

katávti	'I wrote'
katávta	'you (masculine singular) wrote'
katávt	'you (feminine singular) wrote'
katáv	'he wrote'
katvá	'she wrote'
katávnu	'we wrote'
kətavtém	'you (masculine plural) wrote'
kətavtén	'you (feminine plural) wrote'
katvú	'they wrote'

b. What are the Hebrew suffixes for the following words?

I	we
you (m. s.)	you (m. pl.)
you (f. s.)	you (f. pl.)
he	they
she	

c. What are the three Hebrew allomorphs of **wrote?**

The Level of Syntax

Speakers are rather free to apply the rules of compounding. It would cause no particular surprise to hear one person ask complainingly of another *When was his most recent goof-off?* making a noun out of what already exists as a two-word verb, *to goof off.* But if he does this very often, and particularly if he creates words for which the way has not in part already been paved, the result may sound abnormal: *The royal ship-off he got was a real emotional stir-up* might be understood but the speaker would be put down as someone with strenuous mannerisms. On the other hand *Their shipping him off so royally really stirred him up emotionally* would not surprise anyone nor would—as a third possibility—*The royal send-off he got was a real emotional shake-up.*

The difference in our reactions to these sentences stems from crossing the border between morphology and syntax. In making the first sentence the speaker was behaving as if compounds could be thrown together as freely as phrases. But compounds, like other coinages, are tied to a time and a place. When they are used again they are felt to be repeated—they are additions to our vocabulary; *send-off* and *shake-up* are now stock compounds.

Phrases, unlike words, are at the level of syntax: they can be assembled at will. None of the following contain a precise term for an astronautical landing, but any one of them is suitable for referring to it:

The astronauts touched down in the vicinity of Barbados.

The astronauts came down at 6 P.M.

The astronauts let themselves down from their capsule.

The astronauts plunged down.

The astronauts got down.

The astronauts splashed down.

The fact that other things or persons have been said to touch or slip or flop down does not bar these expressions from use with astronauts. But on the morphological side there is no such freedom. The astronauts may touch down, but this is not a *touchdown,* nor is it a *comedown* nor a *letdown.* These are *terms,* preempted for other uses. To find a term for the astronauts' landing it was necessary to look elsewhere. The splash was only incidental, but *splashdown* was chosen.

Of course, phrases and even whole sentences can be frozen and then come to resemble words, as we saw with accidental compounds like *as is.* This happens especially when an occasion is oft-repeated and its phrase or sentence keeps recurring, as with *How do you do?,* which has come to be scarcely more than a synonym of *Hello.* We would call this an idiom.

Nevertheless, the essence of syntax is freedom. It is the airiest stratum of language, where elements unite and separate in the white heat of communication. The speaker has almost unlimited means at his disposal for building sentences, provided he builds them according to certain expectations of his hearer — expectations in the form of syntactic rules.

The concept that underlies all of syntax, which means etymologically 'a putting together,' is that things belonging together will appear together. The togetherness may be no more than a nearness in time if a message is spoken, a nearness in space if it is written; or it may be some kind of physical envelope, such as an intonation curve, that wraps one element up with another. Mere closeness in a series like *Sick John mad me* is enough to suggest a meaning — perhaps 'when John is sick I'm mad' — if the speakers know the separate meanings of the words and the meaning of the whole is a reasonable guess under the circumstances. Togetherness is a necessary but not a sufficient condition for syntax. Without something more, language would be intolerably ambiguous. Even with just three words side by side one needs to know how to rank them and group them.

Among the traffic signals that give this information we find the familiar function words and other system morphemes, plus such other devices as characteristic types of emphasis or pause or pitch and characteristic arrangements. Together they can be called *operators.* They tell the hearer what goes with what, how close the connection is, what is subordinate to what, where an utterance begins and ends, and so on. They are language turned inward on itself.

As was noted earlier with the possessive *'s,* not all system morphemes are pure traffic signals. Some refer to facts in the real world. The same is true of other operators such as word order: In **red brick** versus **brick red** the arrangement tells us which word is the modifier and which is the head. But in **A hundred dollars that mistake cost me!** the word order conveys an emotion; the matter-of-fact statement is **That mistake cost me a hundred dollars.**

How different operators play on different aspects of a sentence can be shown by two sets that get the same result by different means. In **I saw Mary and John together; the former was talking to the latter** the function words **former** and **latter** direct the hearer to select the first and second items just mentioned, in that order. In **I saw Mary and John together; she was talking to him** the function words **she** and **him** direct the hearer to select personal nouns with the semantic feature "female" and "male" respectively. The overall meaning of both sentences is the same.

The more complex a sentence is, the more we depend on the operators to tell us which way to go. If the operators are omitted or garbled, the total sense is lost no matter how clear the content words may be. But if the operators are preserved and nonsense words substituted for the content words, some intelligent guesses can still be made. John Algeo and Thomas Pyles illustrate both situations with the following sentences:

> Oll considerork meanork, ho mollop tharp fo concernesh bix shude largel philosophigar aspectem ith language phanse vulve increasorkrow de recent yearm engagesh sho attentuge ith scholarm.
>
> In prefarbing torming, we cannot here be pretolled with those murler dichytomical optophs of flemack which have demuggingly in arsell wems exbined the obburtion of maxans.[2]

Though in the first sentence we recognize **consider, mean, concern,** and several other familiar words, we have no idea what to do with them. We might think of a foreign language that happened to share a number of cognates with English. But with the second we are back home; perhaps it is just from some scientific treatise in an unfamiliar field; if we met the writer on the street we could pass the time of day with him.

Exercise 9

Many sentences seem alike because they do not have explicit operators to tell them apart, yet they are related to other sentences that are clearly distinguished by their operators. Consider the following example:

1. She was driven to the airport.
2. She was flown to Cuba.
3. She was opposed to the plan.

The difference between 3 and the others can be seen when we try to add a *by* phrase (*by John*)—*She was opposed to the plan by John*. The *by* phrase of agency can be thought of as a missing operator. In the following sets, pick out the sentence that does not match the two others by rewording so that one or more operators appear. For example, in *a*, see if an object can be added after the verb: He reads _____ well. In *b*, see if something can be done to the adjectives to make them explicitly modify the subject or the verb—can *-ly* be added?

a. 1. He reads well.
   2. He writes well.
   3. He seems well.

b. 1. Mary is anxious to graduate.
   2. Mary is eager to eat.
   3. Mary is easy to tease.

c. 1. The boy fell into a puddle.
   2. The tadpole turned into a frog.
   3. The family moved into a house.

d. 1. John impresses Bill as incompetent.
   2. John regards Bill as incompetent.
   3. John identifies Bill as incompetent.

e. 1. She decided to play.
   2. She wanted to sleep.
   3. She ran to school.

f. 1. They're afraid to run.
   2. They're able to play.
   3. They're ready to use.

g. 1. The doctor's house was surprising.
   2. The doctor's arrival was surprising.
   3. The doctor's departure was surprising.

h. 1. The king's banishment was unjust.
   2. The committee's appointment was unjust.
   3. The patient's complaint was unjust.

i. 1. John promised his mother to drive carefully.
   2. John persuaded his mother to drive carefully.
   3. John expected his mother to drive carefully.

Word classes

Some words can replace others without changing the structure of the sentence. If A says *Joe went to Nevada* and B replies *Joe went to California,* B shows, by de-emphasizing everything except *California,* that he intends it to be the same except for that one item. Words treated in this fashion have the same function and belong in the same class. B could have replied *Joe went from Nevada,* de-emphasizing everything but *from* which belongs to the same class as *to.*

The traditional name for classes like these is *parts of speech,* and there would be no reason to call them anything else except that the classical parts of speech have been limited to a very few broad classes — noun, verb, adjective, adverb, pronoun, preposition, interjection, and conjunction — and the term is apt to suggest that classification stops there, when actually it must go farther.

The adverb is a good example of the over-inclusiveness of the traditional classes. It is defined in grammar books as a word that "modifies a verb, an adjective, or another adverb." Yet one can easily find adverbs that fit one form of modification and not others. Take *very: He came in very fast, It's very good,* but not **He eats very; very* is obviously a modifier of other modifiers and not a modifier of verbs. Or consider *aside: He turned aside,* but not **an aside tasty food; aside* modifies only verbs. Many adverbs do straddle: *He worked unnecessarily, It is unnecessarily elaborate, They stayed unnecessarily long.* But this no more justifies ignoring the differences than one can justify lumping nouns and verbs together in a single class of "nerbs," on the strength of words like *run, walk,* *reach, play,* and *strike,* which can belong to either part of speech.

Less obvious classes can be identified by refining the same procedures that led to identifying the obvious ones. The test is whether or not an utterance is "grammatical," and its crudest application is in terms of whether something can or cannot be said. No native speaker of English accepts a sentence like **I'm going to machinery the factory,* even though it would probably be understood to mean 'I'm going to supply the factory with machinery'; but *I'm going to equip the factory* is normal. The two sentences form a minimal pair, like the ones that were useful in testing for phonemes. They mean the same, which proves that neither is rejected because it is nonsense; and they are identical in all respects except the use of one word. The trouble must lie in the use of the word *machinery.* A test frame like this confirms the suspicion that there is at least one class of words, to which *machinery* belongs, that cannot be used in the same way as the class that includes words like *equip.* The two classes are of course noun and verb.

Native speakers reject many utterances that do not violate the norms of the familiar parts of speech, and these, contrasted with similar utterances that they accept, are the key to more refined classes. Most speakers of English would approve a sentence like *The truck collision damaged the cargo* but reject one like **The truck collision damaged the driver,* though both are normal in terms of the parts of speech, with a subject noun, a transitive (object-taking) verb, and an object. The rejection obviously has something to do with the verb *damage,* for one can replace it with almost any synonym and avoid trouble: *The collision hurt the cargo (the driver), The collision harmed the cargo (the driver), The cargo (The driver) suffered as a result of the collision,* and so forth. A native speaker will soon detect what it is about *damage* that makes it so temperamental. It is normally used with inanimate objects, not with animate ones. One can damage a car, a shipment, a reputation, or a carcass, but not a whole person or whole living animal: *It damaged the beef, *It damaged the cows.* Since people are animate, *damage* is ruled out.

So it appears that there must be classes of animate nouns as distinguished from inanimate ones, and also, more than likely, classes of verbs that go only with animate or inanimate nouns, since the verb *damage* is not likely to be unique. And there must be a good deal of overlapping between classes, as the broader acceptability of *harm* and *hurt* seems to prove.

Unfortunately, what can or cannot be said, taken alone, is not a reliable test of grammatical classes. Speakers have more than one reason for rejecting utterances and it is often hard to tell them apart. Both *The eraser magnified the driver* and *The eraser magnified the cargo* are sure to be rejected. Is it because there is a class of nouns naming things that can be magnified, to which *driver* and *cargo* do not belong, or perhaps a class naming things that can magnify, to which *eraser* does not belong? Pursuing this line of reasoning might lead to a class of nouns including *microscope, reading glass, lens, beer bottle,* and a few more that could occupy the subject slot in *X magnified Y* — nouns that have nothing in common that is not shared by *eraser* except the fact that all can go with this one verb. Nothing much could be said about the object slot — one can magnify a picture, a tree, a star, a fear, or a passion. Such clues to classes are a blind alley. Apparently the basis for rejection here is different. It is *semantic incompatibility*. We chew with organs of mastication, kill with what is deadly, and magnify with what is capable of magnifying. *The eraser magnified* is rejected because the meanings — the semantic features — of *eraser* and *magnify* are not congruent with each other.

Semantic incompatibility is different from ungrammaticalness. The first depends on the meanings of individual words, the second on the behavior of classes of words. Every word has a set of features: *semantic* features, which are its individual meanings as a dictionary would define them, and *grammatical* features, which are the labels of the classes and subclasses to which it belongs. The word *boy* has "young" and "male" among its semantic features, "noun" and "countable" among its grammatical features ("countable" means that it can be pluralized: compare *poems* versus *poetries*).

If behaving as a class is what distinguishes classes, then grammatical features ought to be statements of how classes behave toward one another. One set of features of verbs should be the ways they relate to nouns. And since relationships are made explicit by system morphemes and other operators, these can be used in part to mark the classes.

So we find that the class "verb" is marked by the various ways in which its members react to system morphemes. If a word form is a verb, the following will be true, almost without exception:

1. Either it will carry no inflectional morpheme at all (this is true of the imperative or infinitive) or it will carry one of these four: past, perfective (usually *-ed* or *-en,* as in *has studied, had stolen*), third-singular present (*-s* in *works*), and *-ing* (*working*).

2. It accepts *to* and the auxiliaries *can, may, will,* and so on, before it when in the uninflected form (*to work, can work*).

3. It has an emphatic form with *do* or *did* (*He does like it, He did go there*).

More could be added, though additional hedging would be required.

Once the first class is established, others can be referred to it. Thus the features of nouns include, besides their own behavior toward system morphemes (being modified by *the* or *a,* taking as a rule some plural ending, being normally required as the last member of a prepositional phrase, and so on), a relationship of concordance with verbs: when a noun picks up a plural ending, the verb following it loses its third-singular ending if it had one: *The girl talks, The girls talk.* Adjectives in turn have their own acceptances of system morphemes plus a relation to nouns. The scheme interlocks so tightly that most classes can be identified in a variety of ways, which leaves no doubt that they exist in the language and in the minds of speakers.

Subordinate classes have fewer distinguishing marks. The class of verbs that take inanimate objects — including, besides *damage,* such verbs as *devalue, invest, publish, cash, leach, unfurl, prorogue,* and so on — reacts in a characteristic way with the function words called pronouns: *it* may be used as their object, but not *him, her, me,* or *us.* There is a class of "human" verbs, however, that can take these pronouns but not *it: convince, persuade, convict, amuse, anger, dishearten.*

Other marks of classes

English almost never marks its classes by some peculiarity of internal form. To imagine what this would be like, we could think of some sound that always appeared with nouns but never with any other class of words — say, a doubling of the first vowel and insertion of a glottal stop, so that a verb *walk* would be matched by a noun *waʔalk*, a verb *interest* by a noun *iʔinterest*, an adjective *green* by a noun *greʔeen*, and so on.

Instead, classes are marked only indirectly by the potential for combining with system morphemes or by their behavior toward one another. Nevertheless, there is at least one small tendency toward internal marking. Many verbs have final syllables that are more prominent than the final syllables of related nouns and adjectives — when the words have more than one syllable, that is. The last syllable of the adjective *intimate* has a reduced vowel, -/ət/; that of the verb *to intimate* is full, -/et/. The same change occurs in the noun-verb *prophecy* (verb spelled *-sy*) and the noun-verb *supplement.* With the noun-verb *discharge* and the noun-verb *address,* the complete shift of stress to the last syllable makes the difference all the more striking. Not all speakers agree on all items (with *graduate,* for example, some make the distinction noted here, others use -/et/ for both noun and verb), but for many of us there is a reshuffling whereby more and more nouns and verbs are distinguished in this way — a speaker who started out saying *to mánifest* may find himself saying *to manifést.* This tendency has become most entrenched in the *teach in* (verb) versus *téach-in* (noun) contrast. In itself it is little more than a curiosity in the present stage of English, but it does prove the reality of the class — speakers seem to have a feel for "verbness."

Exercise 10

a. Opposite is a list of transitive verbs. Using the first as an example, match the verbs with the noun phrases on the right to produce grammatical and acceptable sentences. You will note that although all the verbs are transitive, there are certain syntactic and semantic restrictions on what each one may be paired with. Match each verb with the appropriate numbers. (People differ in their attitudes as to the acceptability of some sentences.)

I consider	1, 3, 5, 6, 7, 10, 11, 13	1.	his abilities as a musician.
I know		2.	the daylight out of him.
I admire		3.	him impossible to comprehend.
I find		4.	very little fish.
I keep		5.	her trustworthy.
We prefer		6.	her to be trustworthy.
You terrify		7.	him president.
You eat		8.	it in the garage.
I force		9.	him stealing bread.
We'll try		10.	him to be a scholar.
We'll elect		11.	fighting policemen.
We caught		12.	myself to eat liver.
We avoid		13.	the truth.
I want		14.	to persuade him to stay.
I take		15.	no credit for this.

b. What is the difference in syntactic requirements between *consider* and *know?* (Consider the choices with 5, 6, 7, and 10 above.)

Exercise 11

In the passage following, called "Political Speech," the choice of words to fill the blanks is rather predictable if the context is known. However, if the context is unknown and one fills the blanks with random words of the proper parts of speech, the passage becomes nonsensical and sometimes funny. Games such as "Mad Libs" depend on this principle of semantic incompatibility for their special humor. In the passage, ask someone to provide you with words of the particular parts of speech that you name (these are written below the lines). Do not let him see the paragraph until he has finished. How do you account for the fact that if this exercise were done by a number of people who saw the passage as they filled in the words, they would agree on their choice of many of the words?

Ladies and gentlemen, on this _____ occasion it is a privilege to address
                                adjective

such a _____ looking group of _____. I can tell from your smil-
        adjective   _plural noun_

ing _____ that you will support my _____ program in the coming elec-
     plural noun   _adjective_

tion. I promise that, if elected there will be a _____ in every _____.
                                                  noun   _noun_

And two _____ in every garage. I want to warn you against my _____
         plural noun   _adjective_

opponent, Mr. _____. This man is nothing but a _____ _____. He
               name of person in room   _adjective_ _noun_

has a _____ character and is working _____ in glove with the criminal
       adjective   _noun_

element. If elected, I promise to eliminate vice. I will keep the _____ off
                                                                   plural noun

the city's streets. I will keep crooks from dipping their _____ in the public
                                                           plural noun

till. I promise you _____ government, _____ taxes, and _____
                     adjective   _adjective_   _adjective_

schools.

Roger Price and Leonard Stern, _Son of Mad Libs_ (Los Angeles: Price/Stern/Sloan Publishers, 1959). Copyright 1959 by Price/Stern/Sloan Publishers, Inc. Reprinted by permission of the publisher.

Tagmemes and syntagmemes

Classes of words exist to perform functions. Some classes perform only one. There is a class of correlative conjunctions, a very small class, including just the two words **and** and **or** (perhaps **either, neither, nor,** and **whether** should be added too), that serves just one purpose: to join together elements of equal rank. Usually the two things joined are themselves members of a single class: **Mary and John,** two nouns; **to be or not to be,** two verbs; **It's slimy and wet,** two adjectives.

More often, a class performs two or more functions. Then it becomes necessary to name the syntactic operations both in terms of the class that performs the function and the function that it performs. In a sentence like *The man saw the boy,* *the man* performs one function, that of subject, and *the boy* another, that of direct object. Both are nouns: an equally correct sentence is *The boy saw the man.* To describe these sentences, it is necessary to recognize noun-as-subject and noun-as-direct-object. In the sentence *The father gave the man his daughter, father* is noun-as-subject, *daughter* is noun-as-direct-object, and *man* is noun-as-indirect-object.

The combination of class and function is sometimes called a slot-class correlation, and the term for it is *tagmeme.* Tagmemes are the particles of syntax. The adjective in *one sure thing, one thing sure,* and *The thing is sure* occurs in three different tagmemes, since each of those positions represents a different function—the meanings are not the same. The adverb *clearly* in *Clearly he can't see* and *He can't see clearly* occurs in two tagmemes: adverb-as-sentence-modifier and adverb-as-verb-modifier.

As with other levels, particles are ranged in strings. A typical string in syntax is noun-as-subject plus verb plus noun-as-object: *Monkeys love bananas.* Syntactic strings are called *syntagmemes,* that is, tagmemes taken together. Besides noun-as-subject plus verb plus noun-as-object, a number of other simple sentence syntagmemes can be mentioned: noun-as-subject plus verb (*The prisoners escaped*); noun-as-subject plus linking verb plus adjective-as-complement (*Lead is soft*); interrogative pronoun-as-complement plus linking verb plus noun-as-subject (*Who is that man?,* an inversion of *That man is John*).

Syntagmemes are the different syntactical patterns that a language provides for. Besides sentence syntagmemes there are subordinate syntagmemes, like noun phrases and prepositional phrases. In the prepositional phrase *by the author* we find an additional noun tagmeme: noun-as-prepositional-object. In the noun phrase *the visible stars* we find adjective-as-premodifier, whereas in the noun phrase *the stars visible* we find adjective-as-postmodifier: the functions are different because normally the first means 'stars whose magnitude is great enough to make them visible,' while the second means 'stars that can be seen because conditions (the weather, for example) are favorable.'

Identical tagmemes can be arranged in different syntagmemes. The result then "means the same" but the "style" is different: *I didn't see John* and *John I didn't see* contain the same noun-as-direct-object, but it occurs at the end of the first sentence and at the beginning of the second. *The gate is strait* and *Strait is the gate* are different syntagmemes with identical tagmemes in reverse order.

Phrasing and embedding

The most remarkable thing about syntax is its power to use the resources of tagmemes and syntagmemes to expand the syntactical classes and make each one reflect all the others in a potentially infinite regression, like a hall of mirrors. With this power—termed *recursive power*—the class of "noun" is freed from the list of nouns that a dictionary can enumerate more or less exhaustively and is expanded to include syntagmemes of various kinds—for example:

> *Noun phrase:* **Your early arrival** would be no surprise to me.

> *Infinitive phrase:* **For you to arrive early** would be no surprise to me.

> *Gerund phrase:* **Your arriving early** would be no surprise to me.

> *Clause:* **That you should arrive early** would be no surprise to me.

The class "adjective" can be expanded to include *-ing* phrases, infinitive phrases, prepositional phrases, and clauses:

> The only river **navigable** is to the north.

> The only river **permitting navigation** is to the north.

> The only river **to be trusted for navigation** is to the north.

> The only river **for navigating** is to the north.

> The only river **that is navigable** is to the north.

This expansion of classes into strings can be called *phrasing*.

Phrasing throws the doors of language open to utterances of indefinite length by the process of *embedding*. Embedding follows automatically from phrasing in that, if a string can replace a class, the classes in that string can be replaced by other strings, their classes by still other strings, and so on:

I went {yesterday}

I went {after [somebody] telephoned me}

I went {after [somebody (special)] telephoned me}

I went {after [somebody (that I really wanted to see)] telephoned me}

I went {after [somebody (that I really wanted to see/right then/)] telephoned me}

I went {after [somebody (that I really wanted to see/as soon as I could/)] telephoned me}

There is no linguistic limit to the process, though there may be a psychological one. Most readers are annoyed at having to thread their way through embeddings as complicated as the following:

> For literary works may not vent ideas of importance if punishment of suppression be the author's or publisher's reward from juries of average men instructed to cast a ballot of indictment upon their judgment as to whether a particular work is patently offensive to, and appeals to the prurient interests of, other average men.[3]

Syntax and invention

The study of syntax has been developing so quickly in the past decade that no faithful picture of it can be drawn; the outlines change as the words are written.

If the traffic department of a large modern city wants to find out in the most painless way whether some proposed change in the direction, signaling, speed, number of lanes, and lane width of a flow of traffic will move the cars and trucks more smoothly or jam them up, it resorts to a simulation: the conditions are pre-set and a computer sends pretended vehicles along imaginary streets to reproduce the movements and interferences that would occur in reality. It is not necessary to erect the signals, re-route the lanes, and alter the face of the city to find out if the new arrangement will work.

The mechanism of syntax is like the computer. In our advance scheming for good and bad ends, we try out alternatives in a simulated program to see how close we can come to predicting what the results would be if the plans were actually carried out. In part this is possible because we can pre-set the words in the program and then sit back and watch the fun. Will the semantic features clash or blend? Will they weave themselves into amusing or startling or suggestive patterns? What we think of as the free play of ideas is to some extent pure frolicking with the semantic features of words, which the syntax of our language permits us to do.

The bars to incompatibility then are let down—but not, as a rule, those of ungrammaticalness, which correspond to the built-in characteristics of the computer: you punch this button first and turn this crank last, because the machine is made that way; but within those limits you can go where you please.

Dreams are perhaps the extreme of this free-wheeling use of language—the restraints on semantic features are lowered but most of the grammatical ones remain intact. One attested dream sequence was the following: *How to write* (not *ride*) *a creeping doorcan bicycle.* Everything here is according to rule—*how to* is a normal beginning for a set of directions, *write* follows in the normal spot for a verb, the *-ing* form *creeping* is used in its normal way as a modifier, *doorcan* is a normal compound on the order of *doorway* or *ashcan* used normally as a modifier, and *bicycle* occupies the normal slot for the noun. The design of poetry is similar, except that it is contrived and not random. The poet may even alter some of the less secure grammatical features. He is not concerned that the verb *unfurl* takes inanimate objects when he describes a lanky and attitudinizing man as *unfurling himself.*

Being able to "think together" things that do not belong together is a first step to invention. The verb *to fly* has as one of its semantic features the possession of wings. Human beings have no wings, but that was no bar to simulating them verbally and in the end concretely.

Exercise 12

a. Give two examples of each of the following syntactic strings, or *syntagmemes.*

1. Noun-as-subject and verb-as-predicate
2. Noun-as-subject, verb-as-predicate, and noun-as-object
3. Noun-as-subject, linking-verb-as-predicate, and adjective-as-complement
4. Noun-as-subject, verb-as-predicate, noun-as-indirect-object, and noun-as-direct-object
5. Interrogative pronoun-as-complement, linking-verb-as-predicate, noun-as-subject

Give another example of a syntagmeme in English.

b. Replace each numbered unit in the sentence below with a phrase or a clause.

$$\underset{1}{\text{The dog}} \ \underset{2}{\text{chased}} \ \underset{3}{\text{my car.}}$$

c. Identify the embedded sentences in the following sentence:

"A magazine the authorities considered dangerous has been suspended since its editors were arrested while they were putting out the issue that contained revelations which would have proved the authorities to be corrupt."

Begin with the sentence *A magazine has been suspended.*

Exercise 13

The following sentences are ambiguous as they stand. Rewrite them to remove the ambiguity, preserving one of the meanings. For example, in **The jockey dismounted from the horse with a smile,** the ambiguity is removed if **with a smile** is placed at the beginning: **With a smile the jockey dismounted from the horse.** You may need to expand certain syntactic classes by *phrasing.*

a. John was angry at the time.
b. Mary likes music better than Susan.
c. John and Mary visited me.
d. My father drag races with red and gold convertibles.

e. That girl's cooking made me sick.
f. John enjoys entertaining women.
g. The dress comes in pink, yellow, and green on white.
h. Draw more simple designs.
i. He composed music for a play that is hard to understand.
j. Certain reactions to given stimuli are inherent in the human animal.
k. The boy feels strange.

chapter 5

The Evolution of Language:

courses, forces, sounds, and spellings

Flux and Change

A few hours in the life of any speaker of English will turn up curiosities like the following:

He has just said *No talking aloud* but changes it to *No talking out loud.* Even though he ordinarily favors *aloud,* he realizes after the words are out that he was afraid of its being misunderstood for *allowed.*

He sees in a magazine the phrase that he had always visualized as *still and all* but had never seen written, only now it is spelled *still in all.* He realizes that for the meaning 'nevertheless' this spelling makes more sense, and wonders which is right.

These little events and millions like them are instances of language in the process of change. Whether or not they add up to any significant alteration in the language depends on how many people they affect. If enough of us are bothered by the confusion between *aloud* and *allowed,* a word may be lost. ***Still and all*** is typical of countless phrases that become stereotyped in meaning and lose the significance of their individual parts, thus creating new expressions.

Cumulative Changes

There is no question that language changes. But is this change evolutionary? Evolution implies more than a history of unrelated accidents; it implies a trend, a direction, almost a purpose. But our lives are too short for us to see this process entire. Only rarely do we glimpse in a series of changes the tokens of some larger shift. One example is what continues to happen to the adjective forms based on the names of our states. We no longer call peanuts grown in Virginia ***Virginian peanuts;*** we call them ***Virginia peanuts.*** At the same time, we unhesitatingly call pineapple grown in Hawaii ***Hawaiian pineapple.*** An earthquake in California is never a ***Californian earthquake,*** though one in Alaska might be called an ***Alaskan earthquake.*** The ***Iowan landscape*** is impossible, but the ***New Mexican landscape*** seems natural. What we are witnessing is a gradual restriction of the meaning of this form of the adjective to a person who lives in the state: an Iowan, a Californian, a Virginian. With the newest states this has not yet been fully accomplished. A few generations ago we spoke of ***Californian gold*** just as we speak of ***African gold*** today.

But if it is hard to see how language is changing now, it is easy to see how it has changed in the past. When we read a speech delivered fifty or sixty years ago, we are aware that a lot of windiness has gone out of public addresses. Reading the King James version of the Bible, and experiencing difficulty with some of its passages, we appreciate the changes in words and structure that have taken place in a little over three centuries. Most of all, when we are told that the ancestors of the English and those of the Germans spoke the same language, we can see the great change that results when a language divides.

The comparative linguist measures and codifies this kind of change by comparing a language with its earlier stages and with other languages or dialects. At present, he can do the former only in languages for which written records exist, though future linguists will have at their disposal the recordings that we are able to make of live speech. Where the written record shows, as we read it backwards, that English, say, comes to resemble German more and more, and the German record, read in reverse, shows an increasing resemblance to English, the conclusion has to be that the two languages were once the same. This tracing of languages into genealogical trees is the branch of scientific linguistics that developed first and has gone farthest. Much that could not be read in the record can nevertheless be worked out by theory with the result that a good deal is known about many prehistoric or "proto" languages of which there is no record at all.

It is the existence of systematic kinships among words in widely scattered languages that makes this sort of projection backward in time possible. Two such word families, proving that Greek, Latin, Sanskrit, Germanic, and Slavic are all descendants of a single original language or group of dialects, are those with the meanings 'brother' and 'eat'; note their similarities in the following table.

Greek	phrắtēr	édomai
Latin	frāter	edō
Sanskrit	bhrắtā	ád-mi
Old English (representing Germanic)	brōðor	etan
Old Church Slavonic (Medicval Russian)	bratŭ	jadętŭ ('they eat')

This outline and the one on page 108 are adapted from Winfred P. Lehmann, *Historical Linguistics* (New York: Holt, Rinehart and Winston, Inc., 1963), pp. 89 and 84.

Using such correspondences, comparative grammarians have reconstructed the parent language, Proto-Indo-European, and certain intermediate languages of which there was also no written record, such as Proto-Germanic. Now and then an archaeological find brings to light some written record that confirms and corrects the theoretical constructs. Greek scholars were until recently confined to texts in Classical Greek and to inscriptions when they theorized about what the language was like in the centuries before Homer. In 1953, many of their suppositions were confirmed with the deciphering of tablets from Knossus and Mycenae inscribed in a form of writing that had been called Linear B and that no one before had seriously taken to be Greek. These tablets extended the written record of Greek to 1450 B.C., four hundred years before the earliest date attributed to Homer.

The method comparative linguists use to trace kinships between languages can be illustrated by one instance on the large scale of Proto-Indo-European and by another on the smaller scale of Proto-Romance (Vulgar Latin). In both cases, the first step consists in setting side by side the obviously related forms of two or more sister languages. Suppose we want to reconstruct the verb *to be* in Proto-Indo-European. We proceed to match the forms of this verb in widely separated branches of the Indo-European family.

	Sanskrit	Lithuanian	Greek	Gothic
'I am'	ásmi	ēsmi	eimí	im
'he is'	ásti	ēsti	ésti	ist
'we are'	smás	ēsme	esmén	sijum

(The student of Latin will recognize *sum, est,* and *sumus* as forms of the same verb.) It seems obvious that forms so closely related must stem from a common ancestor, and the problem is to devise hypothetical forms that will yield each of these descendants in accordance with what is known about the historical changes in each language. If Proto-Indo-European had had the forms *ésmi, ésti,* and *smés,* these would have developed into the forms given in the table. Each change from the original is confirmed by what is known about other words—for example, all instances of assumed *e* in Proto-Indo-European have *a* in Sanskrit. There is no way to confirm the deductions positively, since Proto-Indo-European has left no records. But it is safe to say that a great deal is known about the phonemic structure of the language, if not about how the phonemes were pronounced. With Proto-Romance we are in a better position because of the abundant literature of Classical Latin. The ancestor language of the present Romance tongues of the southern half of Europe was not Classical Latin; it was a later form of the same language, but it resembled Classical Latin so closely that when a form reconstructed – projected backward in time – on the basis of known Romance forms is found to agree with a Classical Latin form or differ from it in ways that can be accounted for, it is substantially confirmed. An example is the word for the human *chest* in the Romance languages: Sardinian *pettus*, Rumanian *piépt*, Italian *pétto*, Rhaeto-Romance (Northeast Italy and Switzerland) *péč*, Old North French *píc*, Old Provençal *piéits*, Catalan *pít*, Old Spanish *pecos*. A hypothetical, Proto-Romance form *péktus* will account for all these forms in terms of the regular sound changes in each language, and *péktus* also coincides with the Classical Latin *pektus*.

One way of viewing the history of languages is deceptively simple: to take genealogy literally and diagram the developments as a genealogical tree. One diagram that has been offered for the parent stock that underlies our present Germanic languages looks like this:

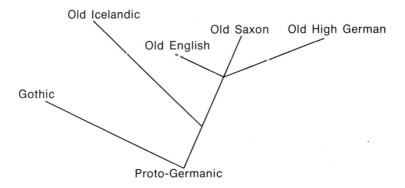

Adapted from Charles Hockett, *A Course in Modern Linguistics* (New York: Macmillan Co., 1958), p. 519.

But the tree is misleading because it suggests an abrupt separation from language to language. Our knowledge of the dialects that make up every living language tells us that the seeds of change are present even while speakers are still in active communication with one another. The striking differences between Northern and Southern dialects in our own country are sometimes inconvenient, but they do not, as a rule, seriously interfere with understanding. But let a break occur in the channel – a political separation, a migration, an invasion of a hostile people that divides the territory and cuts off one area from another—and the resulting isolation removes the checks on independent development. What were once dialects become mutually unintelligible languages.

The tree is misleading in another sense. It suggests that until a separation occurs the language remains uniform. Change, however, is unceasing. There is about as much difference between Modern English and Old English as between Modern English and Modern Dutch, after a period of more than a thousand years. But languages need not grow away from one another any faster than they change internally. Often they develop along more or less parallel lines; two languages may tend in the course of their history to lose a complicated set of inflections and so come to resemble each other more, at least in that respect, than either resembles an earlier period of itself. Moreover, always in the past and increasingly in the present, commercial and other relations have been maintained, and the closer the contact, the greater the resemblance.

Exercise 1

Consult a good dictionary or encyclopedia and indicate whether or not each of the following languages is a member of the Indo-European family. If it is, name the subfamily of Indo-European to which it belongs. Identify those languages which are no longer spoken. The ten commonly recognized subfamilies of Indo-European are: Albanian, Armenian, Balto-Slavic, Celtic, Germanic, Hellenic or Greek, Hittite or Anatolian, Indo-Iranian, Italic or Romance, and Tocharian.

Albanian	Finnish	Italian
Aramaic	Flemish	Latin
Armenian	French	Norwegian
Basque	Gothic	Pahlavi or Pahlevi
Bengali	Greek	Persian
Bulgarian	Hindi	Polish
Czech	Hindustani	Portuguese
Dutch	Hittite	Prussian
English	Hottentot	Russian
Estonian	Hungarian	Sanskrit

Exercise 2

Read the following passage from *The French Schoolemaister,* written in the sixteenth century by Claudius Desainliens (who used the pseudonym Claude Hollyband), and answer the questions that follow. You should be able to read this Early Modern English text without much difficulty. A brief lexicon is provided at the end of the selection.

I had rather thou shouldst be shent, than I should be either chid or beaten: Where haue you layde my girdle and my inckhorne? Where is my gyrkin of Spanish leather? Where be my sockes of linnen, of wollen, of clothe. Where is my cap, my hat, my coate, my cloake, my kaape, my gowne, my gloues, my mythayns, my pumpes, my mayles, my slippers, my handkarchief, my poyntes, my sachell, my penknife, and my bookes. Where is all my geare? I haue nothyng ready: I will tell my father: I will cause you to be beaten: Peter, bring me some water to wash my hands and face. I will haue no river water, for it is troubled: geue me well, or Fountayne water: take the ewre, and powre uppon my handes: powre high.

Lexicon:

shent	harmed or disgraced
girdle	belt or sash
pumpes	low-heeled, slipperlike shoes
mayles	bag
inckhorne	ink container
gyrkin	jerkin, a close-fitting waistcoat
kaape	cape
poyntes	strings or ribbons fastening the hoson to the doublet
geare	apparel
ewre	ewer, wide-mouthed pitcher or jar

a. List the words in the paragraph that are spelled differently today.

b. The speaker, Fraunces, is a young man. Are there words in the text that might lead you to think Fraunces is a woman? Find other words in the text that exist today with slightly different meanings or implications.

c. How does the *be* in "where be my sockes" differ from the *be* in "thou shouldst be shent"? What would we say today instead of "where be"?

d. Translate the entire paragraph into contemporary idiomatic English.

Forces of Change

Never a word is spoken but language becomes a bit different from what it was, however microscopically. What we say displaces what we might have said and strengthens those words at the expense of others. Not even the same sounds in the same setting are ever quite the same twice; each minute difference changes a phonetic atom here or there. We ourselves are creatures in flux. We have marvelous memories, keen hearing, and agile tongues — virtues that make language possible. But each of these has its fault. At times our memories are short, our hearing is bad, and our speech organs are clumsy. The resulting damage is always repaired somehow, but things are not quite the same afterward.

Not all the forces of change are within us. Some are imposed from without. A convicted man is thrown into a prison which has strict rules forbidding conversation at certain periods. He soon acquires the habit of speaking out of the side of his mouth and suppressing the movement of his lips. This distorts the sounds of his vowels and his labial consonants, /p b m f v/. There is little danger that prison life will affect the speaking of those on the outside, but more drastic changes in the life of a society do have their effects. When the Norman invasion brought to English many words containing the phoneme /v/ — *vile, very, vale, vain, venial, venom* — English altered its phonetic system just enough to turn the sound of [v], which it already had as an allophone of /f/, into a new phoneme. The same thing happened with /z/.

Other forces of change are neither within nor without, but exist in the language mechanism itself. When we speak, several things go on at the same time. We organize our sentences into patterns of sound that signal to the hearer how he is to decode them so as to represent the individual words and their connections in his mind. To this we add an intonation contour, with peaks of accent, to convey our feelings and our sense of the important. Around this we wrap a gestural envelope: a facial expression is often our only clue to the difference between a statement and a question. Sometimes these levels interfere with one another.

For example, a certain amount of friction exists between the generally fixed lexical stress of words and our ability to shift intonation in sentences for certain effects. A change in word stress may result, as when someone says *Now wait a MIN-ute*, shifting the accent from its normal position in *wait* to overaccent the first syllable in *minute.* One particular characteristic of intonational rhythm in English is that of placing a major accent close to the end of a sentence. Sometimes this leads to alternating pronunciations of the same word or even—with words most often used at the end of a phrase—to a permanent change. Examples are the words *detail* (pronounced *de'tail* and *detail'*) and *advertisement* (pronounced *advertise'ment* and *adver'tisement*).

It is impossible to enumerate, let alone treat, all the forces of inner and outer change. All that can be done is to identify some of the major forces and explain their effects.

Borrowing

Languages are contagious. No two can come in contact without a swift interchange between them, though often it goes more in one direction than the other. The speaker of a language regarded for any reason as socially or culturally superior does not feel under any compulsion to learn a language he encounters which is regarded as inferior, though he may condescend to pick up an occasional word that saves him the trouble of inventing one himself. That is often the fate of languages that have been brought low by conquest. English shows little trace of the dozens of Indian languages that were once—and in many cases still are—spoken between the Atlantic and Pacific, except for the numerous geographical names such as **Mississippi, Oklahoma, Topeka,** and **Shawnee,** and a few names for material objects like **tobacco, chocolate, hammock, potato, skunk, raccoon, lagniappe** — and even these were often taken through French or Spanish, which borrowed them first. Nothing so deep within the structure of the language as a pronoun or a verb ending or a phoneme or a particular order of words was affected in any serious way. On the other hand, borrowings *from* English in the lands under British and American rule have been vast, if not devastating. Words have been taken up wholesale, and here and there the deeper levels have been affected. In Chamorro, the language spoken on Guam, the phoneme /r/ has been introduced from English, as have certain consonant clusters that were not previously permitted and shifts of accent to vowels that could not formerly carry an accent.

Such changes sound more sweeping than they are. As long as a language is spoken, its core remains largely impervious to the direct impact of borrowings from another language, which is just another way of saying that the core *is* the language and that the new words that stud its outer layer have only incidentally been mined from some other language and could just as well have been taken from pure imagination, as long as they satisfied the need of the speaker to name new things and concepts. The core may eventually be eaten into, but usually that only occurs when the collision of two languages is a part of the collision of two cultures.

The deepest penetration occurs when two languages coexist on an almost equal footing, in such intimate contact that large numbers of speakers on both sides find it convenient to become bilingual. The Norman conquerors of England ended by speaking the language of the conquered, considerably modified but still more Anglo-Saxon than Gallic. Unlike the colonists in America, who encountered a widely scattered Indian population and never tried seriously to assimilate it, the Norman French moved into a compact little island where they were considerably outnumbered and set about governing rather than annihilating. The language of the field, the kitchen, and — most significantly — the nursery was English. English had already received some influence from Latin and was not, to begin with, radically different from French in its structure. Bilingualism was relatively easy, and children grew up knowing English as well as French. In time the social stigma of the language of the conquered was lost, and English triumphed.

Dialect borrowing

Loan words from a foreign language usually ride in on a kind of cultural wave. The wave may be an inpouring of commercial goods with their inventories, assembling instructions, and service manuals packed with terms that have no equivalents in the native language but must be adopted if the goods are to be put to use. Or it may be a new religion or philosophical system employing concepts difficult to translate and accordingly imported unaltered. Such borrowing is close to the top on the scale of consciousness. Most of it is premeditated. Farther down on the scale is a homelier variety: borrowing from one dialect into another. Often what the speaker borrows is a word that is already in his vocabulary but with a different pronunciation. He may assume that the unfamiliar-sounding form has a special meaning and in the process unconsciously creates a new word:

> "He's an igernut, durn fool," said the mountaineer when my sister mentioned a local character.
> "He certainly sounds ignorant," she agreed, thinking to correct his pronunciation diplomatically.
> "Oh, he ain't ignorant," the man retorted. "Lotsa folks is ignorant and can't help it. But he's just plain igernut. He don't want to learn nothin'. Them's two different words, you know."[1]

Probably no American west of the Alleghenies speaks a variety of English that is not to some extent a patchwork of dialects. One result is an enrichment of vocabulary, "doublets"—variant forms of a single word—like **girl-gal, curse-cuss, burst-bust, parcel-passel, vermin-varmint, saucy-sassy, creature-critter, ordinary-ornery, hoist-heist, rearing-rarin', shaken up/shook up, greasy-greazy, slick-sleek, stamp-stomp.**

Exercise 3

By referring to your desk dictionary, identify the etymological source of the following English words:

air	gusto	okra	tonic
babel	hallelujah	orangutan	traffic
barbecue	halo	pajama	typhoon
blouse	hustle	penguin	uvula
buffalo	ill	persimmon	veneer
bungalow	judo	polo	veranda
canasta	kabob	posse	vizier
cocoa	kamikaze	punch (drink)	wing
cola	khaki	raccoon	yacht
custom	kiosk	robot	yogurt
delivery	mammoth	shebang	zebra
guerrilla	mohair	slim	
gull	mugwump	spy	

The Confusion of Sounds

A noted philologist has said that ignorance builds a language. The majority of superficial changes in language are mistakes, born of someone's unawareness of an earlier practice or clumsiness with it and carried on by imitators who are also unaware or indifferent or who, as we saw with *ignorant* and *igernut*, unconsciously sense an advantage in the new changed form and are quick to exploit it.

The most commonplace of all mistakes are the losses, additions, and shiftings caused by some difficulty in hearing or reproducing a string of sounds. What we need is not so much a classification of mistakes as more knowledge of the physiological and psychological conditions that lead to them, for then we could predict them. But, lacking that, we must be satisfied to list a few of the things that happen.

Loss   For most Americans *láboratory* is *lábratory*, while for most Britishers it is *labóratry* (compare what the Portuguese have done to the same word stem in *Labrador*). For practically all of us the addition of *-ing* to *tickle* does not give *tickle-ing* but *tickling*, the syllabic /l/ being reduced.

When the environment of a sound makes it hard to hear, the sound is liable to be lost.

Two powerful forces making for complete loss are vowel reduction and lack of stress. In *laboratory* we can be sure that the syllable *lab-* will survive. The unstressed syllable next to it is in peril, as the pronunciation *lábratory* attests; similarly, we often hear *cabnet* for *cabinet.*

The loss of a sound or syllable generally takes place between generations. A child who says *sherf* for *sheriff* is imitating what he thinks he hears. Young children are our best harbingers of the future; they habitually drop syllables with reduced vowels: *'pression* for *expression* or *'raff* for *giraffe.* Most of our nicknames—*Fred* for *Frederick, Will* for *William, Angie* for *Angela, Chris* for *Christopher*—are the happy result of childhood's refusal to carry a burden of unnecessary syllables. We tolerate a great deal of such pruning, so long as it does not interfere too much with sense.

Assimilation   Our phonetic habits often lead to making sounds resemble each other. In *grandpa* there was first a loss, giving *granpa.* When /n/ and /p/ were thus brought together, the /n/ molded itself on the /p/, giving an /m/· *grampa.* Two sounds made on the lips are easier to pronounce together than one made with the tongue and one with the lips. This kind of change is called assimilation. The word *government* shows a series of losses and assimilations in the pronunciation of many people: *government* → *govermment* → *goverment* → *guvment* → *gubment.* Many speakers say *hap-past eight* for *half-past eight.* These are "contact" assimilations. We also find "distance" assimilations, like *Counfound it!* for *Confound it!,* where the influence of one sound on another overleaps the sounds between them. The actor who muffs his line and says *I slaw Sloane* instead of *I saw Sloane* is guilty of a distance assimilation between /s/ and /sl/.

Dissimilation   There is a tendency to avoid repeating certain sounds within a single word, which affects /r/ and /l/ especially. The word *grammar* has two /r/s, and for many speakers of Middle English this was unsatisfactory so they changed it to *glamor.* The word *purpre* also had two /r/s and was changed to *purple.* Often the dissimilation results simply in a loss; this happens for most speakers, at least part of the time, with the first /r/ of *February.*

Metathesis   A sound changes its position, as when someone intending to say **snap-shots** comes out with **snop-shats.** Usually such deviations are killed on the spot, but a few manage to survive. This is most apt to happen with combinations of sounds that are a bit difficult to say, causing many speakers to make the same adjustments. The word **uncomfortable** is commonly pronounced **uncomfterble,** with the /r/ moved to the following syllable. The clusters /ks/ and /sk/ are typical shifters. Many speakers say **ax** (**aks**) for **ask.** The two words **tax** and **task** go back to the same source and still show a certain similarity in meaning: *They taxed him with his failures = They took him to task for his failures.*

Addition   Another way of dealing with a difficult cluster is to put another sound in the middle. There was a time when many people said **ellum** for **elm,** preserving the /l/ by separating it from the /m/ by a vowel. Some speakers still say **athalete** for **athlete.** Other additions come about accidentally: the speech organs, in passing from one position to another, move through the home territory of an intermediate sound. Many English words ending in *-mble* acquired the /b/ in this way, the /m/ having originally been in direct contact with the /l/: **grumble, fumble, humble.** The /d/ of **thunder** and **tender** has a similar origin.

The ways of change are infinite. We could add more classes to the five listed above but there would be little gain in doing so. Too often, even with these few, it is impossible to decide what kind of change is occurring. Was the speaker who said *That sounds rather silted* when he meant to say *That sounds rather stilted* dissimilating the first /t/ of **stilted** from the second, or assimilating the /st/ to the /s/ of **sounds?** When we say **habmt, sebm, sebmty,** and **elebm** for **haven't, seven, seventy,** and **eleven** are we making the /v/ like the /n/ or the /n/ like the /v/? Undoubtedly we are doing both, pulling them from their old positions to a new one somewhere between.

Most confusions of sounds wither before a second speaker has a chance to pick them up. We simply reject them as foreign bodies in our language system. To have a chance for survival, many of them must tend in a common direction. The American who says **gof** for **golf** follows a pattern of previous change (**sov** for **solve**) and makes **golf** resemble highly frequent words like *cough, soft,* and *off.* In all likelihood he will not be aware of having done anything to the language.

Exercise 4

Besides changes due to cultural contacts, there are others that occur within a language and do not depend on any contact with other languages. These changes are: loss (***sherf*** for ***sheriff***), assimilation (***grampa*** for ***grandpa***), dissimilation (***purple*** for ***purpre***), metathesis (***revelant*** for ***relevant***), and addition (***ellum*** for ***elm***). The following is a list of words displaying these changes. Copy this list and place L, As, D, M, or Ad beside each word pair that displays one of these processes. Some pairs may seem to display more than one process.

a. probly for **probably**
b. sebm for **seven**
c. athalete for **athlete**
d. sump'n for **something**
e. gimmi for **give me**
f. panacake for **pancake**
g. ekscape for **escape**
h. punkin for **pumpkin**
i. idear for **idea**
j. larnyx for **larynx**

k. scant, historically from **skammt**
l. ran, historically from **arn**
m. Cuber for **Cuba**
n. nucular for **nuclear**
o. bird from Old English **bridd**
p. captol for **capitol**
q. acrosst for **across**
r. thorol for **thorough**

Can you think of influences from other words that might have helped the process along in some of these? (For example, numerous words beginning with *ex-* probably led to one of the changes here.)

Spelling Pronunciations

When someone pronounces *pulpit* to rime with *gulp it,* it is a fair inference that he did not acquire the word from hearing it. Learning words from the oral tradition offers the opportunity, though not the guarantee, of saying them as they are customarily said. Guessing at them from reading, in a language that uses an alphabetic system of writing, provides as many chances of breaking with this tradition as there are unreasonable spellings. Left to guesswork, *hypocrite* will come out sounding something like *cryolite,* and *epitome* like *metronome.* This is the penalty for not spelling them *hippocritt* and *epitomy,* for those are the more regular spellings of the sounds in question and, left on our own, we inevitably regularize.

Of course, if the writing system is not alphabetic — if it is as divorced from the sound as it is in Chinese — false associations of precisely this kind do not occur. English spelling might conceivably be so remote from pronunciation that we would throw up our hands and look for no connection at all. As it is, it is just remote enough to insure a maximum of interference between the two.

The influence of writing on the spoken language is a condition of literate societies. Universal literacy is too recent a phenomenon to reveal long-range effects, but it seems reasonable to suppose that one such effect will be to stabilize language to a certain extent. Reading is more widely shared over a longer period of time than any form of listening: we "hear" an author of a hundred years ago as clearly as we hear one today, if we read him, and the cultivation of classics insures that we will. Words, images, and turns of phrase that might otherwise pass from the scene acquire a firmer hold, and become the property of all who share the culture. The separation of societies into cultural rivulets, each going its own way, is more and more a thing of the past.

Within this broader tendency toward uniformity, spelling pronunciations are both a confirmation and a contradiction. When spellings serve as reminders of how things are pronounced today, pronunciation is less apt to change: when we see *policeman* we are not so inclined to say *pleeceman.* Here spelling is merely conservative. When spellings lead to the revival of a pronunciation long since given up, their force is not conservative but reactionary. In Southern Britain the word *often* is coming more and more to be pronounced with a [t] and with the *o* of *odd.* When a spelling leads to a pronunciation that never existed, its influence is neither conservative nor reactionary but subversive. Many words that had long been spelled and pronounced with simple *t* were respelled with **th** by writers who enjoyed showing off their etymological erudition. One by one such words have taken on a pronunciation that they never had, suggested by the **th: theater, Catholic, author, Theodore** (the nickname **Ted** persists uncorrupted). The latest addition for many speakers is **thyme.** Somehow **Thomas** managed to escape — no doubt because there were more Toms among the common speakers and fewer among the idle intelligentsia.

A number of spelling pronunciations reach back to the beginnings of general literacy. The written diphthong **oi** is often cited. One still finds now and then, in dialect writings, **jine** for **join, rile** for **roil,** and **pint** for **point.** These dialect spellings represent a pronunciation that, except for the influence of the spelling **oi,** would probably be standard today. Here are some more recent examples of changes caused by spelling pronunciations:

1. **gynecology** like **guy** rather than as in **misogynist**

2. **conjurer, constable, wont,** like **don** and **con** rather than like **son** and **honey; hover** like **rover** rather than like **cover**

3. **dour** to rime with **sour** rather than with **boor**

4. **diphtheria, naphtha, diphthong** misread as containing simple **p** instead of **ph** pronounced [f]

5. **thence, thither** to agree with **thin** and **thick** rather than with **then** and **there**

6. **chiropodist** like **cheerio**

7. **short lived** as if it had to do with the verb **live** rather than the noun **life**

The spread of popular education in America insured that spelling pronunciations would assert themselves more vigorously than in other parts of the English-speaking world.

With a little change here and a little change there, instead of spelling accommodating itself to pronunciation, pronunciation accommodates itself to spelling.

Exercise 5

The pronunciation of the following words is commonly different from what the spelling would suggest. A foreign speaker or a child not already familiar with the words from hearing them would very probably attempt to make a spelling pronunciation. After looking up the pronunciation of these words in the dictionary, transcribe in phonemic script your own pronunciation and the common spelling pronunciation. Consult the list of phonemes on page 291.

ballet
bases (pl. of basis)
cupboard
forehead
handkerchief
Lethe

necklace
palm
perusal
subtle
toward

chapter 6

The Evolution of Language:

meanings, interpretations, and adjustments

By itself, the confusion of sounds is hardly more than a problem of transmission. A few sounds are crossed up or crossed off here and there, but the main signal remains the same. The speaker who says *golf* and the one who says *gof* are saying the same word.

Matters become more complicated when, in addition to these minor mechanical shifts, there are also changes in meaning. In the first section of this chapter we shall see how meaning can bring about changes in form. In the second section, we shall see how changes result from differences in point of view between one speaker and another since each of us has his own inner world of meaning and grammar. In the third section, we shall see how the language system adjusts itself to such changes and keeps working in spite of all the mischief we make with it. Finally, we will evaluate these changes in terms of "progress."

Confusions of Sense

Confusions of sense come in two varieties: those due to knowledge and those due to ignorance. Knowing too much or too little can both cause trouble with the forms of words.

The trouble with knowing too much is that it puts at our disposal a *choice* of words, and in deciding (as a rule unconsciously, of course) among the choices we often mix words up. Whereas in the previous chapter we saw that confusions in sound occur when we have difficulty hearing or reproducing a particular sound if it comes before or after another particular sound, we now discover confusions among those sounds and others that *might* have occurred in the sentence if we had selected one synonym rather than another.

Suppose, for example, someone were about to say: **A spurious scarcity of goods led to high prices.** (**Spurious** means, in this use, 'falsely-created.') In the part of that sentence reproduced below, the vertical list of synonyms beginning with **scarcity** represents the selection of words available to the speaker which have more or less the same meaning.

A spurious (a) scarcity of goods . . .
(b) shortage
(c) sparseness
(d) lack
(e) dearth
.
.
.

If, instead of what he wanted to say, the speaker comes out with *a curious sparcity of goods,* it is because he has confused the words **spurious** and **scarcity,** two of the words which he wanted in his sentence. This is little more than metathesis. If, however, he says *a spurious sparsity,* he has said **spurious** properly, but has created in **sparsity** a combination between **scarcity** and **sparseness**—two words he might have chosen from his list of synonyms, but only one of which he could use at one time in the sentence. Indeed, so many speakers have confused these words that by now **sparsity** is recognized as a word in its own right (**sparseness** appeared in the early part of the nineteenth century, **sparsity** in the latter half).

It may well be that this process of selection is necessary for the creation of sentences. How do we think of the words we want to say? Our mental scanners seem to sweep over vast networks of words and phrases with deep and invisible connections. Normally this is done with lightning speed, but sometimes we have to make an effort to remember and then we can observe the process in slow motion. Let's say you have forgotten a certain synonym of *heartless* and *indifferent,* which you simply must have in order to make the sentence you want. First you think of something that seems altogether irrelevant: *girl who wears her heart on her sleeve.* But that leads to *impressionable, impressionable* leads to *susceptible, susceptible* leads to its negative *insusceptible,* and finally you have it: *unfeeling.* It is no wonder that confusions occur.

The resulting alterations in language may not survive the context in which they occur — like *curious sparcity* — or they may be perpetuated and even incorporated into written language — like *sparsity.*

Sparsity is an example of the most typical kind of alteration, called a *blend.*

When a member of the family says that a singer has a *sachrymose* voice, it is clear that *saccharine* has been crossed with *lachrymose.* When a motorist rails at a *blatted* bridge that is out and keeps him from crossing a stream, we dissect *blasted* and *dratted.* Where the forces that make for blending are strong enough — and they are strongest when there is already some resemblance in form in addition to the resemblance in meaning — the result is apt to be a permanent addition to the language. On reading a news dispatch one might be surprised to learn of "atrocities by *rampacious* American soldiers" and suspect a blend of *rampageous* and *rapacious,* only to discover that this blend was recorded by dictionaries half a century ago. One may even find three-way blends.

The blends most likely to stick are the ones that bring whole phrases together, for the larger the segment the less we are apt to notice and correct a slight change in it. A popular magazine says "a psychiatrist *rarely ever* saw those patients," combining *rarely* and *hardly ever.* Clauses with *if* are crossed in curious ways: "*If we all do* alike *it makes for* better relations" combines "Our all doing alike *makes for* better relations" with "*If we all do* alike relations will be better." Multiple blends can be found: *Neither candidate had any comments on the issue* combines *made any comment, had any comment to make,* and *had any opinion.*

Unconscious blending, according to one linguist, may be the source of many—if not most—of the words now listed in dictionaries with "source unknown."

It often happens that a speaker mistakes one word for another that sounds almost like it but means something quite different; when this happens, it is known as a *malapropism.* A distinguished proponent of the form is Mayor Richard Daley of Chicago, who has come out with such memorable mal-apropisms as "*harassing* the atom," and "rising to higher *platitudes* of achievement" (in the latter perhaps we can detect a blend: *planes + altitudes*). A political writer says: "A man *aggregates* to himself the right," intending *arrogates.* A weather man predicts "Five below zero, *nominally* a safe temperature for driving," intending *normally.*

The odds against widespread acceptance of any of these pieces of false coin are high, but now and then we are fooled, and where there is a hint of blending, chances of survival are better. *To careen* for *to career* meaning 'to rush headlong' is an example; since a vehicle careering down a road is apt to careen (lurch from side to side), *careen* has replaced *career* for most American speakers of English.

Exercise 1

Consulting your desk dictionary, find the sources of the following blends. In cases where the dictionary does not provide the answer, your own ingenuity will be your guide; for example, knowing *motel,* you should have no difficulty in discovering the blend in *boatel.*

  a. brunch   *h.* transistor
  b. boatel   *i.* travelogue
  c. chortle   *j.* Stewardess to passengers
  d. dumfound   on UAL flight:
  e. fantabulous   "I hope you have a
  f. medicare   pleasant *flip.*"
  g. simulcast

Exercise 2

Identify the correct forms to replace the following malapropisms.

a. The issue would be more quickly *enjoined.*
b. I made them a sincere offer but they *flaunted* it.
c. He lives in *Pepsi Cola,* Florida.
d. She couldn't get into that college because they refused to *waver* the requirement.
e. America is *compromised* of many states.

Interpretative Change

A child comes into a store on an errand for his mother, buys something, and asks, "Will I get any change back?" The storekeeper says yes and completes the transaction; he is unaware that the child understands *changeback* as a compound noun, like *turnaround, shakedown, mixup,* or *sendoff,* and that he is asking, essentially, "Will I get any *change?*" He is unaware of it, that is, until one day the child tells him tearfully, "I lost my changeback." The child's confusion in this situation is more complex than the confusion of sense that we examined in the previous section. His association of *back* with *change* is based on an interpretation of the language different from that of the storekeeper, who associates *back* with *get.* The child is mistaken in this situation, but such individual interpretations of language can be the basis for an endless process of creative change which continuously enriches the language. Our own interpretation of language will in turn help to determine how others will shape *their* language, and any bit of interpretative creativity on our part must be reckoned as a force of change. Thus, a loving father, learning of his child's amusing mistake, might start a tradition of calling change *changeback* as a joke. (The entire Compson family, in William Faulkner's *The Sound and the Fury,* call the mother's mother Damuddy—obviously a tradition that started when some child could not pronounce *Grandmother* properly).

Interpretative corrections: folk etymology

A person encounters an unfamiliar word or phrase and assumes that something else was meant by it, something with which he is familiar. He corrects it to what he thinks is right before he passes it on. Sometimes the false correction sticks. His individual interpretation or use of language may be perpetuated for the use of all speakers. The first American hearing a French trapper in Colorado refer to the **Purgatoire River** judged that what he heard was **Picket Wire** with a foreign accent. Young children often make such substitutions. For one six-year-old discussing **chicken pox** with another, the name was **chicken pots;** for the other it was **chicken fox.** To many children, on first acquaintance an **ice cream cone** is an **ice cream comb;** here the substitution of the familiar for the unfamiliar is aided by the tendency to assimilate the two nasal sounds and make **cone** end like **cream.**

It is not necessary that substitutions make sense; it is only necessary that they be familiar. But if they make some kind of sense, all the better. This is what has given the name "folk etymology" to the phenomenon: to linguists it appeared as if the "folk" were giving themselves airs as etymologists in looking for associations of meaning, analyzing a word in a spurious way. Thus, many people who heard the term **renegade** applied to some sort of outlaw and who lacked the verb **to renege** as part of their vocabularies established instead a connection with **run** and **gate** ('road, way'), for renegades were generally fugitives; **renegade** became **runagate.**

Now and then a folk etymology makes such good sense that it crowds out its rivals. The past tense form **shined** was once looked upon as substandard, but enough people have assumed that it ought to be related to the noun **shine** (as in 'to give a **shine** to') so that now it is respectable to distinguish between **The sun shone** and **He shined his shoes.**

Evidence for folk etymology is sometimes roundabout. When someone calls for a **slam** or **belt** of liquor we can guess that he has thought of **slug of liquor** as if **slug** were the **slug** of boxing and not from the Irish **slog** 'swallow.'[1] The extreme case is found where there is no difference in form at all and we are unaware of any change until we see it written. There is no audible difference between "to give something **free rein**" and "to give it **free reign**," but the latter, rather common, spelling reveals that a change in interpretation has occurred in the writer's mind.

Exercise 3

In many cases of folk etymology, the spelling of the word changes to accommodate the new sense that it is to bear. By referring to your dictionary, note the change in spelling and determine the earlier etymology of the words on the left. Select the correct earlier meaning from those in the two columns to the right.

a. hangnail	aching nail	hanging nail
b. female	a male's companion	little woman
c. shamefaced	bound by shame	face reflecting felt shame
d. crawfish	crawling fish	crab
e. greyhound	a hound	grey-colored hound
f. Jordan almond	imported almond	garden almond
g. Jerusalem artichoke	girasol	imported vegetable
h. acorn	corn	nut
i. chaise longue	lounge chair	long chair
j. couch grass	living grass	synthetic sofa cover

Fusion

When a boy of seven says *He shot his bow and arrow at me,* pronouncing *bow and arrow* as if it were *bow narrow,* we know that for him this phrase is fused so that *bow* and *arrow* are not separately meaningful.

Similarly, we use the word *skyscraper* with no consciousness of the logic that went into the fusion of *sky* and *scraper.* The two or three units in a fusion lose their original force and are reinterpreted as a single unit. The single, set meaning that it then carries is enough for us; the source no longer counts.

Fusion seems to be more prevalent in some languages than in others. Many German words, particularly nouns, are fusions for which the corresponding word in English or French would be a simple noun. The German word for *thimble, Fingerhut,* is a fusion of the words for *finger* and *hat.* The English word, *thimble,* reveals nothing about its etymological source in *thumb,* but we have no reason to believe that

Germans are any more conscious of origins with *Fingerhut* than English speakers are with *thimble.*

Once a meaning is set we forget the original associations. We may even be surprised when someone points them out to us. "It is common experience that the user undergoes a psychological shock when his attention is directed for the first time to the transparency of certain words which he has been *using* for years," one linguist points out.[2]

It is not only the underlying sense of compounds that eludes us in words like *barefaced, crackpot, telltale, stockstill,* but sometimes that of the most obvious phrases: *to be tied up* and unable to keep an appointment, *to have one's hands full* with an assignment, *to keep one's shirt on* when there is need for patience.

Fusion is not necessarily accompanied by a change in form, but it often is, and that is the best evidence of what has happened. When we say *Yes, truly* we make the comma break loud and clear; when we say *Yes, indeed* we drop it. Compounds give various signs of fusion. One is speed: the more fused it is the faster it goes; we say *borderline* more quickly than we say *border zone.* Another is vowel reduction: *mailman* is more fused for most speakers than *trashman,* with audible effects on *man.* Another is the regularizing of grammatical forms: *baby-sitted* instead of *baby-sat, pinch-hitted* and *broadcasted* as the past of *pinch-hit* and *broadcast,* and plurals like *snow mans* and *sweet tooths.* Still another is our reluctance to break up the compound. If one goes to the counter in a library, hands a borrowed book to the librarian, and asks to have it renewed because one wants to "make a *book report* on it," we can be sure that *book report* is a unit, for otherwise it would have been more natural to say "make a *report* on it" — under the circumstances, *book* is obvious.

The most extreme case of fusion, reaching so deep in history that speakers are no longer able to dissociate the elements, is that in which one of the fused parts becomes a mere attachment on the other. This is the source of many inflections, especially those of verbs. The French *finirai* 'I'll finish' was originally *finir + ai,* from Latin *finire habeo,* 'I have to finish.'

It is to our advantage that we no longer think of *chilblains* as 'blains caused by chills,' or *How do you do?* as an inquiry about how one does, of **never mind** as an injunction not to notice something. New associations create new meanings, and old meanings are a clutter.

Exercise 4

Write the words from the following phrases that demonstrate fusion. Specify the context in which you would be likely to hear them used as instances of fusion. In making your decision, apply the criteria of speed, vowel reduction, regularizing of inflection, and reluctance to separate the words.

a. law and order
     (*as used in politics*)
b. law and authority
c. black and white
d. silver and black
e. black and blue
f. bread and butter

g. butter and jam
h. life and happiness
i. life and death
j. assault and battery
k. generator and battery
l. forecasted
m. drug addict

To which stage in the child's acquisition of language can fusion be compared? (See Chapter 1.)

Change of meaning: synthesis

A first look at **ticket** and **etiquette** reveals no similarity in meaning, though the similarity in form is obvious; yet both go back to a common Germanic source that survives almost intact in the English verb **to stick.** French borrowed it to make a verb, **estiquer,** and out of that came a noun, **etiquet,** which was re-borrowed into English as **ticket**—a label or poster, something tacked up or stuck on a surface. Spanish also borrowed the French noun in the same sense to make **etiqueta,** and in the early part of the sixteenth century this was extended to posted rules of conduct at court and diplomatic functions, thus coming to mean 'the prescribed thing to do.' French borrowed back the new meaning, and it passed once more, as **etiquette,** to English. No one could have foreseen these wanderings, and the deflections of meaning would have been as hard to predict as the direction of a ricocheting bullet. To hold to this analogy for a moment, we might say that the bullet remains more or less intact, flattened a bit but in this case with the element *-tik-* still quite identifiable, while the meaning, the direction the bullet takes, reflects not only the direction it has on impact but also the surface it happens to hit. The person, the occasion, the need, the moment's fancy, all are factors that can deflect it toward the unknown. This is typical of meaning. It is far less stable than form.

A deflection in itself is not a change of meaning. It is only the raw material of change. Court ceremony called for doing things "according to the ticket," or posted rules. A ticket was still a ticket. But speakers kept hearing **You have to act according to the ticket.** Before long the "have to act" part, the notion of prescribed behavior, overshadowed the reference to written instructions, and *etiquette* took on a full-fledged new meaning. We are constantly weighing and measuring the semantic data in this way, to yield the best interpretation.

Of course, the circumstances themselves may change. Groups of speakers are exposed to altered data and forced to reinterpret accordingly. The social environment is in constant flux. Ordinarily we think of a *happening* as something accidental; but when in 1965 and 1966 these "accidents" came to be deliberately staged, *happening* began to take on somewhat the same secondary meaning as *incident.* The scientific environment is in flux too. Take the word *light.* Light was, by definition, that which made things visible. At one time such an idea as "invisible light" would have been an absurdity, like gay funeral marches or circular squares. But when the physical basis of light became known, it was natural to transfer the meaning to the *energy* that produces light, and from there to the "same" energy that lies beyond the range of the visible; with the discovery of infrared and ultraviolet, *invisible light* was no longer a mystery.

More often, it is our personal experience with words that changes their meanings. We do not encounter, or perhaps we simply ignore, part of the data. Mr. Abbott's mental computer adds up the contexts of *segregate* and Mr. Maguire's does the same, but the sum is different: Mr. Abbott is used to contexts like **Segregate the stuff from those old files before 1929 and throw it away,** while Mr. Maguire has met only references to segregating the races, and for him *to segregate* means something like having inferior accommodations for Blacks. Mr.

Abbott, afraid that Mr. Maguire and his friends will misunderstand him, begins to refrain from using **segregate** in a broader sense, which appears less and less and is finally lost.

Many of the expressions that we call idioms have acquired their meanings in the same way. When leftovers are consigned as bird feed it does not take long for the association in our minds to pass from the purpose to the value; hence **It's for the birds,** 'It's worthless.'

Our reinterpretation is often simply bound up with the passage of time. Time can either restrict the meaning or it can broaden it. During World War II a great deal was said about **postwar** conditions. Since these conditions were pretty much idealized during that period, **postwar** gradually took on the sense of 'ultra-modern,' and later, during the actual postwar period when these hopes were not realized, **postwar** continued to be used for 'ultra-modern' or 'futuristic.' In 1947 a soap company offered a **postwar kitchen** as a contest prize. But the favorable sense soon faded. Nowadays, **postwar** is associated not with the hopes but with the disappointments: **postwar conditions** of political turmoil, **postwar housing** of shoddy construction, and so on.

Our reinterpretations lead not only to the synthesizing of new meanings for old words but to the unintentional creation of new words. It is tempting to think that new words are made by sitting down and coining them. Occasionally they are, especially in the trades and sciences when a new product or compound comes along and someone has to name it. (Even this bit of linguistic novelty is not spun from air; no one can invent words as if all past linguistic experience were a blank. But the degree of originality will vary.) More generally a new word is borrowed from another language, or appears by accident (by blending, for example), or is born when originally interchangeable forms of a word acquire distinct meanings: we call this phenomenon *bifurcation.*

There comes a moment in every phonetic change when some speakers are using the older form and some the newer. This is the potential source of bifurcation. If I use **burned** as the past of the verb **to burn** and you happen to prefer **burnt,** and our conversation turns on the subject of something charred and you refer to it as burnt, I may suspect that you are in possession of a formula that I lack, whereby a thing gets burned and ends up burnt. It is as if I said to myself, "He is using a different form; it must mean something different." Perhaps my impression is supported by the length of the words—*burned* takes longer to say, it sounds like something going on, while *burnt* is short, like something finished. No more than this may be needed to balance our calculations in favor of a shift of meaning, if we start with the suspicion that any difference in form must be intentional. Our minds immediately go to work to assess the slightest difference in context or association, to interpret what the difference is.

At any moment there are probably dozens of latent distinctions in the back of our minds, ready to crystallize into unmistakable bifurcations once enough speakers develop similar leanings. Suppose you are in the habit of saying *C'mere* as a familiar way of asking someone to approach. This would be a normal phonetic reduction of *Come here* spoken on home grounds, where everyone already half-knows what is going to be said and where there is no need for ceremony. Equally normal under the same circumstances would be a sentence like *Tell her to c'mere.* But one day your friend mentions a relative in Maine or California who plans a trip but is undecided where to go, and you say *Tell her to c'mere.* Something sounds wrong, and you correct it to *Tell her to come here.* On reflection you realize that *c'mere* is not appropriate for a two-thousand-mile trip. *Come here* in the altered form *c'mere* has been reinterpreted in your mind as the kind of coming that requires no more than a trip across the hall.

Not all reassortments of meaning pass quite so unnoticed as bifurcation. It would be simpler if we could speak of conscious changes and unconscious ones, but nobody knows where to draw the line; we seem to be half-awake to what is going on about as often as we are wide awake or dead asleep. Still, some of the things that we do to meanings are closer to daylight than others, and they, as much as the forces that work in the dark, lead to reinterpretations by the speakers who come after us. Among these are certain figures of speech and certain ways of avoiding misunderstanding.

Metaphor   A couple of hundred years ago some sailor likened long-winded storytellers to spinners of yarn; generations of patient listeners have loved his idea and repeated it. This is how a figurative *He likes to spin yarns* was reinterpreted as meaning literally *He likes to tell yarns* and *yarn* became a synonym of *story.* Countless present meanings are embalmed metaphors: *to lie low, to walk out on something, to raise the roof, to go ahead full steam.* Most of our abstractions are borrowed metaphors from Greek or Latin: *to insult* means 'to jump on,' *eccentric* is 'off center.'

Euphemism   A name for something unpleasant produces the same qualms as the unpleasant thing itself, and tends to be avoided. But the time always comes, taboo or no taboo, when the thing has to be mentioned, and then we look for a milder substitute which we call a euphemism. If we hesitate to call someone a liar, *prevaricator* will do. The word *Jew* has been used unfavorably by so many of the world's big and little defamers that it is sometimes avoided even at the expense of grammar. A Sunday supplement discloses that "Refugees were aristocrats during the French Revolution and Jewish in Hitler's era" — matching the noun *aristocrats* with the adjective *Jewish.* If such a word already has some other strike against it, the result is oblivion. To refer to a woman aviator as an *aviatrix* sounds quaint nowadays, and even *actress* is sometimes dropped in favor of *actor* — mention of sex seems inappropriate except for humor or insult. This has spelled the end for the words *Jewess* and *Negress;* they join *popinjay* and *Papist* as historical relics.

Hyperbole   Offer someone his choice between a cannon and a pistol and he will choose the cannon. We strive for effect and like the word with the biggest bang. We call such language *hyperbole:* it comes from the Greek words *hyper* and *bole* meaning, literally 'a throwing beyond'; a hyperbole is an extravagant statement not meant to be taken literally. Of course, the power of a word or image derives from the powerful associations that the word has had in the past, and once these are trivialized it fizzles out. Hence the ruination of many good words. *Elegant* is only now recovering from having once been inflated to a general synonym of *excellent.* Sports writers have so long used *crippled* as an exaggerated equivalent of *lame* that for some persons *lame* is now the stronger word. *Straw potatoes* was a term once used for potatoes of the best quality grown under straw on the surface of the ground; it was vitiated by dishonest dealers who applied it to any crop of potatoes, and in the course of time was dropped.

A milder form of hyperbole consists in piling up modifiers unnecessarily. The result is that two words in themselves powerful may combine to produce a weaker effect. A *disaster* is the ultimate in mishaps, but a *serious disaster,* by trying to say more, says less.

Conflict of homonyms Some reinterpretations are the result of interference. When two words once different in form come by phonetic change to sound the same, speakers may avoid one of them lest they seem to be saying the other. Most of the time homonymy does not bother us — two identical-sounding words are tolerated because we are not really listening to the words by themselves but to the phrases that contain them, and these may be totally different; we no more avoid one because of the other that we avoid saying *Helen* because the first syllable is the same as *hell.* But sometimes the phrases too are similar, and then we are in trouble. About two centuries ago the words *queen* and *quean* coincided phonetically. *Quean* originally meant 'woman,' and as a result both words appeared in many identical phrases: *She is a queen (quean).* But *quean* had also come to be used for 'harlot.' It would have been difficult for two such words to coexist for long, and *quean* was dropped. A century ago a *saloon* was 'a large hall,' especially one for receptions or exhibits. But the proprietors of grog shops in the United States began to call their establishments saloons to raise them in the public esteem. The effect on the word, of course, was the opposite — it was lowered. As a result, one sense of the word has been relegated to history (including television westerns) and the other has been replaced by the French cognate *salon.*

Conflict of synonyms As we saw in the case of *burned* and *burnt,* reinterpretation usually has the effect of diversifying meanings. Sometimes, however, reinterpretation may have just the opposite effect, eliminating rather than creating a distinction; this may even result in the loss of one of the now synonymous words from the language. For example, the Old English word for the left-hand side of a ship looking forward was *backboard,* but there was also another: *ladeborde,* possibly meaning 'lading or loading side.' In time the latter was reinterpreted to eliminate any reference to loading, and the two words became synonymous. *Ladeborde* was transformed into **larboard,** perhaps to match **starboard,** and **backboard** fell out of usage.

The subsequent history of **larboard** is one of conflict of near-homonyms: eventually, their similarity proved to be a nuisance, not unlike the problem of a driver asking his companion, who is watching the signs, whether to turn left and getting the reply **Right,** meaning 'That's correct.' There must have been quite a few nautical accidents before a newly reinterpreted word, **port,** entered the competition and eliminated **larboard.**

Exercise 5

By resorting to a thesaurus or a synonym list (such as *Webster's New Dictionary of Synonyms*), find words that might be applied to the same person by two other individuals, one viewing the person or trait favorably, the other unfavorably. As you complete these, consider whether the words have always had a positive or negative connotation. The etymological information in the dictionary will be helpful in most cases.

   Trait
   (neutral)

a. liberal   *example* (unfavorable = **pinko;** favorable = **progressive**)
b. careful
c. saves money
d. loves his country
e. reserved
f. independent
g. resolute
h. levelheaded
i. phlegmatic

Exercise 6

Expansion, the widening of the scope of meaning, is also called *generalization. Restriction,* a narrowing of scope of meaning, is also called *specialization.* The word **dog** (Middle English **dogge**) once referred only to dogs of native breed, whereas *hound* (Old English *hund,* akin to German *Hund*) was the general term for all dogs. The word *dog* has generalized while *hound* has specialized. With the aid of your desk dictionary, determine which of the two processes each of the following words has undergone. Write E or R to denote the process, and specify the earlier meaning.

meat	fee
layman	wealth
deer	meander
assassin	doctor
cattle	affection
diaper	bonfire
zest	mansion
fable	thing

Exercise 7

Group I is a list of words that are related to the words in group II. They not only look alike but are also of the same origin. Like *burned-burnt* and *struck-stricken,* they are examples of bifurcation. In some cases the distinction in meaning that developed was subtle; in others a similarity of meaning is apparent only through the words' etymologies. Pair the words in I with their etymologically related words in II, and give the form they go back to.

I.				II.	
chamber	host	pauper		poor	guest
chart	hostel	poison		fragile	grammar
dike	hotel	royal		shirt	card
frail	leal	shatter		camera	loyal
glamor	legal	skirt		scatter	potion
hospitality	major			ditch	hospital
				regal	mayor

Exercise 8

The words *egregious, dependent,* and *precocious* are of metaphorical origin in Latin with the meanings of 'outside the herd,' 'hanging from,' and 'ripe before the natural time' respectively. Specify the metaphors in the following expressions.

a. **blanket** legislation	*f.* **foot** of a mountain
b. a **dull** speaker	*g.* wage **freeze**
c. a **sharp** rebuke	*h.* **goose** step
d. wage **ceiling**	*i.* **rat** race
e. **grasp** a meaning	*j.* road **bottleneck**

Exercise 9

a. How many euphemisms can you think of that mean 'insane'?

b. Are there as many euphemistic expressions for 'nausea'? Are they as elaborate? Discuss the implications of your observations.

Exercise 10

a. Look up the etymologies of the words **rogue, mischievous, naughty** and **rascal**. In light of what you find, comment on the change in usage today.

b. **Awfully** is often used as an adverb in a sense approximately the same as **very**. What is its original meaning? List some other hyperboles which have approximately this same meaning.

c. Which of the following words are examples of hyperbole? **certainly, remarkable, carefully, charming, excessively, amiable, outasight, shocking, enormous, incredible.** Remember that in hyperbole the figurative meaning of the word is an exaggeration.

Exercise 11

In the Scottish dialect, the common word for **ear** is **lug.** The word **near** (Old English **neora**), which existed in standard English until the eighteenth century, was used as the word for **kidney.** Since we still have both **ear** and **near** in Modern English, why was one changed? Note that in the Scottish dialect **ear** was replaced, and in the standard English **near** was replaced. (Consider the parts of speech.) What phonetic fact might have served to intensify the need for a change in form?

Exercise 12

The present meaning of the first word in each pair below was shared by the other member at one time. But when there is a distinction in form, language makes use of it with a distinction in meaning. Specify what has happened to the meaning of each word.

   a. animal, deer (German *Tier*)
   b. chair, stool (German *Stuhl*)
   c. girl, maid (German *Mädchen*)
   d. bird, fowl (German *Vogel*)
   e. boy, knave (German *Knabe*)

Change of pattern: analogy and analysis

After a child has heard innumerable combinations like *the man, the fence, the people, the bag, the lights,* he concludes — not consciously perhaps — that a definite noun phrase is formed by *the* plus a noun; give him a noun that he has never heard before and he will try *the* with it — this is a rule of his grammar.

Analogy, multiplied over and over, is the process by which a grammatical rule is formed. The same process appears in word formation, and there it can be studied in sharper outline because the result is often achieved in a single act of creation. A speaker familiar with *macadamize* from *Macadam, mesmerize* from *Mesmer,* and *Hooverize* from *Hoover* sets up a proportion in his mind: *Mesmer* is to *mesmerize* as *Hitler* is to *X,* giving *Hitlerize.* This is not a fully operative rule of grammar, for we do not attach *-ize* to proper names at will; there is no *Churchillize, de Gaulleize,* or *Nixonize.* But the rule of grammar starts with the same kind of proportion and differs only in being enormously extended — not to a few items but to a whole class. *The* goes with the *class* of nouns. If after coining *Hitlerize* the coiner goes on to say *Hitlerized* and *Hitlerizing* he is extending an analogy that already embraces every member of the class of verbs: their participles are formed by adding *-ed* and *-ing.* Of course, it is part of the process to reveal the classes too: items that behave similarly in these analogical proportions are members of the same class.

Grammatical rules call for digesting such enormous amounts of widely available data that there is not much room for differences between one person and another. It is inconceivable that any two native speakers of English would not have as part of their internal grammar the same rule for forming noun phrases with *the.* Still, deviations are possible on a small scale. Speakers may agree by and large on the rules and classes, but disagree here and there on what words or expressions belong to what classes. For example, we have in English grammar the opposing classes "human" and "nonhuman." This distinction is revealed in numerous ways, among them by the interrogative pronouns: "**Who** was it, John or Mary?"; "**What** was it, the clock or the radio?"

The two classes, human and nonhuman, impose subtle restrictions on the way verbs and nouns may combine, even when meanings seem to be the same: *He grew his corn* but *He raised his children.* A speaker who has not heard enough examples of such distinctions to be aware that there is a logic to them may dispense with the accompanying grammatical distinction. For instance, a very small child might say, "The mother grows her children." If enough speakers do this with enough different items, the categories of human and nonhuman will be blurred.

It may also happen that two classes overlap so extensively that a time may come when it seems more logical just to throw them together, making a few minor adjustments. We have in English a class of uninflected verbs that take the infinitive with *to* as their complement: "Help me *to do* it"; "Force him *to pay.*" Opposite this class stands another that takes complements in *-ing:* "Restrain him *from attacking*"; "Prevent him *from leaving*"; "Refrain *from smoking.*"

Looking at these examples we are tempted to make exactly the generalization that many speakers do make: that *to* and *from* mean the same here as everywhere else — *to* refers to promoting something, to moving toward it, and *from* refers to avoiding something, to moving away from it. So the traditional use of *to* in *Forbid him to speak* gives way to *from* in *Forbid him from speaking.* In time perhaps this will spread, with *He refuses to cooperate* becoming *He refuses from cooperating,* and *He neglected to pay* becoming *He neglected from paying.*

It is evident from these examples that we are constantly at work endeavoring to bring order into an otherwise chaotic un-system of individual words and phrases. The linguist ferrets out the formulas and states them as grammatical rules, but ordinary speakers create them. Although at the core of its grammar language is almost immovably regular, at the edges it defies rigid formulation and mocks all rules with a host of exceptions. Indeed, if a language could be subjected to an overall system such as Esperanto or Basic English, it would still spiral off sooner or later like a cloud of gas from the sun.

Exercise 13

Suppose the following words came into English usage. Not having heard the plural of the nouns or the past of the verbs, you would probably form the plural and the past in a way that most other speakers of English would. Write the plural or the past for each of the following words:

bront	meaning	'spider'
wug	meaning	'silver jug'
laysh	meaning	'joy'
mank	meaning	'to hunt'
gade	meaning	'to worry'
ludge	meaning	'to move'

For the noun plurals, you probably selected an allomorph of the plural morpheme, namely, /s z əz/; for the past, the choice was among the past allomorphs /t d əd/. Survivals such as the historical plural forms in *oxen, brethren, geese, mice,* and *sheep,* or new verbs that change the internal vowel to form the past and the past participle as in *sink-sank-sunk* are not prevalent nowadays. What is the most prevalent ending for the past participle?

Most readers would agree on the pronunciation of the fictitious words. Why? What process is involved?

Compensatory Change

We have examined a variety of small and medium-sized forces of change. Do these scattered gains and losses and minor realignments add up to something? Clearly, if changes do not cancel out one another, over the years a movement in a set direction ought to become visible, a slow but engulfing transformation that alters the physiognomy of the language, setting it off from others: "German differs from English in the freedom with which it forms compounds"; "Czech differs from English in the ease with which it shifts the position of words to gain emphasis"; "French differs from English in its comparative reluctance to put a major accent anywhere but at the end of a phrase." These are statistical differences, not absolute ones; every language is such a melange that one can find examples of practically anything in it; but the relative amounts fluctuate, creating a distinctive flavor for each language, an impression that our ear catches and that tells us when a particular language is being spoken even when we cannot understand it.

The linguist Edward Sapir referred to the gradual process by which these different proportions were achieved in each language as "drift." As an example of drift, let us consider the "slope," as Sapir would have called it, that is manifested by word order in English.

As any high-school student of Latin will tell you, the arrangement of words in Latin is comparatively "free." As far as the most vital part of the message is concerned—the bare facts of who does what to whom and when—it makes little difference whether one uses **Pater puellam amat, Pater amat puellam,** or **Puellam amat pater.** The form of the words—declension of the nouns and conjugation of the verbs—puts them in their proper relationship. No such freedom exists in Modern English. **Father loves daughter** and **Daughter loves father** do not mean the same, and *** Father daughter loves** is nonsense.

Old English was different. It had a system of case endings and verbal inflections much like that of Latin, providing the hearer with the clues he needed to make the right word-to-word connections and leaving the order of words comparatively free. But between the tenth and the fourteenth centuries most of the inflections were lost. In part, at least, this was the result of the Scandinavian invasion and settlement of parts of England, which brought speakers of two Germanic languages in close contact with one another. For a foreigner the case endings and verbal inflections are, next to the brute memorization of vocabulary itself, the hardest things to learn. One can guess at syntax. *People many candy ate* is not English, but if you heard it you would probably take it to mean 'Many people ate candy' — and the sounds can be mastered in a few days; but inflectional endings are infuriatingly arbitrary, especially those of the "irregular verbs" most often used. We can imagine a Dane communicating with a speaker of Old English and trying to make himself understood with the bare stems of words shared by their two languages. One thing that no doubt aided comprehension was a particular sentence order — probably that of subject-verb-object — already so highly favored that both speakers could comfortably use the first noun as subject even if it lacked the proper ending.

The second event that limited the freedom of English word order was the Norman Conquest. The Norman French spoke a language much less closely related to English than that of the Danes. They contributed hosts of new words not easily fitted with English sounds or English inflections.

To compensate, English reorganized itself both phonetically and grammatically. On the phonetic side, one major problem was that of stress. English words were typically stressed on the first syllable, French words on the last. The result of the blending was a new stress system in which the old rule of stressing the first syllable was partly relaxed. English now has a fairly stable pattern of nouns like *mascot, creole, format, topaz,* and *furlong,* where the typical stress on the first syllable has asserted itself but the former stress can still be discerned in the full vowel of the second syllable. A more important result is that the breakup of the old rigidity has made possible the growing distinction between nouns, with stress on the first syllable, and verbs, with stress on the last. Most people now say *cómbat* for the noun, *combát* for the verb. Other examples are *áddress, addréss; súrvey, survéy; álly, allý.*

The reorganization of grammar was equally sweeping. When the Old English inflectional endings gave way, their functions were largely taken over by prepositions and word order. Instead of determining the nominative case by an ending, we now determine it by its relative position — it is the noun or pronoun immediately preceding the verb, the **John** of the utterances **John can see Mary, Mary John can see** ('As for Mary, John can see her'), **What John can see.** Instead of marking the indirect object by an ending, we now mark it by its position relative to the direct object: **John gave the dog the fish; Show me it.**

The disadvantage of the English system of word order is difficult to see if we think of the word order of Latin and Old English as entirely "free." **Pater filiam amat** and **Pater amat filiam** do not really mean the same thing. The first answers the question "What is the father's attitude toward his daughter?" (It is one of *love* — the pivot word, **amat,** comes last.) The second answers the question "Toward whom does the father manifest love?" (Toward his *daughter* — again the pivot word comes last.) The word order told something more than who did what to whom. If this seems too subtle a distinction to bother with, the fact is that English, in spite of its relatively rigid word order, still bothers with it on a sizable scale. We are still eager to put the pivot in the end position, if we can. One place where it is possible, in fact quite easy, is in the order of clauses: **After he ate he left the house** answers the question, "What did he do after he ate?"; **He left the house after he ate** answers the question "When did he leave the house?" The pivot expression comes last. A nicer example is the "introduction," where we are presenting something for the first time on the mental scene: **Around the corner ran two dogs** brings the dogs into view more effectively than does **Two dogs ran around the corner.** So with **Into my face blew a gust of wind, Over the radio came an alarm, Out of the night sounded a scream.**

Many languages use this device of putting the known first and the unknown or unexpected last. English must resort to various stratagems to communicate the sentence dynamism that has been partially lost by the stiffening of word order, and these are among the factors in the distinctive syntactic appearance of English.

One such stratagem of English syntax is that it makes a heavier investment in the passive voice. Suppose we have a sentence like **Goethals built the Canal.** This serves very well in response to "Tell us about Goethals," but less efficiently for "Tell us about the Canal"—for the latter, we are apt to say, "Well, *it was built* by Goethals, it took ten years to build," and so on. Had it not been for the loss of inflections, we might today be saying something like *Built it Goethals.*

Another device is an increase in the number of sentences with indefinite subjects. To answer "What's a haberdashery?" one might say, "In the United States, it is a place where *they sell* (or *you buy*) men's clothes," with indefinite *they* or *you.* English sentence structure forces us to express a subject, but we have no reason to mention any particular one. The passive voice, which might otherwise enable us to eliminate the doer of the action altogether (*clothes are sold*—we don't have to say by whom), will not work, because it prevents us from putting *clothes* where we want it, at the end—we can't say *where are sold clothes.*

A third recourse is the greater reliance on intonation. In place of *It was built by Goethals,* we could say, putting the kind of accent on *Goethals* that calls for raising it to the highest pitch,

$$\text{We}^{\text{ll,}}\ \text{G}^{\text{o}^{\text{e}}}\text{thals}\ \text{built}\ \text{i}^{\text{t}}\cdots$$

And with the *clothes* example we could do the same, now using the passive voice for the sake of its actor-eliminating function:

$$\text{It's a }^{\text{place}}\text{where}^{\text{men's}^{\text{clothes}}}\ _{\text{are sold.}}$$

Written English, of course, lacks this last resource. One result is that the pivot word of a sentence cannot be highlighted by a freely-placed intonational peak. To make up for this, writers tend to do the next best thing and put it as close to the end of the sentence as possible, which is where speakers put the peak anyway when they have no special plans for it. Readers come to expect it there and are confused if it is placed anywhere else. In answer to *Couldn't you tell Jane by her green dress?* if we wrote *Mary wore the green dress* we would probably be misunderstood, though in speech

$$M^a$$
$$ry \ wore \ the \ ^{green}$$
$$dres^{s.}$$

would be perfectly intelligible. In writing we must put *The green dress was worn by Mary* (or use another syntactic trick to show where the highest pitch comes: *It was Mary who wore the green dress*).

Exercise 14

If the sentences *I saw the boy* and *George tore the boy's book* are combined into *I saw the boy whose book George tore,* the subject-verb-object order of the second sentence is changed in the combined sentence to object-subject-verb. Give other examples of such inverted order.

Exercise 15

When the accent sign ^ occurs over a French vowel, it often signifies the loss of a following *s* from an older form. Give the English cognate which has preserved the following *s.* Give the Spanish and Latin cognate in the last two words.

fête *(example)* fest, feast	hôtel
île (in spelling)	hôte
forêt	côte
conquête	mômo (Spanish)
bête	nôtre (Latin)

Progress

To speak of "the forces of change" is to picture them as beyond human control. It is important to recall, however, that everything in language is manmade.

The area where creativity is most obvious is that of the invention of new words. We know a little about composition as a source—the combining of words to make a word, such as **wave** + **length** to give **wavelength**—and about derivation—the addition of affixes to stems such as **auto-** + **intoxication** to give **autointoxication.** But about other kinds of change that might be brought about intentionally, such as what resources are available for making a new grammatical contrast should the need arise or for constituting a new phoneme or salvaging an old one, we shall continue to be wise after the fact for some time to come.

In Chapters 10 and 11 we shall meet again, in a different guise, the problem of whether men control language or language controls men. For the present, we shall ask a very general question: Is change for the good (which it ought to be, if human beings are to guide it and guide it sensibly)? We like to think of ourselves as moving onward and upward. Is there evidence that the broad shifts in form that language undergoes over long periods of time betoken progress toward a "better" state?

To become better later implies that something must have been worse before, and this suggests that we ought to be able to look over our language and find flaws in it. We say, "Of course—look at English spelling. What a mess!" But spelling is comparatively exterior to language as a system of spoken communication, and faults of a different sort make better examples.

Pronunciation is hard to judge, because speakers sail over difficult combinations of sounds without noticing them. Yet some combinations are undeniably more difficult to pronounce than others: **mulcts** and **bursts,** for example.

At the level of words, most of us feel frustrated at one time or another because we are unable to get a convenient term for our meaning. Usually this is just because we forget, but sometimes the lack is real and the fault is not ours. We even make jokes about some deficiencies, such as the favorite of old-time vaudevillians: **Take one pill three times a day.** There is no single satisfactory word for "one's given name": we have to use a phrase. Usually the circumstances and the context conceal the bad coin so that we are unaware of it until some finicky speaker insists on his due, like the jaywalker who told the judge that the sign said **Don't walk** and that he had a perfect right to run; there is no one term in English that means "to locomote with the feet."

But lack of particular words is hardly more than a blemish on the surface of something with strata as deep as those of language. A bit farther down we encounter a defect that caused us no end of struggle when we were children (and would infuriate us now if we were learning English as a foreign language)—the lack of consistency in the forms of various classes of words. There would be advantages if all verbs, for example, were regular, on the model of **like-liked-liked, hate-hated-hated,** rather than **do-did-done, see-saw-seen, sell-sold-sold;** and many verbs have in fact regularized themselves, for example **work,** which has discarded **wrought** in favor of **worked.** But quite a few have gone in the other direction, **digged** turning into **dug, sticked** into **stuck,** and, for many speakers, **dived** into **dove.** The difficulty with "progress" in these morphological caverns is that rival standards are set up: while one speaker is busy trying to level **sped** into **speeded,** another is trying to level **speeded** into **sped,** and a third, wondering what the argument is about and offered a choice between them, blithely uses them both with a difference in meaning, thereby destroying any chance of eliminating the inconsistency (**He sped down the road** 'went fast'; **He speeded down the road** 'drove his car fast'). The would-be regularizers unconsciously defeat each other.

A language, then, has a hard time achieving consistency. To the extent that it succeeds, it makes progress of a sort, but by an outside, objective standard it is rather sterile progress, like repairing an old organism instead of evolving a new one. Nevertheless, this kind of progress is fascinating to watch, for it gives us our best understanding of language as a system —an integral whole in which nothing can happen in one chamber without echoing in another. An example often quoted is the phenomenon known as the Great English Vowel Shift. Somewhere in the Middle English period, speakers began to alter the sounds of the long vowels, pronouncing them with a higher position of the tongue. It probably started with just one of them, but that set off a chain reaction: as the /a/ of **name,** for example, was pushed up into the territory of the /e/ (producing the modern pronunciation /nem/), /e/ moved toward /i/ to make room, as in the shift of Middle English *shene* (/e/) to Modern English *sheen* (/i/); this threatened /i/, but /i/ was already the highest vowel and could not easily move higher; eventually it moved to a dipthong, as when *wif* (/i/) became in Modern English, *wife* (/ay/).

Thus, as various parts of a language change, some adjustment must generally be made throughout the system. In the Great English Vowel Shift, a change in the pronunciation of one vowel required adjustments among all the vowels in order to retain audible distinctions between words. Another change in the English language occurred when the /g/ sound was lost at the end of *sung, king,* and *fang;* speakers could no longer rely on that sound as a means of distinguishing these words from *sun, kin,* and *fan.* But the sound of the allophone of /n/ before /g/ ([ŋ]) was still there and sufficed to maintain the distinction. What formerly was just an automatic variant of /n/ before /g/ or /k/ (try saying *sun-kissed* fast and see if the [n] is not apt to turn into [ŋ]) became a new phoneme. Needless to say, speakers do not decide that they need a new phoneme and consciously select one. The process is unconscious.

We see that a language in making "progress" toward internal consistency does little more than catch up with its constantly appearing variations, and this is hardly progress in a real sense. Can we, recognizing that our language is not all that we would like it to be, apply some other standard that would enable us to say that some languages are better than others, hence have "progressed more," and therefore hold out the hope of progress to their lesser brethren?

This is a judgment that most linguists are reluctant to make. With memories of the cultural snobbery that has colored opinions about superiority in the past ("French is the most logical language, Italian the most musical, German the most scientific"), and with their discoveries of the beautiful intricacies of supposedly "primitive" languages fresh in mind, they have rejected the idea that any language is intrinsically better than any other, from which it follows that fifteenth-century English was just as good as twentieth-century English, and there has been no progress. Linguists are willing to admit that there is a constant, though slow, evolution toward greater fitness of the tool to the needs of its time, but point out that this again is just an instance of catching up — the needs are evolving about as fast as the language is, and the gap between them remains the same. Of course, this is progress of a sort: as the needs themselves grow more complex, a language in catching up with a progressive culture may itself be progressing.

Another conception of progress in language has to do with discarding redundancies — particularly in languages like English and Chinese. When we say *Mary is the sweetest, dearest, liveliest girl I know,* we express the one superlative idea three times, in the suffix *-est,* as can be seen by factoring it out and saying instead *Mary is the most sweet, dear, lively girl I know.* In the latter construction, supposedly typical of a later stage of language growth, we do not require an explicit superlative each time, but get the same results through the larger organization of the sentence. This is really a reversal of the older argument that Latin was a superior language because it was highly inflected.

This idea of nonrepetitiousness as a sign of superiority has been demolished by another trend of thought stimulated by information theory, the discipline that deals with codes and message-sending and serves, among other things, to measure the efficiency of our telephones. It turns out that if language actually did express a particular bit of information only once, it would not be intelligible unless all the channels of communication were functioning perfectly, free of noise and with undistracted attention on the part of the listener. If the idea of 'most' in the example above is given just once and that once happens to be obscured by noise, the message is lost.

Redundancy goes much deeper than out-and-out repetition of words or suffixes. Take the simplest case, the way languages use so many phonemes. Why, for instance, do we keep *superfluous* instead of reducing it to *sperfl?* The fleshing out of a word with more than the minimum it needs makes things easier for the listener. He has more cues. If he correctly hears either *superf-* or *-erfluous* he can get by. Or a word may be so obvious in a given position that almost any audible part of it is enough. In a sentence like *I'd just as soon Jerry stayed* *away; he's superfluous around here anyway,* so few words other than *superfluous* would make sense in that spot that hearing just the first syllable betrays it. We catch our signals from sounds, contexts, situations, facial expressions, and our knowledge of what to expect—each repeating the other to some extent. Languages have to be redundant, and while particular redundancies might be done away with to some advantage, their loss in general would not spell progress.

So it seems that languages get better only in a relative sense, in shifts, as the culture changes and the language moves to close the gap between the new culture and the traditional language. Efficiency is irrelevant since progress only makes sense in terms of the progress of the culture as a whole. To claim that a language is getting better is to claim that its culture is getting better, and that is a bold claim.

Exercise 16

One theory has it that "progressive" language is increasingly efficient in eliminating redundancies from the language. Do you think Lincoln's famous phrase "of the people, by the people, and for the people" would be more efficiently organized as "of, by, and for the people" ? Think of the context in which the phrase was used (in concluding the Gettysburg Address, delivered to commemorate soldiers killed at the great Civil War battle at Gettysburg) and discuss why Lincoln chose that organization. Which form would be more effective in a piece of informational prose, such as legal prose?

chapter **7** *Dialect*

Dialect and Language

Linguistic history records sweeping changes that affect vast bodies of speakers over long periods — some abrupt, even cataclysmic, so that everyone is conscious of what is happening, others so gradual that speakers may be unaware of them during their lifetimes. Dialectology looks upon the differences that set one community apart from another and characterize the individual speaker even when they do not necessarily interfere with communication. There is no clear separation of what one speaker does that others of his community do not do; nor is there any between what communities do that makes them different from one another or what it is that distinguishes one language from another. Techniques of discovery may differ — historical linguistics has elaborate strategies to hypothesize what cannot be observed because the evidence has long since vanished, whereas dialectology may be contemporary, capturing many of its facts almost as they happen.

The facts in both fields are the same; the size of the bite is what distinguishes them.

But size makes a difference in our appreciation, for dialect differences are cut to the measure of our comprehension, while differences between languages may overwhelm us. Comparatively few persons are truly bilingual, but every speaker is multilingual in the sense of understanding more than one dialect. And most speakers command different styles of speech which, if they are not to be called different dialects, are denied the name only because we want to reserve it for contrasts that are more pronounced. Whenever we speak in a more "reserved" or "decorous" manner, whenever we strive to avoid "grammatical mistakes," we pass from one dialect to another.

Every speaker speaks as many dialects as there are groups among which he moves that have different modes of speech. Some groups are biologically determined. Others are formed by more or less voluntary association. Here are some important ones:

Profession   The speech of the minister differs from the speech of the merchant. Each occupation has its own things to talk about. But the difference goes beyond merely having different words for different things. It often embodies a variety of names for the same thing: the soothsayer has his *augury,* the weather man his *forecast,* the doctor his *prognosis,* and the scientist his *prediction.*

Sex   Men's talk differs from women's talk. This line is somewhat blurred in our society, but it remains legible. Adjectives like *dreadful, precious, darling* are more apt to be encountered in women's speech than in men's—in fact, women are more liberal with adjectives in general. In some levels of society men are less inhibited in their choice of words than women. Women are less inhibited in their intonational range.

Age   The infant differs from the child, the child from the adolescent, the adolescent from the adult. The most extreme case is baby talk, which, in the sense that its speakers are physically unable to speak otherwise, is not really a dialect, but it becomes one when its forms are imitated—and sometimes fabricated—by adults and used by them with young children. As with all dialects, forms from this one may be picked up and broadcast; a recent instance is **bye-bye,** which is heard more and more as an ordinary friendly farewell, not necessarily an intimate one. At the other extreme is the dialect that time imposes on us all: older speakers do not always adopt newer ways of speaking, and the older they grow the more quaint their speech becomes. Nor is the process always purely automatic—a transition between age levels may be made consciously. Among the Ainu of Japan, there is a kind of "old speech," characteristic of the older people, which does not grow old and die out but persists and is adopted by the younger people as they mature.[1]

Occasion   Even the most careful speakers permit themselves a style of speech at home that is different from the one they use in public. Many societies set up—not by legislation but by tacit consent—a standard dialect that is used on formal occasions and that serves as a kind of inter-lingua, available to any speaker when he wants to identify himself with speakers at large rather than with speakers at home. The standard dialect takes on the local color of the speaker but is nevertheless different from the relaxed style used with friends, family, and neighbors. It is more neutral and as a rule is more generally understood, but intelligibility is not essential to its authority. In some countries, any relaxation of the formal standard in occasions that call for it is resented even if, as happens sometimes, speakers have difficulty understanding it (this may be likened to the reactions of some people in our own culture to attempts to make the Bible more intelligible by modernizing the English). In India, formal Hindi is stiffened by generous doses of Sanskrit. In Chinese, a formal lecture and a conversation may even differ syntactically: the idea that one group of officials (A) is more numerous than another group (B) is expressed in the lecture as

A	dwō	yú	B
A	numerous	than	B

and in the conversation as

A	bǐ	B	dwō
A	compared to	B	numerous[2]

The standard in English is not clear-cut (it is never entirely so anywhere), but certain tendencies mark it off. The obvious ones are in the choice of words. Where a university press, announcing a competition, reserves to itself the *"first refusal* of manuscripts," the intent is not to be candidly pessimistic but to avoid the more accurate but too colloquial *first chance at.* At a graduation one hears *All seniors will please rise* (or possibly *stand*); a relaxed occasion would call for *get up* or *stand up.* Certain contractions are avoided on formal occasions: the easygoing *'em* harmonizes with *show* in *Let's show 'em* but would hardly be used with the stiff verb *reveal: Let's reveal them.* In the supremely formal atmosphere of the church, even *let's* may be avoided: *Let's pray* would sound secular, if not sporting.

There is practically no limit to the number of social affinities revealed in differences of language. To age, sex, occupation, and occasion it would be necessary to add religion, politics, lodge affiliation, preference as to sports or amusements, and any other circumstances under which people meet and speak. But overshadowing them all are two coordinates laid on every society that determine far wider differences than any thus far mentioned. One is horizontal, as on a map: Bostonese, for example, differs from the speech of the rest of New England, and the speech of New England differs from that of the Coastal South; geographical dialects are inevitable, because people do more talking to their neighbors than to those who are farther away, and where more is shared, differences are fewer. The other is vertical, as with layers: in stratified societies people are born to a social class; nothing marks a class more indelibly than its language, and differences in speech are often cultivated for this very purpose.

Probably because they touch us in a tender spot, the vertical and horizontal differences are the ones that come first to mind when dialects are mentioned. Geographical differences have ties with our loyalties to home, town, and state. Social differences are nourished on feelings of superiority and inferiority, and to some extent color all other differences. In a society where women and farmers are regarded as inferior, sex differences and occupational differences become class differences. As for differences due to occasion, inability to handle the standard dialect when the occasion calls for it is especially likely to be taken as a class difference, for the dominant social class is the one whose traits of speech are most fully embodied in the standard.

The linguist and the sociologist are selective in different ways in their attitudes toward dialect. The linguist focuses mainly on the horizontal coordinate. Differences from region to region are the specimens that attract him most, probably because they are the same, though on a smaller scale, as the ones already familiar to him from language to language. When he speaks of dialectology it is almost always in this sense, more specifically referred to as "linguistic geography," or "dialect geography." The sociologist focuses mainly on the vertical coordinate. He is interested in how social groups interact within a single speech community, in how language influences our opportunities and our behavior. He views language as a series of codes by which the individual acts out his roles in society.

Exercise 1

a. In a brief essay, note some differences that you have observed between your own speech and that of other social groups in your community. Relate them to the group of speakers they characterize — perhaps "young adult" as against "adult." Consider whether groups that are distinctive in physical or cultural respects are also distinctive in their language — to what degree does their language distinguish them?

b. Are there dialect differences among ethnic or regional groups in your public school system? Write a brief composition in which you try to identify a few of them. They may be phonological (*house* pronounced [həʊs], *pen* pronounced like *pin*), morphological (verb forms like *dove* or *might could*, or switching of preterit and participle forms like *He done it, He seen them, They had went, Somebody had stole it*), or syntactic (adjectives used as adverbs, as in *He did it easy;* nonstandard clauses, as in *This is a recipe that if you don't do it right you won't like it;* interchange of cases, as in *Him and me don't like it,* or its opposite, by overcompensation, *It's for he and I*). Where are the speakers from? Are the forms they use standard in those areas? Do you use similar forms sometimes (for example, *Whom shall I say is calling,* an overcompensation)?

Linguistic Codes

The language of a profession, say that of law, is social distinction in its crudest form. It is part of an economic order in which everyone's way of earning a living somehow influences his speech because of the need to manipulate a certain set of objects and concepts that are the tools of the profession. But ordinarily it goes no deeper than the choice of terms to match the objects. What really counts for the sociologist is how the lawyer interacts with his banker and his grocer, and how the banker's son and the grocer's son are able, through having certain models to emulate in their parents, teachers, and others, to define themselves and by so doing to open or close the doors to growth and change of status.

The sociologist Basil Bernstein distinguishes two types of code that are socially significant: restricted and elaborated. A restricted code allows one to interact with one's fellows in a highly predictable way. It is associated with a certain social set or activity where only a limited number of things can be done. They are not necessarily prescribed in a particular order, as they would be in a game, but the choices are few. An example is a cocktail party where the nature of the language used and the nature of the things talked about is known in advance and what one learns about new-made acquaintances is transmitted not so much by language as by look and gesture. The conventionality of the language enables speakers to relax in one another's company and communicate in other ways, much as the set movements of a dance remove the necessity of deciding what to do next. In a restricted code, individuality is submerged. The speaker and listener are in a well-defined relationship with each other, with verbal routines laid out in advance. There is not much choice of what to say simply because there is no need to say much, and the little that is said carries a heavy load of implicit meaning. There is room for a bit of ad-libbing but little more.

In an elaborated code, the speaker and listener are acting parts in which they must improvise. Their standing with each other is such that neither can take much for granted about the other. Intentions and purposes have to be brought into the open and defined. What the speaker will say is hard to predict, because it is not about commonplaces but about something more or less unique, related less to some foreseeable role and more to him as an individual. He is wearing not a comic nor a tragic mask but his own face, and that is harder to put into words. An example would be that of a man told to do something by his boss and having to explain why it is impossible for him to comply.

All speakers communicate with both restricted and elaborated codes, but not all speakers are able to switch codes with the ease that is needed to interact to their advantage. If a speaker is forced to operate with a restricted code because he has never had any other models to imitate, his communication will probably be only with other speakers who use the same code—it becomes self-enforcing and self-perpetuating. One of the tasks of education is to lead to an awareness of the limitations of one's code and to a large amount of practice with elaborated codes, where the speaker is forced to become conscious of his language, in Bernstein's expression, to "orient towards the verbal channel." This is the individual's road of escape from the confinement of his every act by restricted codes laid on him by the social structure without regard for his individuality, capacities, or intelligence.

Educated adult speakers of English command a number of different *styles* of speech, each suitable for a different occasion. One, termed "consultative" by Martin Joos, is for communication between strangers, or for discussion of serious or complicated matters.[3] In such a conversation a relationship of familiarity is lacking and the speaker makes up for it by supplying background information. The listener participates continuously, if by nothing more than nodding his head to show that he is listening. The following passage is in what Martin

Joos calls the consultative style. It was recorded from a phone line in Ann Arbor, Michigan.[4]

> I wanted to tell you one more thing I've been talking with Mr. D—in the purchasing department about our type-writer (yes) that order went in March seventh however it seems that we are about eighth on the list (I see) we were up about three but it seems that for that type of typewriter we're about eighth that's for a fourteen-inch carriage with pica type (I see) now he told me that R—'s have in stock the fourteen-inch carriage typewriters with elite type (oh) and elite type varies sometimes it's quite small and sometimes it's almost as large as pica (yes I know) he suggested that we go down and get Mrs. R— and tell her who we are and that he sent us and try the fourteen-inch typewriters and see if our stencils would work with such type (I see). . . .

The "casual" style is used among friends and acquaintances in small groups or pairs. Little background is needed or given. There is much in-group slang and jargon. Formulas are common, such as those of utterance 7 in the passage below.[5] Their function is to signal the casualness of the communication as well as its meaning. (The lines on the exclamations show intonation levels.)

1. A— I don't know whether you let B— go out during the week do you suppose he could come over tonight while we go out to dinner
2. Well the difficulty is J— that he got back in his lessons
3. Oh│oh
4. And in his last report about two weeks ago he was down in two subjects his father hasn't been letting him do anything
5. Well that's a good idea
6. I'm awfully sorry
7. Well that's all right thanks A— to tell you the truth I don't want awfully badly to go you know what I mean
8. M│hm

"Formal" style is marked by a lack of participation of the audience; it is designed to inform; it is essentially dominating; it expects the listeners to remain silent till the end of the speech. What the speaker says can be arranged in sentences and paragraphs.

Exercise 2

The following example sentences cannot show all the characteristics of each style, since they are isolated from context, but there are characteristics of vocabulary and syntax that mark the styles even within the sentences. Translate the utterances below into the other styles. The translation of the consultative utterance of sentence **c** will sound strange when put into formal language. Can you explain why?

consultative: *I don't understand this.*
casual: *Hey prof, that doesn't reach me.*
formal: *The subject is beyond comprehension.*

a. formal: We request the honor of your presence for luncheon Tuesday next at 12:00.
b. consultative: I would like two hamburgers and one order of French fries.
c. consultative: Please fill up the gas tank.
d. consultative: I'm completely exhausted.
e. casual: He's full of beans.

The Horizontal Imposed on the Vertical

When a rubber manufacturer in Akron, Ohio, employs low-wage laborers from West Virginia, he unwittingly turns a geographical dialect into a social one. The newcomers are readily identified by their strange forms of speech, and they are poor and uneducated. No matter how carefully they dress and conduct themselves, they cannot change their dialect quickly enough to merge with the rest of the community, and the result is that the one trait that marks them most distinctly is taken as a badge of their "class."

Or, to make things more complicated, the new employees may speak a dialect that was socially nonstandard even in the place of origin and is still further out of line with the standard speech of the new area. The most radically different form of speech likely to be encountered in this country echoes African dialects spoken by traders, African and European, in the early part of the eighteenth century on the West African coast, and was probably carried to the plantations of the South and used by African slaves who were not allowed to use their native languages.[6]

This transplanting, as American dialectologist Raven McDavid points out, has happened and continues to happen all over the United States, and constitutes a grave social problem. For the fact is that nothing more thoroughly excludes a person from a social group than a manner of speech that has come to be identified as uncultivated. And, given the fact that the most extensive recent migrations have been from the poorest rural areas, especially those of the South, to the most tightly structured urban societies, those of our large cities, one understands how much language has contributed to the creation or deepening of class lines.

The best solution seems to be an enlightened "bi-dialectalism," fostered by the schools, where the basic job of integration has to be done. The form of speech approved by the local community is taught not as something that must be acquired and used under all circumstances but as something useful for general communication, while the "imported" speech is respected in its place on the playground, in the home, and in relaxed conversation.[7] "The first principle of any language program is that, whatever the target, it must respect the language that the students bring with them to the classroom."[8] The schools will need to be more sophisticated in their teaching of English. This calls for helping teachers to see that when students come to them limited to a nonstandard dialect what they need is not to be corrected in supposed mistakes but to be introduced to a new and in many ways different but related system, no better and no worse than the old one, but more useful in their new contacts.[9] It might even be wise to teach some of the nonstandard dialect to the speakers of the standard. Acceptance, not just toleration, implies both knowledge and use.

Exercise 3

A common opinion about language is that there is such a thing as a single correct pronunciation of a word. The manuals of "correct English" used to tell their readers what these pronunciations were. It is not an uncommon experience of English teachers to be asked for the "right" pronunciation.

Read the following summary of the regional and social variations in pronunciation of the word *aunt.*

> *aunt* In the Northern, Midland, and Southern speech areas, except for Eastern New England and a part of Tidewater Virginia, /æ/ is nearly universal at all social levels. The vowel /a/ as in *pot* is predominant in most of Eastern New England, though there are instances of /æ/ everywhere. "No social prestige seems to attach to /a/ in this area; in fact, some speakers regard /a/ as old-fashioned." This pronunciation is a prestige form in Connecticut, New York City, and Philadelphia, and is found only in cultured speech there. In a part of Tidewater Virginia dominated by Richmond, /a/ is the usual pronunciation at all social levels. Elsewhere in Virginia, this pronunciation is a prestige form "almost exclusively in cultivated city speech—as in Alexandria, Winchester, Charlottesville, and Roanoke. As a prestige pronunciation, it has also been adopted by better educated speakers on Albemarle Sound, N. C. The few instances of /a/ recorded in *aunt* from Charleston, S. C. southward occur in folk speech (four of the six in the speech of Negroes). Here cultured speakers avoid /a/."[10]

Answer either of the following two questions.
1. What is the correct pronunciation of *aunt?*
2. Rephrase the first question so that it could be briefly and reasonably answered. What is your answer?

Exercise 4

A common myth about language in this country is that dialects other than the "establishment" dialects are erratic and disorderly, and thus lazy and inexpressive. Actually, they are consistent and patterned. Consider the following statements from one fourteen-year-old black student in a Washington, D. C., poverty area.

1. Every day last winter when they would come by to get me I would be busy.
2. Tomorrow morning when my mother get up I will be busy.

3. Every day, in the morning, when the others get up at my place I be busy.
4. Every day, in the morning, when you come I be busy.

He refused to substitute *I'm busy, I will be busy, I would be busy,* or (a dialect form) *I busy* for *I be busy* in 3 and 4. He would use these suggested substitutions knowledgeably at other times, but said he would not use them in these two contexts. He would not say *I be busy right now;* for him the correct wording was *I'm busy right now.* If a person saw him on the street during the week and asked him why he had not been going to church Sundays, he might say, **Sunday I be busy.**

What does *I be* in *I be busy* in 3 and 4 mean in this dialect? Does it mean action in the present, action carried on from the past through the present, an action taking place occasionally?

Linguistic Geography

In the United States the model for serious investigation of geographical dialects has been the *Linguistic Atlas of New England,* directed by Hans Kurath and published between 1939 and 1943. Other regional atlases covering most of the country have been drawn up as part of a *Linguistic Atlas of the United States and Canada,* still in preparation.

As the name implies, a linguistic atlas is a collection of maps showing the prevalence of particular speech forms in particular areas. What the dialect geographer most often selects to mark off a dialect area is simply its preference for certain words. Differences in pronunciation or syntax yield a more reliable measure, but words are easier to work with; information can even be gathered by mail through a questionnaire that asks what words a speaker uses for particular meanings: is a field enclosure made of stone called a *stone wall,* a *stone fence,* a *rock wall,* or a *rock fence?* Are drains that take rainwater off a roof called *eaves troughs, water spouting, gutters,* or *rain spouts?* For greater accuracy, detailed phonetic information is needed. Trained interviewers must be sent to the scene and may spend hours with a single informant. Does he pronounce *soot* to rime with *boot* or with *put?* Is his final consonant in **with** like that of **bath** or that of **bathe?** Does his pronunciation of **tomato** end with the same vowel sound as **panda** or is it like **grotto?** The Swiss German atlas, published in 1962, was based on a questionnaire containing 2,600 items, which took from four to eight days to administer. Its phonetic discriminations were exquisite — as many as twenty-one different tongue heights, for example, in front unrounded vowels. The items chosen for a questionnaire to test differences in vocabulary, pronunciation, and syntax are the ones most likely to reveal the peculiarities of everyday speech: names of household objects, foods, parts of the body, weather phenomena, numbers, and so on.

American dialect geography

Unless he is combining his interest as a linguist with an extracurricular one as a folklorist or sociologist, the dialect geographer is less concerned with the items in a questionnaire for their own sake than as indicators of where to draw the boundary lines and how to trace the routes of speakers as they migrated from one area to another. The latter — the fanning out of dialects from their original centers and their crisscrossing and blending as the wave moves outward — is of special significance in a country like the United States, with its extraordinarily mobile population.

Boundaries are set by mapping the farthest points to which a given form has penetrated. When a line — termed an *isogloss* if it has to do with words, an *isophone* if with sounds — is drawn connecting these points, it is usually found to lie close to the lines drawn for other forms — for instance, the same speakers who say **snake feeder** for 'dragonfly' are also apt to pronounce the word **greasy** as **greazy.** The interlocking lines form a bundle of isoglosses (or isophones) and represent the frontier of the dialect in question.

American English divides rather clearly into three grand dialect areas in the eastern part of the country. They reflect the settlement of these areas by early migrants from England who brought their dialects with them. One such dialectal transplant from England is the vowel in words like **half, bath, aunt, glass,** and **laugh.** We easily recognize one way of pronouncing these words as a feature of cultivated speech in the

East and of overcultivated speech elsewhere. It is by no means uniform (in eastern Virginia, for example, it will be heard in **master** and **aunt** but not in many other words), and represents one side of a split that took place in the eastern counties of England before the American Revolution. The /a/ was transplanted from those counties as folk speech by immigrants to New England, but it also took root in London and so became established as fashionable speech in the parts of the country that maintained the closest ties with England.[11] The map on page 167 shows the three areas (plus subdialectal sections) known, from their geographical position, as Northern, Midland, and Southern.

As the population spread westward the boundaries became more and more blurred. The earlier, more gradual movement extended them fairly evenly as far as the Mississippi. Maps 2 and 3 show the northern limit of certain Midland terms and the southern limit of certain Northern terms, as this rather complex bundle of isoglosses traversed the states of Ohio, Indiana, and Illinois. By the time the migrants had flowed up against the Rocky Mountains, the three tides had broken into a series of rivulets and eddies. Where a given area was settled mainly by speakers of a given dialect, that dialect of course prevailed. The area around Hayden, Colorado, was turned into a kind of Northern island by a group of women schoolteachers who came out from Ann Arbor, Michigan, and married ranchers there. Later, as younger speakers grew up and intermarried, Northern and Midland traits were blended. The shaded areas of Map 4 show this for Colorado.

Two metaphors describe the extremes of diffusion. One is the relay race, the other the cross-country. In the first, a speaker picks up something from his neighbor to the east and runs with it as far as his neighbor to the west, always staying between them. In the second, a speaker breaks loose from the paternal neighborhood and travels to all points of the compass, picking up pieces at each stop and dropping them all along the way. The latter is the kind of diffusion that makes dialectology a hazardous business. As Robert Louis Stevenson wrote in *The Amateur Emigrant,*

> I knew I liked Mr. Jones from the moment I saw him. I
> thought him by his face to be Scottish; nor could his accent

ADAPTED from Hans Kurath, *A Word Geography of the Eastern United States* (Ann Arbor, Michigan: University of Michigan Press, 1949).

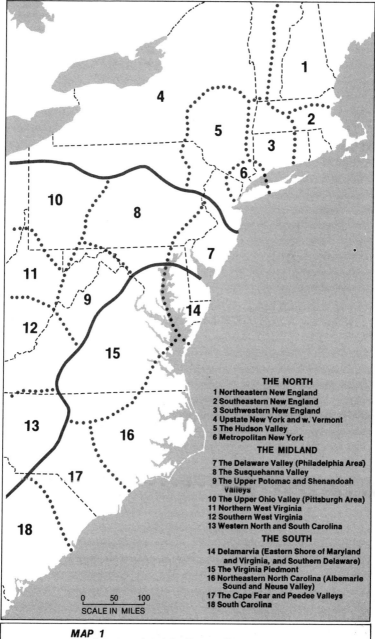

THE NORTH

1 Northeastern New England
2 Southeastern New England
3 Southwestern New England
4 Upstate New York and w. Vermont
5 The Hudson Valley
6 Metropolitan New York

THE MIDLAND

7 The Delaware Valley (Philadelphia Area)
8 The Susquehanna Valley
9 The Upper Potomac and Shenandoah Valleys
10 The Upper Ohio Valley (Pittsburgh Area)
11 Northern West Virginia
12 Southern West Virginia
13 Western North and South Carolina

THE SOUTH

14 Delamarvia (Eastern Shore of Maryland and Virginia, and Southern Delaware)
15 The Virginia Piedmont
16 Northeastern North Carolina (Albemarle Sound and Neuse Valley)
17 The Cape Fear and Peedee Valleys
18 South Carolina

0   50   100
SCALE IN MILES

MAP 1
Word Geography of the Eastern States

MAP 2 MIDLAND TERMS, NORTHERN LIMIT

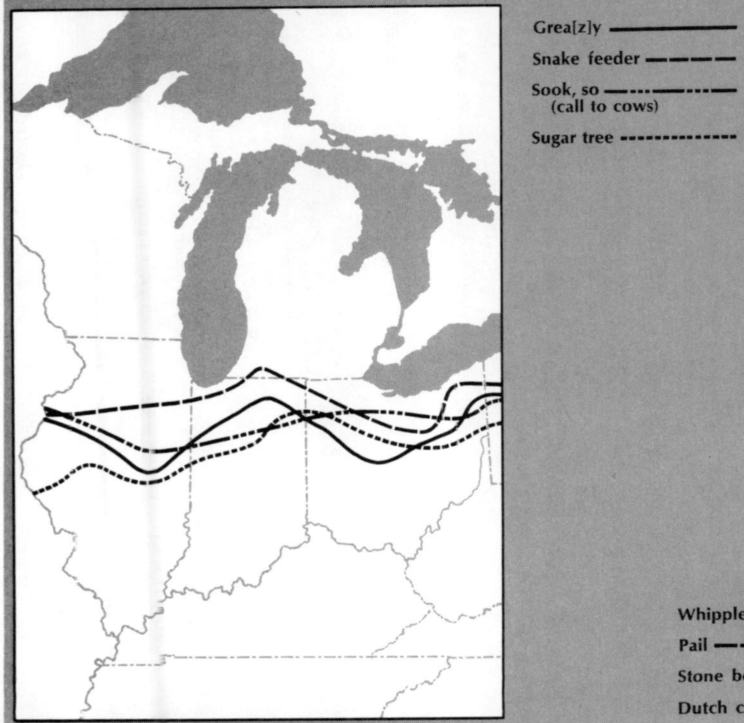

MAP 3 NORTHERN TERMS, SOUTHERN LIMIT

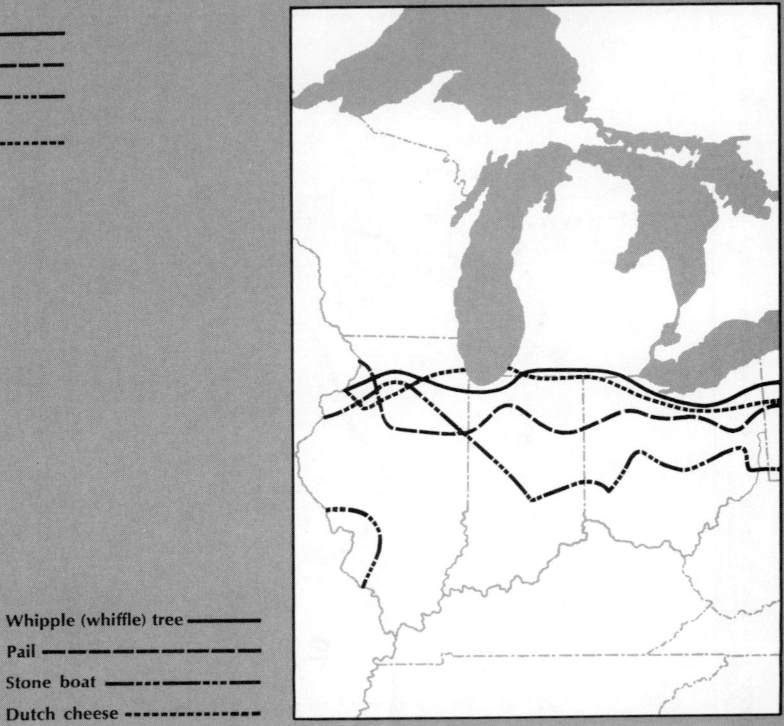

Grea[z]y ————————
Snake feeder ——————
Sook, so ——·——·——
(call to cows)
Sugar tree ··············

Whipple (whiffle) tree ————————
Pail ——————
Stone boat ·············
Dutch cheese ——··——··——

ADAPTED FROM Albert H. Marckwardt, "Principal and Subsidiary Dialect Areas in the North Central States," *Publications of the American Dialect Society* 27.10–11 (1957).

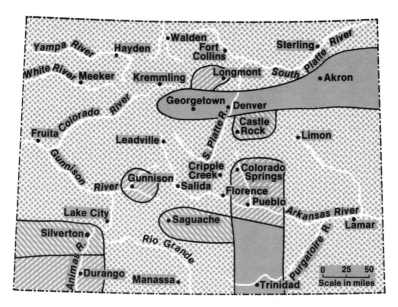

MAP 4 **NORTHERN-MIDLAND MIXTURE, YOUNGER INFORMANTS**

12 or more Midland responses   11 or more Northern responses

ADAPTED FROM Clyde T. Hankey, "A Colorado Word Geography," *Publications of the American Dialect Society* 34.24 (1960).

undeceive me. For as there is a *lingua franca* of many tongues on the moles and in the feluccas of the Mediterranean, so there is a free or common accent among English-speaking men who follow the sea. They catch a twang of a New England port, from a cockney skipper, even a Scotsman sometimes learns to drop an *h;* a word of a dialect is picked up from another hand in the forecastle; until often the result is undecipherable, and you have to ask for a man's place of birth.[12]

But geography is not all. The fading of differences is accelerated by social pressures. Where a normalized, cultivated speech gains in favor—and this, we should remember, was until recently the largest single result of formal schooling —everything with a pronounced local or, especially, rustic flavor tends to be rooted out. Thus, in the area of northern Illinois already mentioned the cultivated forms *I ran home yesterday, He did it, I'm going to lie down* are replacing the uncultivated — whether Northern or Midland — *I run home yesterday, He done it, I'm going to lay down.*

Exercise 5

a. Take the expression *hot cake.* As a folk term, in the East this expression is centered in eastern Pennsylvania. But somehow it has found its way into formal English: "In parts of the Middle West . . . one is likely to make *pancakes* at home, but to order *hot cakes* in a restaurant."[13] In California, *hot cake* is more general than *pancake.* Is it more likely taken from the Pennsylvania or from the formal usage? In a state such as California, populated by persons from all areas to the east, what competing forms are likely to be the most successful, those widely and generally used elsewhere or those restricted in their distribution?

b. In Chapter 5, page 115, it was noted that dialect borrowing enriches vocabulary. Of the following pairs of competing dialectal terms, it may be that you use only one from each pair or that you use neither, but if you use both, consider whether they mean exactly the same or have come in your speech to represent different shades of meaning: *pancake, flapjack; roasting ears, corn on the cob; angleworm, earthworm; window blinds, window shades.*

c. Test your reactions toward some other dialect of English. If you are a Northern (or Southern) speaker do you find a Southern (or Northern) accent irritating? How do you react toward a speaker of British Standard (Southern British, or "Received Pronunciation")? Does it make a difference whether the other speaker is of the same sex as you? Or the opposite sex?

d. If you distinguish the vowels /a/ and /ɔ/ in words like *sot-sought, tot-taught, stock-stalk, sod-sawed,* but have only /ɔ/ in *ma-maw, rah-raw,* and in all one-syllable words ending in -/g/ such as *log, frog, dog,* consider whether this may be partly because disregarding the distinction in the latter words creates fewer conflicts. If conflict of homonyms can result in a loss, can it also be a factor in preserving something?

Exercise 6

Regional dialect boundaries are drawn on the basis of information gathered from speakers of the region. Field workers interview informants who learned to speak in the area and are still living there; the data is then entered on maps. Map A on page 172 is such a map. Each circle means that one speaker in that area used the form indicated. Maps B and C show what is usually done next: the area of predominance of a form is marked off by a line. Map D shows several such lines and gives an idea of how a number of lines can reinforce each other on one map. When enough lines come together, they may mark off a dialect area. The goal of this exercise is to use the information contained in the first four maps to draw a dialect boundary on a fifth map. The dialect boundary in question separates what traditionally has been called the Northern and the Midland speech areas. Remember that a line that shows the extent of use of a word is an *isogloss;* one dealing with a sound is called an *isophone.* Maps A and D deal with words, and Maps B and C with sounds.

Draw in the isogloss of the word *see* on Map A. You are only interested in the area of the map where the isophone of Map B lies. Then, combining the isoglosses and isophones from the first four maps into a group, draw the Northern-Midland dialect boundary on Map E. What words and sounds characterize each region?

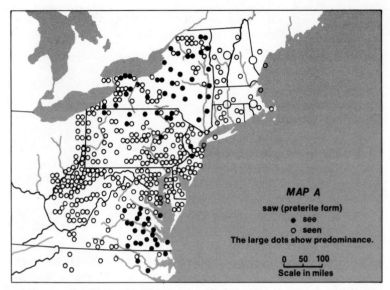

MAP A

saw (preterite form)
• see
○ seen
The large dots show predominance.

0   50   100
Scale in miles

Adapted from E. Bagby Atwood, *A Survey of Verb Forms in the Eastern United States* (Ann Arbor, Mich.: University of Michigan Press, 1953), Fig. 17. Copyright 1953 by University of Michigan Press. Reprinted by permission of the publishers.

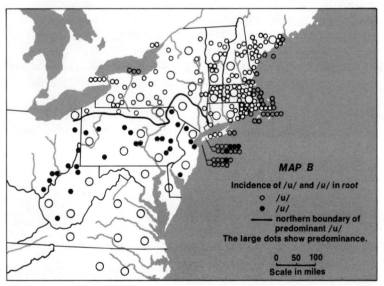

MAP B

Incidence of /u/ and /u/ in root
○   /u/
•   /u/
──── northern boundary of
      predominant /u/
The large dots show predominance.

0   50   100
Scale in miles

Adapted from Hans Kurath and Raven I. McDavid, Jr., *The Pronunciation of English in the Atlantic States* (Ann Arbor, Mich.: University of Michigan Press, 1961), Map 113. Copyright 1961 by University of Michigan Press. Reprinted by permission of the publishers.

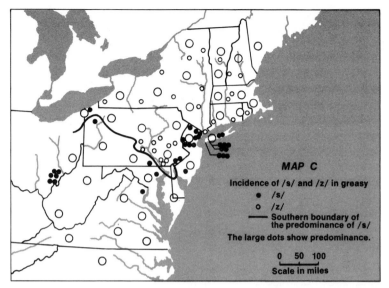

Adapted from Hans Kurath and Raven I. McDavid, Jr., *The Pronunciation of English in the Atlantic States* (Ann Arbor, Mich.: University of Michigan Press, 1961), Map 171. Copyright 1961 by University of Michigan Press. Reprinted by permission of the publishers.

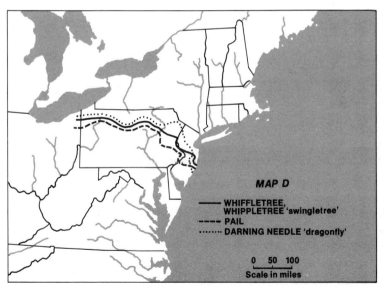

Adapted from Hans Kurath, *A Word Geography of the Eastern United States* (Ann Arbor, Mich.: University of Michigan Press, 1949), Fig. 5a. Copyright 1949 by University of Michigan Press. Reprinted by permission of the publishers.

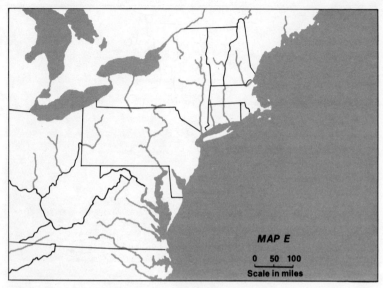

Adapted from Hans Kurath and Raven I. McDavid, Jr., *The Pronunciation of English in the United States* (Ann Arbor, Mich.: University of Michigan Press, 1961), Map 1. Copyright 1961 by University of Michigan Press. Reprinted by permission of the publishers.

chapter 8

Writing

The Correspondences Between Writing and Speech

If the Aztecs before the time of Columbus had had schools with classes divided according to subject matter, a child taking instruction in language would have been taught the correct way to recite the texts of an oral tradition and might have been lectured on avoiding the Aztec slang of his day, but he would never have had to hand in a written composition and would never have been scolded for a misspelling. Writing, such as it was, would have been taught in his art class, and misspellings would have been impossible because there were no spellings.

Pictures, then as now, could tell a story. But they did so in their own way, not as marks that represented particular words or sounds. A picture of a man or of a man's head, or a stylized figure of a man, meant a man, a male being, an old boy, an adult person of the male sex, or a man by any other name one might choose. The symbol pictured the meaning directly, with no particular sounds as intermediary, unlike the written drawings in our modern culture, where the letter signs *m + a + n* stand for a particular construct of sound that means one thing in the word *man* and something else in the word *mansion.*

Our own experience in school is so different that we are prone to think that writing *is* language and that speech is only a sort of replay of what is written, like a tape recording that is language in solid form but can be turned into sound if fed into a machine. We learned to speak so long ago that all the details have been forgotten, even if we could have been self-conscious enough at that age to observe what we were doing. Our "language" class, therefore, did not teach us the sound or structure of English but concentrated on teaching us how to write; this is our most vivid recollection of language instruction, and it colors our notions of what constitutes language.

Yet the convergence of speech and writing—the use of writing to mediate *language* rather than to mediate ideas directly—was a process that took thousands of years and that even now many of the world's cultures have not undergone. Advanced as the Aztec culture was when Cortez invaded Mexico in 1519, it was centuries behind that of Europe in the development of writing and only a little more advanced than that of the nomadic tribes of Indians inhabiting what is now the United States and Canada. The Aztecs and Mayas were great artists, but they were cut off from the written art of other lands where the flow and counterflow of communication implanted the little innovations that led the cultures of the Old World to make great forward leaps in symbolization.

To understand the past of writing we must begin with the present, which we know best.

Letters and phonemes

Almost all modern writing is *alphabetic.* It uses symbols that with more or less refinement correspond to individual sounds, and the degree of refinement is measured by how close the correspondence comes to being one-to-one. A perfect correspondence, with each letter symbol standing for one and only one distinctive sound, would of course be a form of phonemic writing. Some modern writing systems come very close to this ideal — Spanish, Czech, Finnish. Others, of which English is a dismal example, are so erratic that for a long time educators advocated giving up altogether the teaching of reading by letter sounds, using instead a global or whole-word method in which the child is expected to recognize word shapes but not break them into their phonetic parts. There has recently been a reaction against this approach, which is fortunate because, imperfect as English writing admittedly is, it still is basically phonemic. Unless a reader is taught or develops on his own an ability to interpret the spelling of unfamiliar words, he will be cruelly handicapped. Most such spellings can be interpreted with confidence: we are safe in inferring that *sline,* if there were such a word, would be pronounced to rime with *fine,* not with *fin,* and that *wip* would rime with *rip,* not with *ripe.*

It is hardly a coincidence that one of the greatest successes of linguistics in this century has been what could be characterized as simply a clean-up job on alphabetic writing.

An alphabetic system has the capacity to become completely phonemic, and if it has failed to do so the reason is that writers are not linguists and have other needs and interests than that of making their writing a perfect image of their speech. The needs are practical and the interests are both practical and esthetic. Among the needs are the functions that writing has fulfilled since its beginnings: communication across time (which until the invention of sound-recording devices was impossible for speech), communication across great distance (which likewise was impossible for speech until the appearance of the telephone), and communication to great numbers of people (which was closed to speech until the invention of radio). And in modern times, the vastly greater size of the readership — for many publications, embracing readers of English from Tacoma to Calcutta — has made it necessary for writing to transcend local dialects and adhere to a standard that can be widely understood. A Southerner may say /ðə poə rʊf bʊljd/ and a Northerner may say /ðə pʊr ruf bʌljd/ but both will *write* **The poor roof bulged.**

Even a linguist can find some fault with a purely phonemic writing. Its worst feature is that it does not represent morphemes consistently. In English the spelling of the past morpheme *-ed* is phonemically bad but morphemically good for it is always the same: the identical spelling in **kissed, plagued,** and **faded** has to be transcribed phonemically in three different ways, -/t/, -/d/, and -/əd/. The possessive morpheme is consistently *-'s* or *-'*, where phonemically it has four different shapes: -/s/ in **Pat's,** -/z/ in **Ted's,** -/əz/ in **George's,** and zero in **the boys'.** The word **news** is spelled the same in **The news is good** and **I read the newspapers** even though for many speakers the latter has /nus/ rather than /nuz/. So in some ways a combined phonemic and morphemic or "morphophonemic" spelling is preferable to a purely phonemic one. It is possible that writers sense this, and that some spellings are preserved or changed accordingly.

Other, more trivial, advantages can be extracted from the disadvantages of our spelling. Though **Frances** and **Francis** sound the same, we can tell by looking that the first applies to a woman and the second to a man. What might be ambiguities in speech are thereby sometimes avoided in writing. Of course, writing has other devices more systematic than random distinctions with letters: *my sister's friend's investments, my sisters' friends' investments,* and *my sister's friends' investments* all sound the same but are different in writing.

Esthetic considerations, too, prevent a writing system from becoming fully phonemic. There is hardly a town in the United States that does not boast at least one establishment with the sign **Ye Olde Tea** (or **Pottery** or **Antique** or **Curiosity**) **Shoppe.** Common English names are sometimes regarded as too common, and ambitious parents dress them up with exotic spellings: **Alyce** for **Alice, Bettye** for **Betty, Edythe** for **Edith.** One esthetic attitude in particular has deflected writing away from speech and even created a counter-evolutionary trend: the deference that is felt in all societies, including our own, to the authority of the written word. For the Hindus, the Sanskrit writings embody "the language of the gods," and knowledge of Sanskrit and use of Sanskrit words has long been a prestige symbol in India. In our society a respect for standard spellings is a requirement for social and economic advancement; the person who writes words with bad spellings in a letter of application will find it almost as hard to get a job as the man who has been caught writing bad checks. As a result, all spellings are locked in place and shielded from reform. Long after pronunciations have changed and speakers all over the English-speaking world have agreed on new ones, the old spellings live on: *-tion* for /šən/, **gh** for /f/, the **b** of **plumb, climb, limb,** and so on.

Unwritten parts of language

While the lack of a full correspondence between writing and speech is occasionally to the advantage of writing—as in distinguishing *its* from *it's* or *indict* from *indite*—more often the advantage is on the side of speech, where writing has simply failed to incorporate some element of spoken language. It is good to have homonyms spelled differently sometimes; but homographs—identical spellings of words that do not sound or mean the same—are a nuisance. A writer about to put down a sentence like *Some stamps will be acceptable in lieu of coins,* and intending *some* as /sʌm/, should probably use *certain* instead, for the reader may take him to mean /sm/.

But the worst deficiency of writing is that it never got around to providing a regular way of marking accent (writers can use italics, but good style allows them to use this device only very sparingly), and it has virtually disregarded rhythm and intonation. What a writer intends as

You would have been ^welcome^ if you had said ^nothing at^ ^all.^

could be taken as

wel

You would have been
come if you had said nothing at ^a^l.

There is evidence that in certain medieval manuscripts spaces may have been left where pauses occur within compounds or between words, wider for longer pauses, narrower for shorter. So we might write today *If you see him   when you*

get home   **call me.** But this tradition, if it existed, was lost. Punctuation serves as a rough guide to some of the rhythmic and intonational contrasts in speech, but it leaves too much out and what it puts in suffers from a confusion of two aims: the representations of the breaks that we *hear* and the divisions that logical-minded persons sometimes insist that we *write*. The two usually agree, but not always. Consider the following sentence: *It is common knowledge that, if we are to learn to speak another language well, we must spend a great deal of time practicing it.* There is no comma after **knowledge,** where a pause would normally come, but there is one after **that,** where most speakers would not pause at all.

In all this we can detect the hand of an ancient tradition: that writing never fully symbolizes speech but serves as a *prompter* to what we want to say. The result is that writers have to make many choices that are not forced on them as speakers.

The jockeying necessary to overcome the lack of accent and intonation markings calls for a high degree of skill, which is part of the equipment of every good writer. Sometimes nothing can remedy the defect. Lord Acton's phrase **Compromise is the soul if not the whole of politics** remains ambiguous —we shall never know whether he meant 'is the soul, nay, more, possibly the whole,' or 'if not the whole, at least the soul.' Sometimes a simple repetition—unnecessary in speech —will clear things up. So with the phrase **more or less:** in the question **Are you more or less satisfied with the way things went?** one of the meanings can be pinned down by writing **Are you more satisfied or less satisfied . . . ?** The accommodation most often called for is a change in word order, with or without a change in construction. A speaker wishing to reprove someone for shouting can say **Is shóuting necessary?** and be clearly understood if he puts the main accent on **shouting** and de-accents **necessary;** but if the sentence is written, the regularity with which main accents fall at the end will lead the reader to interpret it as **Is shouting nécessary?** A good writer will change the wording to get **shout** at the end: **Is it necessary to shout?**

In one respect, writing, though visual, lacks a visual support enjoyed by speech. This is gesture. We have seen how paralinguistic gestures help us tell the difference between statements and questions (Chapter 1, pages 18–19). Other gestures, too, cooperate with speech, as when one says *When I was about yea high*, accompanying the demonstrative *yea* with the hand held at a definite height. Writing is compelled to find substitutes.

Now and then we can make capital of a deficiency. Just as a piece of writing can—to advantage—span two or more dialects and so gain in universality, so by its very ambiguity it can at one and the same time embrace two or more actual utterances that we do not care to distinguish, and thereby gain in generality. At check-out counters in stores one often finds containers of free samples with a sign reading *Take one.* Ordinarily this represents the utterance *Táke one.* But if a customer were to help himself to several, the storekeeper might point out that the sign reads *Take óne.*

By its permanency writing enhances the possibilities of style. It is no longer something that issues from the mouth and vanishes with the air but is an object of art to be contemplated and worked upon at length. With less dependence on brute memory, the devices that an orator or a storyteller might have had to use to help him remember and to help his hearer follow become less necessary—such things as rimes, alliterations, and summations. Elaborate language becomes less the province of a few; more intricate ideas can be grasped and more elegant expression attempted by every user of the language. The gap between writing and speech is widened. Writing creates a new environment with internal features unique to it. Some of these result from the display of words in space rather than in time: page references, words such as *former* and *latter* or *above* and *below.* Others reflect the conservatism and formality of writing. In conversation we would be apt to say that someone had *followed us around;* in formal prose this would probably be changed to *followed us about.* Above all, writing is characterized by amplification. One rarely finds parenthetical clauses in speech, but they are frequent in writing: *The President, who as we know has been under great pressure to reduce three of his budgetary requests (the latest having to do with public housing, but excepting the military), finally submitted a revised report, prepared by a specially appointed staff, to the joint meeting of the two committees last night.*

So we see both primary and secondary divergences between speech and writing: primary ones that are simply the lack on one side of some device that is present in the other—a graphic sign such as the apostrophe in writing, or a distinctive sound such as an accent in speech; and secondary ones that are the result of having to make alternative choices or arrangements in order to remedy a primary lack. There are vested interests in both. Writing and speech are like two railroads with overlapping boards of directors that share, over part of the route, a single right of way. At times they seem to be the same, but there has never been a formal merger and their managements have too many ingrained rivalries now to approve one.

Exercise 1

English spelling appears chaotic and orderly by turns. For example, the phoneme /ɪ/ is spelled in a variety of ways. In the words *hit, sieve, England, women, busy, myth,* and *build,* the spellings are *i, ie, e, o, u, y,* and *ui.* Write the spellings of the phonemes /ə/, /ʌ/, /ʊ/, /e/, /g/, /f/, /z/, /s/ as they appear in the following words.

hut	put	does	dungeon
veil	weight	along	villain
blood	porpoise	play	book
would	gauge	give	rough
easily	guard	ghost	none
rate	wolf	obey	trait
steak			

Assuming that the sample is representative, which spellings are more consistent with sound, vowels or consonants?

Exercise 2

a. Various systems of reformed spelling have been devised as solutions to the irregularities of English spelling. The British Simplified Spelling Society published its system in 1940, and Axel Wijk published his system in 1959. The following passage is spelled out twice, once according to each system. The British system is first and the Wijk system next.[1]

We instinktivly shrink from eny chaenj in whot iz familyar; and whot kan be mor familyar dhan dhe form ov wurdz dhat we have seen and riten mor tiemz dhan we kan posibly estimaet? We taek up a book printed in Amerika, and *honor* and *center* jar upon us every tiem we kum akros dhem; nae, eeven to see *forever* in plaes of *for ever* atrakts our atenshon in an unplezant wae. But dheez ar iesolaeted kaesez; think ov dhe meny wurdz dhat wood hav to be chaenjd if eny real impruuvment wer to rezult. . . . But dhaer iz soe much misapprehenshon on dhis point, and such straenj statements ar maed, dhat it bekumz necessary to deel widh dhis objekshon in sum deetael.

We instinctivly shrink from eny chainge in whot iz familiar; and whot can be more familiar than the form ov wurds that we hav seen and written more times than we can possibly estimate? We take up a book printed in America, and *honor* and *center* jar upon us every time we cum across them; nay, even to see *forever* in place ov *for ever* attracts our attention in an unplezant way. But theze ar isolated cases; think ov the meny wurds that wood hav to be chainged if eny real improovement wer to rezult. . . . But there iz so much misapprehension on this point, and such strainge statements ar made, that it becums necessary to deal widh this objection in sum detail.

How do these two systems treat the plural morpheme? Is it spelled according to the allomorphs of that morphene (-/əz/, /s/, and /z/), or with just one symbol for the morpheme? Write all the plural nouns of the passage as spelled by each system. What is the principle that each system follows here?

b. Notice that neither system uses the schwa, ə. This is partly because the public might be alienated from spelling reform by a new symbol. Also, the use of the schwa obscures the relationships between some words. The ordinary spellings give more clues to word similarities than do the phonemic transcriptions.

Write out the phonemic transcriptions for the following pairs of words and explain how the ordinary spelling gives clues to their relationships.

human	injure
humanity	injurious
moral	minister
morality	ministerial
tutor	medicine
tutorial	medicinal

Exercise 3

a. In Chapter 6, pages 133–34, we noted that bifurcations in pronunciation enrich the language with new words. Are there also sometimes bifurcations in spelling, in which a word with more than one meaning comes to be spelled in different ways, though remaining the same in pronunciation? Look up the etymologies of the following pairs of words: *errant-arrant, crumby-crummy, coin-coign, born-borne.*

b. The following sentences are from written sources. Each can be interpreted in two radically different ways. Read them aloud, adding the unwritten elements (accents or intonations) that will make each of the possible meanings clear:

1. *Several cities have imported taxicabs propelled by light diesel engines.*
   Meanings: "possess imported taxicabs"; "have performed the action of importing cabs."

2. *Physics and biology surely provide basic stuff for the critical mind of the humanist; only science, to its own misfortune, is presently out of bounds for him.*
   Meanings: "but science"; "science alone."

3. *He seems to feel that Ramirez himself would never have consented.*
   Meanings: "Ramirez, as far as he himself was concerned"; "not even as important a person as Ramirez."

The Growth of Writing

The forerunners of our written signs were nearly all pictorial or diagrammatic. That is to say, they were *analog*, in the sense explained in Chapter 1, pages 22–23. Primitive pictures conveyed messages in the same way as modern cartoons —the drawing of a man's figure might look more or less like an actual man, but its meaning depended on there being at least some resemblance. A diagram to point out a direction really pointed in the direction intended, relative to the ground or to other points on a map. Notches on a stick to record the number of sheep sheared or soldiers recruited or vessels of oil delivered corresponded to the actual count. What men inscribed on wood or clay or graved on stone was intended to speak to the mind through the eye alone, not through the eye as a stimulus to the ear.

This is not to deny all connection with speech, nor to say that long strides were not taken toward an arbitrary digital system in representational drawing. Drawings could be digital: if notches could represent recruits, clearly circles or dots would do just as well; nothing compelled the artist to include more detail than he was interested in. But always the potential of depicting an actual characteristic was there: a stick figure might be enough to represent a man, but a man with an arm missing would be shown by a stick with a missing arm.

Connections with speech were often close: some designs were drawn to be translated aloud, either as reminders for those who drew them or as messages calling for an interpreter. But they differed from writing in having no fixed correspondence between the design and the language; the interpreter was free to ad-lib. A three-part drawing in which a king was shown first assembling his hosts, then laying waste to an enemy land, then pausing to rest, might be read aloud as *After assembling his hosts and before pausing to rest, he laid waste the enemy land* or it could be read as *In order to lay waste the enemy land he assembled his hosts, and afterward he rested* or perhaps as *Before he rested he laid waste the enemy land with the hosts he had assembled.* There might be any number of readings. The words could vary, and the actions did not need to be reported in the same sequence. Language, with its enormously greater resources, could run circles around the drawing, and this explains why each step toward a symbolization of language rather than a direct symbolization of things and events was bound to mark a gain in communicative power.

The main steps were three: the writing of words, the writing of syllables, and the writing of distinctive sounds. Each stage overlapped the following one. Even modern English writing has a few remnants of word signs and syllable signs: ¶ means 'paragraph' and § means 'section' (we even use the primitive device of pluralizing these by doubling them: ¶¶, §§). And *bar-b-q* uses *b* and *q* to stand for the syllables /bɨ/ and /kyu/, as **OK** stands for the syllables /o/ and /ke/.

Archaeology enables us to estimate the dates of the three steps and credit their first appearance to particular societies, though we cannot be sure, even when a given piece of writing is assigned definitely to a given people, that some later archaeological find will not reveal that the style was borrowed from a near neighbor who invented it a century or two earlier. Thus, while the Phoenicians seem entitled to credit for the second step, it could have been taken first by some other group in their general area. What is fairly certain, in view of a number of finds clustering near one another, is that it did occur in that area.

Word writing

While the interpreter of a pictorial message was usually free to ad-lib, a few of the signs must always have referred to individual persons or things that could be mentioned in speech by just one name. A drawing of a small bear could have been verbalized as *small bear, little bear,* or *bear cub,* but if it designated a person known as *Little Bear* only that reading would have been admissible. A semantic annotation might or might not be added to help the interpreter—say, a figure of a man to which the figure of the cub is attached; the result was necessarily that a particular sign called for a particular word or phrase.

Something similar must have happened with pictorial messages where the interpreter was theoretically free to ad-lib. If the message was to himself—a series of reminders, perhaps, for recounting a story—a timid person no doubt did as he would do today and memorized the text. In that case, when he came to deliver it, using his notes for added confidence, each symbol for a particular meaning would also have stood for a particular word or phrase. It is not difficult to imagine almost from the first a tendency to link a written sign to its meaning, not directly, but via a particular word or words. Any such tendency must have taken hold quickly, for it put all the resources of language at the command of the writer and reader. For the first time writing was *phonetized:* a given sign represented a given complex of sounds.

When this step was first taken is impossible to determine. One cannot tell by looking at the earliest pictorial messages whether they were interpreted idea by idea, with the words ad-libbed, or word by word. The signs might have been direct representations of concrete objects, or figurative representations of one notion through another (sun for 'bright, brilliant, blinding'), or diagrams (an empty circle for 'empty, vacant, hollow')—nothing would prove that a word rather than a meaning was intended. Even an additional semantic indicator like the man beside the bear cub would not assure us that the sample was one of word writing, for the idea might be one that could be expressed by only one word anyway, such as the proper name **Little Bear,** and some semantic indicators would still leave room for ad-libbing: man plus mountain could stand for 'man from the mountain,' hence 'slave,' 'servant,' 'person of low birth.'

But somewhere in the word-writing stage an event took place that proved the word-by-word interpretation beyond a doubt. The pictorial stage would have found it very difficult to express abstract notions like tense and mood in the verb; so if we find **would be** symbolized by a drawing of a piece of wood and a drawing of a bee, we can be certain that the figures no longer stand for ideas. This is the *rebus;* something that we now associate with children's games was proof of the innovation of word writing.

Now nothing stood in the way of applying the same phonetic principle not just to whole words but to parts of words.

Most languages contain words of more than one syllable, and often the syllables are the same in sound as certain one-syllable words. A slight extension of the rebus game enabled writers to use double characters for two-syllable words. In a modern rebus, *fancy* can be depicted by a fan and a sea, or *mumble* by a chrysanthemum and a bull. At first the sign-to-syllable relationship would not have been pure—a three-syllable word like *loggerhead* could have been represented by two signs, one for logger and one for head; but the basis for syllabic writing was laid, and the whole period of word writing was a mixture of word writing and syllable writing.

The earliest developed form of word-syllabic writing was that of the Sumerians in Mesopotamia at the end of the fourth millennium B.C. The Egyptians had their own system within a century or so of this, but were probably influenced by the Sumerians.

Syllable writing

Even after the knack of writing by syllables had been acquired, pure syllable writing was rather long in coming. The older word signs were kept through tradition and inertia, and often a given word could be represented either by its own sign or by signs for its syllables. The second historical step—the discarding of all the word signs and the adoption of a straightforward system of syllable writing—had to be taken by disrespectful foreigners who had no romantic attachments to the old signs and merely borrowed what was practical. These were the Phoenicians. Other borrowers of other systems did the same, but the Phoenicians are most important to us because they stand in direct line with the later development of the alphabet.

The Egyptian table of syllable signs, or syllabary, contained two sets of figures, each representing a different kind of value. The figures of the first set represented particular consonants plus any vowel or no vowel at all; a single sign stood for *ma, me, mi, mu,* or *m,* or for *ta, te, ti, tu,* or *t.* The members of the second set were the same except that two consonants were involved; one sign, for example, stood for *tama, tame, tem, tma,* and so on. The consistent omission of vowels was in line with the nature of the Semitic languages,

THE JAPANESE KATAKANA SYLLABARY

ア	カ	サ	タ	ナ	ハ	マ	ヤ	ラ	ワ		ガ	ザ	ダ	バ	パ
a	ka	sa	ta	na	ha	ma	ya	ra	wa		ga	za	da	ba	pa
イ	キ	ㇰ	チ	ニ	ヒ	ミ		リ	ヰ		ギ	ジ	ヂ	ビ	ピ
i	ki	si	ti(tsi)	ni	hi	mi		ri	wi(i)		gi	zi	di	bi	pi
ウ	ク	ス	ツ	ヌ	フ	ム	ユ	ル			グ	ズ	ヅ	ブ	プ
u	ku	su	tu(tsu)	nu	hu	mu	yu	ru			gu	zu	du	bu	pu
ヱ	ケ	セ	テ	ネ	ヘ	メ	エ	レ	ヱ		ゲ	ゼ	デ	ベ	ペ
e	ke	se	te	ne	he	me	ye	re	we(e)		ge	ze	de	be	pe
オ	コ	ソ	ト	ノ	ホ	モ	ヨ	ロ	ヲ		ゴ	ゾ	ド	ボ	ポ
o	ko	so	to	no	ho	mo	yo	ro	wo		go	zo	do	bo	po

ン (n)

FROM Fossey, *Notices sur les Caractères Etrangers*, p. 314; reproduced in I. J. Gelb, *A Study of Writing*, rev. ed. (Chicago: University of Chicago Press, 1963).

THE CHEROKEE SYLLABARY

This syllabary was invented between 1809 and 1821 by Sequoya (George Guess) and used by the Cherokee people and missionaries working among them. It is partly an adaptation of roman letters.

D	a	R	e	T	i	Ꮙ	o	Ꮕ	u	Ꭵ	ʌ			
Ꮂ	ga	Ꮄ	ge	Ꭹ	gi	A	go	J	gu	E	gʌ			
Ꮓ	ha	Ꮅ	he	Ꭿ	hi	Ꮁ	ho	Γ	hu	Ꮀ	hʌ	ꭰ	ka	
W	la	ꮆ	le	Ꮅ	li	Ꮄ	lo	M	lu	Ꮁ	lʌ	ꮕ	hna	
Ꮃ	ma	Ꮊ	me	H	mi	Ꮇ	mo	Ꮋ	mu			G	nah	
Ꮎ	na	Ꮑ	ne	Ꭵ	ni	Z	no	Ꮕ	nu	Ꮕ	nʌ	ꭰ	s	
Ꮖ	gwa	Ꮝ	gwe	Ꮗ	gwi	Ꮔ	gwo	Ꮘ	gwu	Ꮛ	gwʌ	W	ta	
Ꮚ	sa	Ꮞ	se	Ꮟ	si	Ꮠ	so	Ꮢ	su	R	sʌ	Ꮧ	ti	
Ꮥ	da	Ꮆ	de	Ꮧ	di	Λ	do	S	du	Ꮪ	dʌ	Ꮯ	tla	
Ꮬ	dla	Ꮭ	dle	Ꮨ	dli	Ꮰ	dlo	Ꮴ	dlu	P	dlʌ	Ꮦ	te	
Ꮳ	dza	Ꮴ	dze	Ꮵ	dzi	Ꮶ	dzo	Ꮷ	dzu	Ꮸ	dzʌ			
Ꮹ	wa	Ꮺ	we	Ꮻ	wi	Ꮼ	wo	Ꮽ	wu	Ꮾ	wʌ			
Ꮿ	ya	Ᏸ	ye	Ᏹ	yi	Ᏺ	yo	Ᏻ	yu	Ᏼ	yʌ			

FROM H. A. Gleason, *An Introduction to Descriptive Linguistics*, rev. ed. (New York: Holt, Rinehart and Winston, Inc., 1961), p. 414.

where inflections are shown by internal changes instead of by affixes (like English **man-men** rather than **man-*mans** or **rise-rose** rather than **rise-*rised**); it was possible to sacrifice the vowels without losing the identity of the word, and thus make a saving in the number of different symbols written.

The Phoenicians entered the picture around the middle of the second millennium B.C. They imitated the one-consonant syllabary of the Egyptians, throwing out the rest. By about 1000 B.C. they had developed a completely syllabic form of writing with no word signs and no signs for more than one syllable. The vowels were still omitted, though where needed to avoid ambiguity they were often added in the form of consonants whose features resembled those of the desired vowel. For example, Semitic writing—including Phoenician—had syllabic signs for the semiconsonants /w/ and /y/ (plus a vowel), and used them as makeshifts for the simple vowels /u/ and /i/. There were other such makeshifts. The glimmerings of alphabetic writing were already visible.

Sound writing: the alphabet

It is a bit presumptuous of modern phonology to appropriate the term "distinctive sound" for its phonemes, as if the users of language would never have supposed at each new and successive refinement of the relationship between sound and symbol that they had at last hit upon the phonetic atom. This is dramatized for us now with the theory of distinctive features—what we had thought was the atom, the phoneme, turns out to be a rather complex molecule. Words and syllables must have been felt to be just as distinctively irreducible in their time. So if phonemes continue to be called distinctive sounds—and the phrase is too firmly entrenched to be got rid of easily—we should remember that the term refers to a set of phonetic features, at a certain level of refinement, which actually came into consciousness within the growth of alphabetic writing. For that we can thank mainly the Greeks of some three thousand years ago.

The Phoenicians were the seafaring traders of the ancient world and carried their writing wherever they went as one of the tools of their trade. It was probably in the ninth century

B.C. that the form of Phoenician writing that was to become the Greek alphabet was planted along the western shores of the Aegean.

The Greek innovation—and it was gradual, like all the others—was to do consistently what the Phoenicians had done sporadically: to add the interpretative vowel signs to all their syllables. What they themselves must have regarded still as a syllabary thus became an alphabet by accident. A sign signifying /mu/ (as well as /mi me ma/) would not have needed any /u/ after it if the context made it clear that /mu/ was intended. An English sentence written **Y mst b crfl wth sch ppl** would give us no trouble—**mst** here can only mean **must.** But when the symbol for any **m**-plus-vowel syllable was consistently accompanied by a sign for a particular vowel, it was natural for the next generation of scribes to forget that it stood for the syllable and take it for the consonant alone. Now it was possible to go on to a full specification of all the phonemes. This was the form of writing that took hold in all the major languages of the world, including—with modifications —the Semitic itself, from which it was derived. We can never guess how far the progress and power of the Western world may have been due to the speedup of communication and the accumulation of recorded experience that was made possible when a quasi-phonemic writing that could be quickly learned took literacy away from a select priesthood and put it within reach of the general public.

Yet we need not be overly prideful of our Western accomplishment, for from the standpoint of sheer creativeness it was outdone by the Koreans some five hundred years ago. In 1446 King Sejong promulgated an alphabet—the date is still celebrated as a national holiday in Korea—in which certain strokes of the characters represented phonetic characteristics such as tongue position or force of articulation. The Koreans had had a good deal of practice with word and syllable writing using Chinese characters, and of course the whole evolution of alphabetic writing lay behind them, so they knew pretty much what they were doing in designing new forms; but their "visible speech," to borrow the name given to his own similar system four hundred years later by Alexander Melville Bell, was still a remarkable achievement.

STAGES OF THE DEVELOPMENT OF WRITING

No Writing: **Pictures**

Forerunners of Writing: **Semasiography**

   1. Descriptive-Representational Device
   2. Identifying-Mnemonic Device

Full Writing: **Phonography**

1. *Word-Syllabic:*	Sumerian (Akkadian)	Egyptian	Hittite (Aegean)	Chinese
2. *Syllabic:*	Elamite Hurrian etc.	West Semitic (Phoenician) (Hebrew) (Aramaic) etc.	Cypro- Minoan Cypriote Phaistos? Byblos?	Japanese
3. *Alphabetic:*		Greek Aramaic (vocalized) Hebrew (vocalized) Latin Indic etc.		

FROM I. J. Gelb, *A Study of Writing*, rev. ed. (Chicago: University of Chicago Press, 1963), p. 191.

Exercise 4

Communication through pictures was a preliminary stage in the evolution of the symbolic representation of language; these pictures conveyed only concepts, not particular words. Some pictograms are simple reminders of a name or event.

a.   The example on page 193 was obtained in 1888 from the Passamaquoddy Indians in Maine. They kept records of their trade with the white man; this is a record of one such transaction. Fill in the parentheses in the interpretation with the appropriate letters from the pictogram.

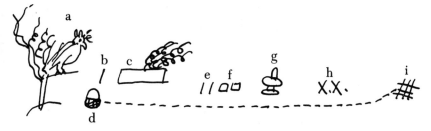

Interpretation: A woman called "Owl" ( ) bought one ( ) plug of smoking tobacco ( ), two ( ) quarts ( ) of kerosene for her lantern ( ), and all this is worth twenty cents ( ). To barter for this, she brings in a basket ( ) and the basket cancels the debt ( ).

b. Consider the development of the Sumerian word for 'hand' from the easily recognizable symbol on the left below to the cuneiform symbol on the right.

Might the complexity of communicating by pictograms have contributed to their being interpreted arbitrarily, that is, being taken to stand for sounds rather than for what they originally pictured? Could the opposite also have happened, a loss of the original meaning leading to a carelessness with the form? Explain your answers.

c. Are there differences among the parts of speech that might make the meanings of the words in one part easier to represent by drawing than those in another? If so, list the differences among adjectives, verbs, and nouns. Between these three parts of speech on the one hand and prepositions and conjunctions on the other, which could be shown best by diagrams?

Exercise 5

Pictograms are not *writing* symbols, since they do not symbolize language. They symbolize the information directly.

One method of writing is with word symbols: each word has its symbol. Unlike pictograms, word symbols make it possible for the exact wording of a message to be preserved.

a. In modern English, 2, &, and $ are examples of word symbols. Give an alphabetic symbol for each of these words.

b. Interpret the following figure, pretending first that you are reading it as a pictogram, then as a word symbol or logogram, then as a syllable symbol or syllabogram. What words might correspond to it as a logogram? What words might it form part of if it were a syllabogram?

c. Transliterate the following words written in the Cherokee syllabary on page 189.

Cherokee	Transliteration	Translation
G W y		Cherokee
Ꮟ Ᏺ ꮎ		Sequoya
S h Z Ꮫ		October, harvest month
Ꮻ Ᏺ ꮅ G		instantly
D l Ꮢ		war club

chapter 9

The Evolving Approaches to Language

Changing Approaches

The growth of linguistics as a science can be traced in five stages, each overlapping the preceding one but at some point breaking rather sharply with it and constituting itself an embattled school of thought. The five stages are traditional grammar, historical linguistics, descriptive linguistics, structural linguistics, and formal linguistics. Though born of conflict, they represent different emphases rather than irreconcilable rivalries; so each lives on. The new is a reassortment of the old to which are added deeper insights plus—for the troops who change sides—the spice of fashion.

Traditional Grammar

To anyone who has gone through a language course since the early 1950's, "traditional grammar" doubtless has a bad sound. Textbooks and teachers using supposedly up-to-date methods in teaching foreign languages or English mention traditional grammar either unfavorably or not at all; it embodies, for them, all the outmoded practices of reciting grammatical paradigms, translating to English instead of learning to speak, and worrying about what language ought to do rather than what it does.

But at the moment there is a renewed interest in traditional grammar, largely inspired by a contemporary group of linguists who find in the traditional grammarians their spiritual predecessors. Early traditionalists held that particular languages are individual forms taken by an underlying oneness common to the race. This notion of universality can be traced to the ancients, but it was encouraged by the linguistic situation prevailing in Western Europe throughout the Middle Ages: Latin was the vehicle of learning, the vernacular was the vehicle of commerce and daily living. Even after full dignity was accorded to each of the common languages and Latin was no longer regarded as superior—well into modern times—the sense of community among European scholars persisted. Their languages, especially the dominant Romance tongues of France, Italy, and Spain, were obviously related through Latin; underneath the superficial differences lay an immutable sameness. Whether universal grammar would have been so generally accepted if Europe had been sharply divided, say, between two languages as unlike as French and Hungarian, no one can say. But what was then perhaps an ill-founded idea comes to us now with a new suggestive power as we compare widely diverse languages and find in them more similarities than differences.

Traditional grammar was at its best in describing the inflections, idioms, and sentence forms of particular languages, especially the differences from language to language in Europe; this had a practical purpose too, for it put the emphasis on what had to be learned if one already knew French and wanted to study Italian—the same principles are expounded in "contrast grammars" today. But there were weaknesses which stemmed from the fact that traditional grammar was neither empirical nor experimental. It assumed that language was a system embodied in the writings of the best authors, something to be sheltered from change. From one standpoint this was useful: the view of individual languages as self-contained systems is essentially correct. From another standpoint it was harmful, because it blinded its advocates to the potential of language to renew itself from generation to generation. The potential for renewal was the all-absorbing interest of the up-and-coming younger generation of linguists at the beginning of the nineteenth century, who were so fascinated with the historical development of languages that they turned away from systematic descriptions. What descriptions had been made were thus cut off from criticism and became self-contained in every sense of the word. They fell into the hands of schoolmen who perpetuated them as stylebooks—not as records of what speakers did but as models of what speakers, especially schoolboys, ought to do. Where usage differed from the books, usage was corrupt. So traditional grammar drew farther and farther away from language as it was, and more and more it became a policeman of correctness.

Every culture recognizes some styles of speech or writing as better than others, at least under certain circumstances. In our culture there is a standard, or prestige, dialect that more or less coincides with the formal modes of expression used among persons who are not acquaintances and who do not belong to the same social class—who are, in short, "not relaxed" with one another when they speak. In writing, it more or less coincides with the style that must be used in a letter to a stranger. As this is not a dialect that is ordinarily learned in the home, it has to be learned later, and its rules of usage are what we generally think of when someone mentions correct speech. Normative grammar is unassailable when it identifies itself with a prestige dialect and honestly recognizes its practical and esthetic aims. It goes wrong when it is taken over by quacks who peddle self-improvement in the form of lessons—in school or out—on how to avoid a few dozen "mistakes." It also goes wrong—at least according to one conception of democracy—when it polishes correctness as a badge of superiority. Thus, slang might be appropriate under some conditions and a form of literary expression under others, but the appropriateness of slang is never viewed as a sign of quality, while that of literary expression frequently is. This, of course, is the linguistic side of social stratification: the speech of superior people is regarded as superior speech.

Exercise 1

The following sentences are samples of "false syntax" found in Samuel Kirkham's *English Grammar* of 1835. The words that Kirkham considers wrong or misplaced are italicized. Some of the same examples still appear in handbooks of English. What are your personal reactions to these sentences? Write 1, 2, or 3 for each sentence to denote *acceptable,* *questionable,* or *not acceptable* respectively.

a. Great pains *has* been taken to reconcile the parties.
b. The sincere *is* always esteemed.
c. The variety of the productions of genius, like that of the operations of nature, *are* without limit.
d. Time and tide *waits* for no man.
e. Patience and diligence, like faith, *removes* mountains.
f. Man's happiness or misery *are,* in a great measure, put into his own hands.
g. The prince, as well as the people, *were* blameworthy.
h. The nation was once powerful; but now *they are* feeble.
i. The multitude eagerly *pursues* pleasure as *its* chief good.
j. Much depends on this *rule* being observed.
k. *Who* did you talk with?
l. *Who* did you give the book to?
m. He is a man *who* I greatly respect.
n. Which of those two cords is the *longest?*
o. I was at a loss to determine which was the *wiser* of the three.
p. Be composed, it is *me.*
q. The French language is *spoke* in every state in Europe.
r. These things should be *never* separated.
s. I shall work today, unless it *rains.*
t. They were all well but *him.*

Exercise 2

The following article by George N. Feinstein, titled "Letter from a Triple-threat Grammarian," represents pointers taught in rhetoric nowadays.[1] As you read it, compare the author's concerns with Kirkham's. To what degree are both sets of rules bound by tradition, and to what degree are they dictated by clarity?

Dear sir; you never past me in grammer because you was prejudice but I got this here athaletic scholarship any way. Well, the other day I finely get to writing the rule's down so as I can always study it if they ever slip my mind.

a. Each pronoun agrees with their antecedent.
b. Just between you and I, case is important.
c. Verbs has to agree with their subjects.
d. Watch out for irregular verbs which has crope into our language.
e. Don't use no double negatives.
f. A writer mustn't shift your point of view.
g. When dangling, don't use participles.
h. Join clauses good, like a conjunction should.
i. Don't write a run-on sentence you got to punctuate it.
j. About sentence fragments.
k. In letters themes reports articles and stuff like that we use commas to keep a string of items apart.
l. Don't use commas, which aren't necessary.
m. Its important to use apostrophe's right.
n. Don't abbrev.
o. Check to see if you any words out.
p. In my opinion I think that an author when he is writing shouldn't get into the habit of making use of too many unnecessary words that he does not really need in order to put his message across.
q. In the case of a business letter, check it in terms of jargon.
r. About repetition, the repetition of a word might be real effective repetition—take, for instance, Abraham Lincoln.
s. As far as incomplete constructions, they are wrong.
t. Last but not least, lay off clichés.

Historical Linguistics

If the intimacy of language is what makes it a late arrival to science, it is also true that the least intimate part, the history of language, is what first took shape as an empirical science. The genealogy and family relationships of languages became a recognized discipline early in the nineteenth century and developed so vigorously and successfully that it took something like a revolution a century later to prove that linguistic science could be anything but historical.

This first great empirical theory—that languages now widely different can be traced to a common origin—was born of the intense interest of the 1800's in evolution, plus something that resulted accidentally from the English conquest of India: the discovery of Sanskrit. The effect of the latter has been described as follows:

> The knowledge of Sanskrit was found to have revolutionary consequences. The mere fact that scholars were unexpectedly confronted with a third classical language in addition to Greek and Latin was sufficient to shake their reliance on the easy-going ways of thinking that had satisfied previous centuries. Latin had been regarded as a sort of corrupted Greek, and the resemblances between Latin and the other European languages had been explained, in the same superficial way, as due to the preponderating cultural influence of Latin in Europe. But a similar offhand explanation of the resemblances between the ancient languages and this new-found Sanskrit was not possible: its home was too distant, and its remote cultural world was entirely independent of both Greco-Roman and modern civilization.[2]

The evolutionary kinship was unmistakable. For the next two or three generations the chief preoccupation of linguists was with formulating it. We have seen how this formulation made it possible to reconstruct languages that are no longer spoken—it is known almost to a certainty what Vulgar Latin was like, for though records are lacking it was captured between Classical Latin and the modern Romance tongues, with records of both. A fair estimate can be made of the language that preceded modern German, Swedish, English, and other Germanic tongues, though there is no record of any close preceding stage. And, as we saw earlier (Chapter 5, pages 106–10), something is known about the hypothetical ancestor of all our Western tongues, Proto-Indo-European.

Since each step in reconstruction had to be based on correspondences among languages that provided a clue to the reconstructed form, and since correspondences are not very often perfect, it became necessary also to explain the differences. Out of these explanations—of why, for instance, Sanskrit had *śatá-m* for 'hundred' but the related word in Latin, **kentum,** showed differences as well as similarities—there developed theories about sound change that eventually grew dependable enough for comparative grammarians to make a sweeping claim: that all change is amenable to law. Exceptions there were, of course, but not because some law of sound had changed its method of operation—rather because many words were late borrowings that had no ancestry within the language or because of accidents such as folk etymologies or blends. This insight—the universality of law and the possibility of arriving at it by scientific methods—was the most pregnant discovery in the study of language during the nineteenth century. But it had to be rediscovered when linguists turned from the evolution of language to its involution, from changes in surface form to analysis of inner form. Once again the history of science repeated itself: what was most intimate resisted formulation.

Exercise 3

Loan words were mentioned among the exceptions to sound laws. Actually, however, the moment a word is borrowed it is exposed to whatever laws are operating at the time, and hence will probably be modified, though not as much as a word that was borrowed earlier. One pervasive law in English affects borrowed nouns in which some other syllable than the first carries the stress: it tends to be shifted to the first syllable. (See Chapter 6, page 144.) Thus Italian **trombóne** has become **trómbone** for many speakers, and French **parlánce** has become **párlance.** Some words go through this process quickly: French **mascótte** was borrowed between 1880 and 1884, but soon became **máscot.** Others resist.

Note how you pronounce the following words and see if others pronounce them differently: **intrigue** (dated 1647 by the *Oxford English Dictionary*), **prestige** (1656), **crusade** (1706), **perfume** (1533), **parakeet** (1581). Now and then one resists indefinitely. About 1915, **gárage,** riming with **carriage,** competed with the pronunciation that is general in the United States today. How do you pronounce **garage?** How might another sound law change *garage* so that a shift of stress to the first syllable will be out of the question? Apply the analogy of *police-pleece.*

Descriptive Linguistics

The person who did most to turn his colleagues away from their absorption with history and toward the investigation of the languages of their own time was the Swiss scholar Ferdinand de Saussure, himself a historical linguist. He envisioned languages as systems in unstable equilibrium, but with emphasis on the equilibrium.

For Saussure, there were two axes of linguistic study which had to be distinguished. One axis was the integral, self-contained and (to individual speakers with their limited perspective) temporally arrested state, termed *synchronic* (with or through a given time). The second axis was the history of a language, termed *diachronic* (across time). "Ever since modern linguistics came into existence," he complained, "it has been completely absorbed in diachrony." This was his manifesto: "Linguistics, having accorded too large a place to history, will turn back to the static viewpoint of traditional grammar but in a new spirit and with other procedures. . . ."[3]

Traditional grammar had been static in a dual sense—not only in dealing with the state of a language and nothing more, but in its unawareness of the forces that work to overthrow the state. How speakers react to the little potential subversions that surround them is part of their linguistic behavior. Their moments of hesitancy, which reflect the language in flux, are as real and as much a part of the language *now* as their moments of certainty, which reflect the language in repose.

The old approach and the new were not really in conflict, though the shift of emphasis made them appear to be. How necessary the two are to each other was pointed out in 1927 by the man whom most linguists today regard as the dean of their guild, Roman Jakobson. Jakobson called for a historical linguistics in which the static viewpoint would play a key role: it was not the successive development of individual sounds that should be investigated but the succession of whole stages, for unless we knew the relationship of a sound to its fellow sounds at a given moment in history, we could never understand why sounds changed the way they did.

But events decreed that in the United States, at least, Saussure would be taken literally, and linguistic science in this century would develop along lines clearly synchronic. Where European scholarship carried on the older tradition that had seen first the attachment of philological study to the study of literature and then its convergence with the study of history, in America a new affinity grew up between linguistics and the aggressive young science of anthropology.

There were two stages in this development. In the earlier one the leading figure was the German-born anthropologist Franz Boas, who spent most of his life studying American Indian cultures and who early realized that the language of a culture was its most distinctive creation. Boas had the luck to acquire as a student Edward Sapir, a poet, critic, and amateur musician as well as a trained Germanist. To the inspiration of these two men was added the desperation of anthropologists to record American Indian languages before it was too late, since many were rapidly dying out. It was no easy task that the anthropological linguists cut out for themselves:

> The New World is unique in the number and diversity of its native idioms. There are probably well over one thousand mutually unintelligible American Indian languages, which are customarily grouped into more than one hundred and fifty different families. In California alone, according to Sapir, "there are greater and more numerous linguistic extremes than can be illustrated in all the length and breadth of Europe. . . ."
>
> A similar diversity may be observed along the Pacific coast from Oregon to Alaska, where languages belonging to twelve different stocks are spoken; on the Gulf coast from Texas to Florida, with seven families of languages; and among the Pueblo Indians of New Mexico and Arizona, where people with remarkably similar nonlinguistic cultures speak languages belonging to four distinct and widely divergent stocks.[4]

It is little wonder that linguists in America were so caught up with the urgency of recording and analyzing native American languages that they had little time or patience for anything else. The anthropological approach to language attained a similar prominence in England, at the School of Oriental and African Studies at the University of London.

The second stage in the development of anthropological linguistics in the United States came in the early 1930's from religious missionaries. A number of Protestant denominations with extensive missions abroad established the Summer Institute of Linguistics, with two principal aims: the linguistic training of missionaries and the translation of the Bible. Since practically all the languages in question were without an alphabet, one of the first tasks the Institute faced was to "reduce the language to writing." The Summer Institute has carried on a veritable linguistic conquest, for it has moved from small outposts among a few American Indian tribes to an operation that extends from Colombia to New Guinea and enlists the cooperation of government bureaus in more than a dozen countries. By 1968 it was conducting work in over four hundred languages, with a staff of more than 2,000 permanent members and about 600 new trainees a year. The leading figure of the Institute is Kenneth L. Pike, whose view of linguistic structure is the tagmemic theory (outlined in Chapters 3 and 4, pages 53–55, 98–100).

Other religious organizations have been active too, though in recent years none with such far-flung interests as the Summer Institute. But, the linguistic endeavors of missionaries go back many centuries. After the Spanish conquest of the Americas, the religious orders were charged with educating the Indians, and numerous grammars of Indian languages were written. In South America, the Jesuits even made two of the more generalized Indian languages — Guaraní and Quechua — their medium of instruction.

Linguistics under the influence of anthropology lived in a constant state of emergency. The anthropological linguists based in the universities were driven by the need to record the languages of cultures *in extremis*. The missionary linguists were driven by their calling to spread the Word. Urgency was stepped up to a frenzy when during World War II the American armed forces found themselves in the fearful situation of having to govern scores of Pacific enclaves with no one able to speak to the inhabitants, and they turned to the anthropological linguists to get a language program moving. Haste was the order of the day, and the climate of the 1930's and 1940's was wrong for profound reflection and all-encompassing theory. But the storehouse of observations was by the 1950's so full that it cried for a stock-taking.

Exercise 4

a. Given an innate capacity for language, the rudiments of language organization, and an intense need for particular forms and amounts of communication, speakers build up the communicative power of their language to the point where it almost exactly balances the need. Relate this statement to one frequently-heard comment that "primitive" languages (that is, those of unindustrialized societies) are inferior.

b. Review the list of language universals in Chapter 1 (page 27). Consider whether some or all of the following traits would be found in all languages; explain your opinion:

1. Some way of distinguishing between what is real (or, more specifically, what is going on now) and what is unreal (what went on in the past). How is this represented in English?
2. Different ways of addressing superiors and inferiors.
3. Comparison — that is, devices for showing "more" and "less."

c. Following are some traits of languages you may know. Consider whether or not they could be universal:

1. In German there is a system of cases (some school grammars used to list *of the table, to the table, O Table!*, and so on, as noun cases in English).
2. In French there is a gender system.
3. In Italian there is a progressive construction, *Essi stavano dormendo* 'They were sleeping.'
4. In Greek, Latin, English, and other languages there is a decimal system of numerals.

Structural Linguistics

American structuralism

The anthropological bias created a turn of mind in the United States that has confined linguistic theory to a rather narrow channel. Consider the first order of business for a missionary who wants to teach an aboriginal tribe to read and write its own language. He does not need to teach the language. The natives already know it; all they have to learn is a representation. As soon as the missionary-linguist has managed to isolate the phonemes, he is in a position to set up an alphabet and his main work is done. What is left after the associations between the written symbols and the distinctive sounds have been established is less imperative, because the previously illiterate native knows the syntax of his language, even if the linguist knows little beyond the phonemes.

This is an exaggeration—more than phonemes must be taken into account to determine the phonemes themselves, and translating the Bible calls for a delicate analysis—but it illustrates where the emphasis in anthropological linguistics was bound to lie. Until the phoneme was attended to, nothing systematic could be done with morphology or syntax. Thus forced to start at the bottom, the anthropological linguist had his priorities laid out for him: he had to analyze first the sounds, then the morphemes, and last of all the syntax.

There was very little in the recent tradition of linguistics to make him question this scheme. The great triumphs in historical linguistics had been in the laws of sound. In the schools it was the same: the learner of a foreign language must—like the anthropologist visiting a new tribe—master first the sound system and then the morphology, and then he can largely guess at the syntax. Language teaching had the same priorities in the same order.

What had started as a combination of practical necessity and historical accident was thus elevated to a theoretical precept: "Do not attempt to deal with syntax before morphology, nor with morphology before phonology; to do so is to *mix levels.*" Since the units of each lower level were the components of the units at the next higher one, it was impossible to move up until the proper foundation had been laid.

Now a great "-eme" hunt was on. The categories of classical grammar were gone — they were good for Latin but not, so it was thought, for Hokan or Chinook. And linguists would have nothing to do with mentalistic notions imposed on language from philosophy and logic — in this they were influenced by the behavioristic psychology in vogue during the 1920's and 1930's. Nothing was left but to find the needed entities within the substance of language itself. The result was a concentration on what has come to be called "discovery procedures." It was assumed that, since human beings could react intelligently to speech, it must be on the basis of sets of signaling units. One such set — the phonemes — had been brilliantly demonstrated. It remained to ferret out the audible units that enabled speakers and hearers to tell how the phonemes were assembled into morphemes — were there phonemes of pause, or stress, that did this? In a language where stress occupied a fixed position in a word, for example, it would be possible to locate the word boundaries by counting syllables to the right or left of the stress. And, at the highest level, were there phonemes of rhythm or pitch that marked the beginning and the end of clauses and sentences? Just enough evidence of this sort of thing did turn up to encourage the hope that the whole pattern would one day become clear.

This was American structuralism, and one of its effects was the continual postponement of the investigation of syntax. But an orphan can be neglected only so long, and syntax was not to be denied. Structuralists brought to it their morpheme-before-syntax method and created a syntax that had the same characteristics of fixed smaller units organized into fixed larger ones that they were accustomed to in their building of phonemes into morphemes. As before, the starting point had to be samples of utterances as they were observed. The principles of organization were in the text, in the spoken segments, not from outside nor from underneath.

What is the first thing that a linguist observes about the organization of a sentence if he approaches it without preconceptions about subjects, predicates, subordinations, and the like? It is that elements that stand side by side tend to belong together. This seems to hold in most human organization. In a filing drawer, the items in a folder have more in common with one another, and especially each with its nearest neighbor, than any item has with those in the next folder, and the folders behind a single guide card are more like one another than like those behind the next guide card, and so on up to drawer-versus-drawer and cabinet-versus-cabinet. One of the main uses of the phonology of the sentence that the structuralists thought they had discovered was this insertion of guide cards to separate a togetherness on one side from a togetherness on the other.

Two kinds of examples illustrate how pervasive the principle of togetherness is in language. One is our resistance to putting something between two things that are more closely related to each other than they are to what is inserted. Teachers find it hard to enforce the rule of interior plurals in forms like *mothers-in-law* and *postmasters general* – speakers want to put the *-s* at the end. They are even more reluctant to say *hardest-working person*, inserting the *-est* between the members of the compound *hard-working;* and though some might manage it there, probably no one would say **farthest-fetched story* for *most far-fetched story.*

The second kind of example shows up when two things that formerly did not belong together come to be viewed as if they did, because they are side by side. The attraction of nearness may even override an intervening pause. For example, the word *frankly,* which was common in half-apologetic statements like *I am, frankly, bored,* has become virtually an intensive modifier of the word that follows: *I am frankly bored.* Something similar has happened to certain prepositions which at an earlier stage were felt (as is customary) to be most closely bound to the following noun, but which have come to acquire a closer attachment to what precedes, as our manner of spelling sometimes indicates: *lotsa* for *lots of, kinda* for *kind of, sorta* for *sort of* (the last two have taken the further step of being used as unit adverbs: *kinda nice*). The pull from two directions – from what precedes and from what follows – can be detected in mistakes that we sometimes make, like **an idea of which he was very fond of,* where the preposition is torn between *which* and *fond.*

Applied to linguistic analysis, this togetherness-by-levels was refined into a technique of identifying "immediate constituents." Given a set of morphemes or words, one can show their interrelationships in this fashion. Take the two words **ungraceful** and **disgraceful** which have different constituent analyses:

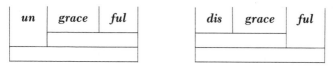

In the first, **-ful** is an immediate constituent of **-grace-** (the two are on the same level and belong together), while **un-** is an immediate constituent of the combination **-graceful;** in the second, **-ful** is not on the same level as **-grace-**, but rather on the same level as **disgrace-:** 'full of disgrace.'

Analysis by immediate constituents is the most effective way of showing how a complex sentence is layered; for example, **He said he wanted to marry her** is analyzed as follows:

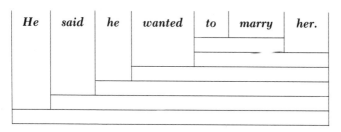

The same relationships are shown by a tree diagram such as the one below.

By itself, immediate-constituent analysis tells us how a stretch of speech is layered, but it tells us nothing about the

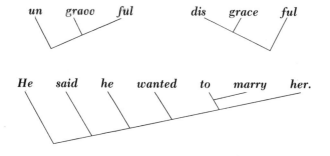

nature of the elements nor the manner in which they are related. For example, *behind the house* and *only a few* have the same constituent diagram,

behind	the	house

only	a	few

but the first is more closely related to *in back of the old stone house on the hill,* whose diagram seems quite different:

in	back	of	the	old	stone	house	on	the	hill

There is an obvious similarity between diagrams of this type and those once used for teaching grammar in schools, and it suggests what is needed to complete the analysis: something about parts of speech, or word classes, and about subjects, predicates, modifiers, or functions of the classes.

The diagram opposite reveals both the layering and the unlimited possibilities of embedding constructions within constructions: *in back of the old stone house on the hill* is a prepositional phrase that contains a prepositional phrase, *on the hill.* And *on the hill* could be lengthened to contain two more prepositional phrases, *on the hill up the river from here,* in which *up the river from here* modifies *hill* and *from here* modifies *up the river* as a unit, explaining how *up the river* is to be oriented.

on	the	hill	up	the	river	from	here

It	grows	in	back	of	the	old	stone	house	on	the	hill.
							Compound noun				
						Noun modified by adjective			Inner noun phrase		
					Inner noun phrase				Prepositional phrase		
		Compound preposition			Outer noun phrase, object of preposition						
	Main verb	Prepositional phrase, complement of main verb									
Subject	Predicate										
Sentence											

Immediate-constituent analysis, plus some form of label-ing for classes and functions (tagmemes and syntagmemes — see Chapter 4, pages 98–100), is the syntactic style of Ameri-can structural linguistics. It carries to a higher plane the buildup of smaller units into larger ones that appeared to work reasonably well at lower levels. It can be carried still farther: In the view of Kenneth L. Pike, human behavior as a whole is structured in the same way, and on top of morphemes and grammatical tagmemes there are "behavioremes," such as the organized activity of a game, a church service, or a meal.

Exercise 5

a. Immediate-constituent (IC) analysis divides a sentence into adjacent parts. Each of these parts is divided into adjacent parts, and so on until no further division is pos-sible. The parts are labeled according to their structure and function. Using the labels from the analysis above and any others you think appropriate, such as *modifi-cation, subordination,* or parts of speech, make an immediate-constituent analysis of the following sentences and phrases.

1. His asking why makes no difference.
2. Usually the train comes on time.
3. Since the car wouldn't start, I had to walk to work.
4. whenever he came into town
5. into the old white house that he had just sold
6. to hit the ball squarely
7. the hunter in the red jacket who was sneaking up on the cow
8. The first of the men left his jacket in the car.

b. Make an immediate-constituent analysis of some particular human activity—a game, a religious service, a meal, a political campaign. What labels will you use? Do the components function the same way as words in a sentence?

Exercise 6

a. The expression **I'm sorry for you (him, John, etc.)**, formerly meant 'For you, because of you, I am full of regret.' The *for* belonged with **you.** But nowadays we link *for* with **sorry,** giving a phrasal verb meaning 'to pity.' A similar shift has taken place, but in the opposite direction, with sentences like **It is easy for him / to do it.** Explain the shift that turned *for* into an empty word introducing infinitive phrases, as in **It would be terrible / for that to happen.**

b. Use immediate-constituent analysis to show different senses of the following: **more competent workers; clean water intake; one horse show.**

Formal Linguistics

In the early 1950's, a certain restiveness began to disturb the calm of structuralism and by the end of the decade had developed into open revolt. The revolt was abetted from other countries—there were European schools with traditions of their own whose influence was spread by visiting scholars—

and from within by increasing contacts between linguists and specialists in allied fields such as psychology, mathematics, logic, and communications engineering. Linguists became conscious of some of the flaws in the structuralist edifice and began to ask themselves questions like the following:

Why should the sequence of phoneme-to-sentence, which might be useful for an anthropological linguist or for a missionary facing a tribe of hostile Indians, necessarily have any relevance to linguistic theory? Why not assume an interrelated system that is simply "there" and no part of which can be fully understood without a grasp of the whole? In diagramming it or writing a description of it one might want for the sake of convenience to scan up or scan down (most formal representations look as if they proceeded from more inclusive to less inclusive), but no priority would be implied. Some structuralists were quite willing to go along with this criticism.

Why should it be necessary to dig up — or even expect to be able to dig up — an audible structural signal for every linguistic class? Why not accept the intuition of native speakers, in whose speech linguistic classes are seen to agree in subtle ways even though there is no apparent physical basis for the agreement, and carry on from there? That is what traditional grammar had always done, and it seemed to work, perhaps because it was close to the inwardness of language.

Why should the basis of linguistic theory be so narrowly defined that it could draw only upon those things that emerged from the field work carried on by linguists, avoiding universals as if they did not exist, and fearing abstract concepts just because they had once been used — and abused — by old-fashioned Latinizing grammar? Other sciences would have been paralyzed without abstract theory.

How could a frame so confined as that of immediate constituents be expected to fit comfortably around the whole of syntax, when there are many important relationships that escape it? The classic example is the relationship between the active and the passive voice: **George sees Mary, Mary is seen by George.** An immediate-constituent analysis of these two sentences tells nothing about their underlying kinship.

Why should all the energies of linguists be spent in gathering more and more examples? The younger linguists had harsh words for specimen-grubbing. It seemed to them that we already had a superabundance of scattered facts and now it was time to fit the facts into a system.

The upshot of these doubts and queries was a cry for an all-encompassing theory of language that would, as theories must, see first the whole and then the parts; that would hypothesize and look for confirmation rather than gather specimens in the hope that broader principles would emerge magically from them. Such a theory—if it were to be a theory of language and not of particular languages—would boldly assume that there were universals in language; and it would have a more flexible apparatus than the mere labeling and chopping that went on in immediate-constituent analysis.

According to such a theory, each language must be viewed as a coherent system, with the possibility of writing a grammar for it that will embrace the whole. Two characteristics of such a grammar are that it is *self-confirmatory* and that it is *automatic*. We need to dwell on these for a moment to grasp what such a grammar is like and to see its relationship to theoretical models in general.

When a scientist makes a "model" or theoretical description of a body of facts, he does so on the assumption that there is an underlying unity in the facts, that they are so intimately related that if something happens to disturb one part of the system there will be an echo somewhere else. Where the facts are as complex as they are in language, the assumption of an underlying system becomes a way of testing the theory. Suppose in our grammar system of English we hypothesize that adjectives in front of their nouns have an underlying relationship to predicate adjectives—that is, that **the red book** and **the book that is red** both "come" from some archetypal structure that is very close in form to **the book that is red,** so that we can, crudely, set up the "derivation" *the book that is red →* *the red book.* Most native speakers would feel intuitively that this is correct, and that is enough for a hypothetical start. But to get from one of these two structures to the other, more than one step is needed. The adjective has to be moved in front of the noun, but before that the *that is* must be dropped. Dropping it gives *the book red,* with which we are not very happy because our hypothesis has predicted the possibility of something that we do not find in English. But we ask ourselves whether the language contains any other closely related structures that *would* fit at this point, and if so, whether they ought to be derived in the same way; perhaps there is some restriction in English that prevents the particular manifestation *the book red* but permits the same manifestation in another form. We find just such a manifestation in prepositional phrases. There is the same relationship between *the book on the shelf* and *the book that is on the shelf* as between *the red book* and *the book that is red.* And this time *the book on the shelf* is as far as we can go—there is no **the on-the-shelf book;* the predicted structure is just what we are looking for. As an extra dividend, we find that we have an explanation for some of the "exceptions" that crop up here and there—adjectives that remain behind their nouns, like *books galore,* and prepositional phrases that jump over to the left, like *under-the-counter sale.* It is not necessary for us to have in our collection any such examples as these last ones. We deduced their possibility from the hypothesis. The advantage of a theoretical model is that just such deductions can be made and confirmations sought.

The second characteristic, that the grammar is *automatic,* is just another way of saying that its rules must be explicit enough for a machine to apply them (assuming that a machine could be built that is vastly beyond our capabilities now). This is the sense in which the word *formal* is used: a formal grammar is one that does not need any intervention from outside to make it work. The best rules in any traditional grammar are the formal ones, the ones that have no exceptions that call for a standby intelligence to decide whether they apply or not. Take a traditional rule like the one stating that when a personal pronoun is preceded by a preposition it will be in the objective case: *from him, from her,* not **from he, *from she.*

A computer can make this selection as efficiently as a human being. Formal linguistics goes beyond traditional grammar in assuming that everything is potentially automatic. True exceptions will be listed in the dictionary (the entry for *galore* will show that it follows the noun); apparent exceptions — resulting from imperfect rules — will call for revising the rules. A proper grammar will account for "all and only" those sentences that a native speaker regards as "well formed." In addition, it will specify how grammatical or ungrammatical a sentence is that does not quite make the grade.

A formal system needs a formal presentation. The disciplines that had already worked out a scheme for handling similar problems were symbolic logic and mathematics, and to them the formal grammarian turned. Take a simple example from mathematics, two number series like the following:

1, 7, 5, 11, 9, 15, 13, 19, 17, 23, 21 . . .
2, 8, 6, 12, 10, 16, 14, 20, 18, 24, 22 . . .

Inspection shows that in each series there are pairs (*1, 7; 5, 11*) that have a difference of 6 between their numbers, and that each such pair is larger than the preceding pair by a factor of 4. One way of describing the series would be to list them, but this could only be partial because they run to infinity. Another way is to pretend that you are *making* the series and to state the rule of operation. Probably the simplest rule here would be "Alternately add 6 and subtract 2." Such descriptive rules in mathematics are termed "generative," and the term has been borrowed for grammar.

As an illustration of the way a generative rule in English grammar is constructed, consider the method of introducing relative clauses. This type of rule accounts for the potentially infinite layering noted on pages 208–11. We know that a noun can be modified by a type of sentence,[5] which we term a *clause*, containing *that, which,* or *who* and occasionally certain other forms. Wherever one encounters a noun phrase, that phrase potentially subtends such a clause. We can write the formula,

NP → N + WhS

"A noun phrase may be manifested by noun plus *which* (or *who-*, etc.) sentence." But we also know that sentences often contain other noun phrases; for example, **who cuts the X** contains the noun phrase **X:**

WhS → Wh + V + NP

"WhS is manifested by **who** plus verb plus noun phrase." Now we can reapply the first formula for the included NP, giving

WhS → Wh + V + N + WhS

"The included noun phrase is manifested by a noun plus its own WhS," so that the whole complex turns out to be something like **the man who cuts the meat that comes from the shop.** The process can be carried as far as native speakers will tolerate the addition of more and more clauses; a classic example is "The House that Jack Built." Rules that can be reapplied in this manner are called "recursive."

Intuition is so important to generative grammarians that one could almost call them the psychologists of language. They affirm an underlying psychological reality, that of the human being's native ability to grasp linguistic form whatever its specific content (from this standpoint differences between languages are trivial) and to infer the rules that will enable him to make his own sentences. There is an "innate mechanism responsible for a child's acquisition of a language." Without such a psychological premise it is difficult to explain "why there should be a certain structure and content found in every language."[6] The structuralists were confirmed anti-mentalists; their psychology, when they admitted any, was behavioristic. The formalists unblushingly admit their mentalism, and find in their theory one way of "seeing" the psychological reality that underlies the human power to communicate.

In its algebra, generative grammar is reminiscent of immediate-constituent analysis, and this kind of analysis does in fact make up a sizable part of generative description—the part that embodies the "phrase-structure rules," which describe the way sentences are broken into parts. The tree diagram is regularly used, but turned upside down, since the progression is from the sentence to the parts. The diagram of **That man lost a dollar** on page 218 can be verbalized as follows:

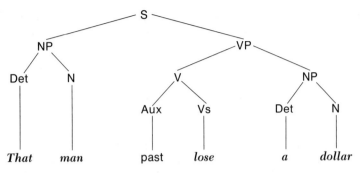

The S(entence) is made up of a N(oun) P(hrase) plus a V(erb) P(hrase). NP is made up of a Det(erminer) plus a N(oun). The Det in this sentence is manifested by **that** (other members of the same determiner class which might have been chosen are **the, this, a,** and **my**). The N in this NP is manifested by **man.** The VP in this sentence contains a V plus an NP, which specifies the verb as transitive, that is, as object-taking (had the sentence been **The man died,** there would be no following NP). V contains an Aux(iliary element) plus a Vs (verb stem). The Aux in this sentence is manifested by just the past tense; it could be the present tense, or it could involve a modal verb like **can, may,** or **must** in addition to the tense. The Vs is manifested by the verb **lose.** The NP is made up in the same way as the other NP.

"**That man** past **lose a dollar**" of course is not an English sentence. It is a representation of morphemes, most of which happen to be representable as words. To get from the syntax to the actual sentence, more steps are necessary. The first step converts "past **lose**" into **lost.** (If we had shown grammatical number separately from **man** and **dollar,** as would have been necessary in a less schematic diagram, this step would also be responsible for turning out the form **man** rather than **men** and **dollar** rather than **dollars.**) The next step decrees that the indefinite article shall have the form **a** and not **an,** and in general it specifies the phonemes, or, if carried further still, the distinctive features, that make up the morphemes. A more interesting example of this last kind of step is the attempt to give rules of word formation—a higher-level form such as /opæk/ giving /opæs/ if specified as noun and /opek/ if specified as adjective, for the words **opacity** and **opaque** respectively.

The illustration shows the completeness that generative grammar lays claim to, embracing the whole of description, from the full sentence to its minutest fragment. Yet why not? If language is a system, and most linguists agree that it is, nothing should be omitted. The only valid criticism is that giving names to barely explored subdivisions may create the illusion of controlling them, which we are far from being able to do as yet.

The area that generativists have worked hardest to bring under control is one that does not reveal itself through a phrase-structure diagram. It is the area mentioned earlier as neglected by immediate-constituent analysis through its inability to give form to the relationships that native speakers feel intuitively between such things as statements and questions, active voice and passive voice, emphatic utterances (*I did tell them*) and unemphatic ones (*I told them*), and so on. An analysis of these relationships calls for a separate component in the grammar, a *transformational component*. It is the conspicuousness and originality of the transformational concept that has led to referring to the entire formal approach as "transformational grammar." The name most closely associated with it is that of Noam Chomsky, whose brief synthesis *Syntactic Structures* was published in 1957 and is regarded even by many erstwhile structuralists as representing the most significant recent "breakthrough" in linguistics.

A transformation is a way of specifying, by rule, the relationship between the structures underlying sentences like *John saw Mary* and *Mary was seen by John.* It can be shown roughly by matching the two:

John saw Mary → Mary was seen by John

But since the relationship applies to the syntactic elements, not just to these particular words, it is expressed algebraically:

$$NP_1 + Aux + Vs + NP_2 \rightarrow NP_2 + Aux + be + en + V + by + NP_1$$

Or, to verbalize: The two noun phrases exchange places, with *by* placed before the one that now comes last. The tense (Aux) remains the same (past *saw* matches past *was*), but a form of *be* is inserted and the verb takes its past participle (*en*) form: *was seen.*

In similar ways it is possible to take a sentence like *John saw Mary* (remembering that the sentence is only the surface manifestation of the underlying structure NP + VP with all its subtended symbols) and relate it to *Did John see Mary?*, *John didn't see Mary, for John to see Mary, John's seeing Mary (was no accident)*, and any other construction in which *John*, *see*, and *Mary* keep the same relationship to one another.

This confers a cohesiveness on grammar that it lacked before. Cohesiveness is essential if a language is to be described as a self-contained system. Transformations seem to account for the complex buildup of simpler constructions into more and more intricate ones better than any other scheme of analysis. The buildup is accomplished by embedding one construction in another, as we saw done with adjective clauses in the earlier example. As another example, the NP object of the verb *to prefer* can be a noun, as in *They prefer pork chops*, or it can be a construction, as in *They prefer that nothing more be done for the present* or *They prefer a specialist to examine John.* If we use X as a dummy symbol for the embedded sentence, the latter can be expressed as a composite:

$$\left.\begin{array}{l}\text{They prefer X}\\\text{A specialist will}\\\text{examine John}\end{array}\right\} \rightarrow \begin{array}{l}\text{They prefer a specialist}\\\text{to examine John}\end{array}$$

The transformational rule here converts the verb to its infinitive form. It does the same when the embedded sentence has already been made passive:

$$\left.\begin{array}{l}\text{They prefer X}\\\text{John will be examined}\\\text{by a specialist}\end{array}\right\} \rightarrow \begin{array}{l}\text{They prefer John to be examined}\\\text{by a specialist}\end{array}$$

This notion of embedding, of viewing certain parts of complex sentences as disguised sub-sentences (sentences that were "understood," as traditional grammar phrased it), goes back at least as far as the grammarians of the sixteenth and seventeenth centuries. Recent writings in generative grammar express it by writing S(entence) an unlimited number of times in a phrase-structure diagram (page 221). For instance, *They saw John* and *They saw that it was John* have the same structure, differing only in that NP₂ is a proper noun in the first and a sub-sentence in the second.

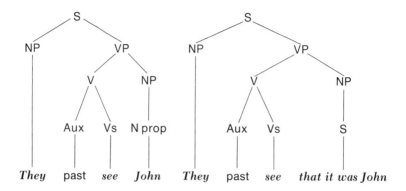

By thus combining active descriptions, or transformations, with static ones, or phrase structures and lexical items, generative grammar aims, in theory at least, to fulfill its claim of accounting for any and all of the well-formed sentences in a language.

Exercise 7

Consider what happens to the NP's of the sentence **Columbus discovered America** when the sentence is transformed to its passive counterpart.

passive
Columbus discovered America. → **America was discovered by Columbus.**

A transformation is symbolized by →. We note that the positions of the NP's **Columbus** and **America** have been interchanged. Since only the NP's interchange, the *passive transformation* can determine the NP constituents of sentences. This is a helpful guide in the case of those sentences that undergo the passive transformation. Some sentences do not.

a. Write out the sentences in which the passive transformation applies. Then write the passive transform.

Columbus suppressed a mutiny $\rightarrow$ A mutiny was suppressed by Columbus.

1. Columbus died a happy man.
2. Columbus died happy.
3. Columbus greeted the Indians.
4. Columbus was a lucky man.
5. Columbus ignored the sailors.

b. Again write out the following sentences and underline the NP's. If you are not sure, use the passive transformation as a guide.

1. The emotional actress divorced the movie magnate.
2. *Webster's Third* heralded a new age of lexicography.
3. The strikers demanded better working conditions.

c. Now consider the sentence **Beauty is in the eye of the beholder.**
The passive transformation does not apply to this sentence. The NP, however, can be isolated by means of another transformation that turns the statement into a question taking "yes" or "no" as an answer, as in **Is beauty in the eye of the beholder?** The shift of the verb **be** has isolated the NP.

Beauty **is** *in the eye of the beholder.*
(NP)

Thus, the *yes-no question transformation* also identifies the NP, in this case **beauty.** Write out on a separate sheet of paper the NP's in the following sentences with the aid of the passive and the yes-no question transformation guides.

1. The clerk at the third counter was happy to cash the check.
2. His discourteous manners and unkempt look could annoy many persons.
3. Winter arrives early in Minnesota.

d. To apply a yes-no question transformation to the third sentence, you had to supply a form of the auxiliary **do** to the sentence. **Does** is the word that moves around the NP. Where does **does** belong in sentence 3 before it is transformed to a question? To find its position, transform sentence 3 to an emphatic or a negative sentence.

Exercise 8

The sentence ***It was unforgivable for the police to arrest the students*** is represented by the following derivation (application of phrase-structure rules) and tree diagram:

1. S ⟶ NP + VP
2. VP ⟶ *be* + Adj
3. NP ⟶ N + S
4. N ⟶ *it*
5. S ⟶ NP + VP
6. VP ⟶ V + NP
7. NP ⟶ Det + N

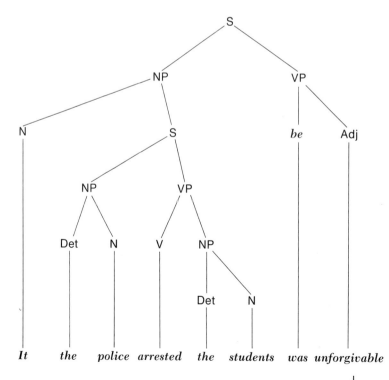

Here we find that the NP consists of an N followed by an S. We say that the S is embedded in the NP.

a. What is done to the sentence represented by the tree diagram to make *It was unforgivable for the police to arrest the students*?

b. Construct a tree diagram from the morpheme string *It Bill pleased the teacher was unusual* and apply the same transformation. What is the sentence you have produced?

chapter 10

Meaning

Making Contact

At what point does language break free? Distinctive features make phonemes, phonemes make morphemes, morphemes words, words sentences, sentences discourses, discourses monologues or dialogues or stories or whatever, and these may be expanded into novels, trilogies, encyclopedias, or still more complex levels of organization. Yet at some point—and it surely is not necessarily the last and highest—language must make contact with the outside world. This contact is what we call *meaning*.

The term *meaning* is used in many ways, not all of them equally relevant to our investigation of language. Saying *I didn't mean to hurt him* is the same as saying *I didn't intend to. Another child means an extra mouth to feed* or *Smoke means fire* signifies an inference. *The German* **Hund** *means* '*dog*' is a translation. And so on. The meaning of "meaning" that, while not itself linguistic, is closest to its function in language is that of the example *A red light means 'Stop.'* This is not quite the same as **Smoke means fire.** We do not make smoke in order to mean fire with it; but traffic lights, like words, are part of a communicative system with arbitrary values. We infer the meanings because we put them there ourselves; we only get back our investment.

It is the same with language. The linguistic counterpart of *A red light means 'Stop'* is *X linguistic form has 'Y' meaning,* for it expresses the value according to the code, the significance that we have provided for. (It may be that psychologically *A red light means 'Stop'* and **Smoke means fire** are identical, the code having been so thoroughly assimilated that we react to the warning of the color red as if it were a natural phenomenon. But this is not a question for linguists.)

Traffic signals have about the same relation to linguistic signs that counting on two fingers has to calculating with a computer. One is simple, the other complex. Traffic signals have a one-to-one correlation: red for stop, orange for caution, green for go. Only rarely do two or more together have a special meaning, as in Massachusetts, where red plus orange means 'Walk.' Linguistic signs are built of units built of units. Not all levels are penetrated equally by meaning.

It is pointless to look for meaning in distinctive features, phonemes, and syllables, for these are members of the phonological hierarchy and are meaningless by definition, though we did observe a curious relationship between vowels and the notion of size. With morphemes we begin to find units to which meanings are attached, and this extends through words and sentences. So the question comes down to which of these levels—from morpheme upward—is the real tie with the outside world.

Our choice depends on how we picture the outside world. If it is seen as a kind of idealized collection of entities that keep their shape no matter what kaleidoscopic patterns they take when they are shaken up, our choice will be morphemes or words. If it is the patterns themselves, our choice will be sentences. This is because a sentence—a particular sentence, not a sentence type—does not have meaning in the same way that words have meaning. The meaning of a word is potential;

it has a "purchasing power," like that of a dollar bill before it is involved in a transaction. The meaning of a sentence relates specifically to something in the outside world at a given time and in relationship to given persons, qualities and objects. The statement **X *word means* 'Y'** predicts how a speaker will use **X** word. To refer to a real event we must use a sentence — an exclamation like ***John!*** when we unexpectedly see a friend or ***Run!*** when danger threatens. The same is true of sentence forms, though not of sentences themselves: the sentences **Boy meets girl** and **Girl meets boy** involve the same forms, including that of **X**-as-subject, which suggests something about who takes the initiative. A speaker will use this or any other form in an actual sentence to match some real event, but the arrangement is only a linguistic potential, a bit of linguistic substance with a meaning that tends to remain constant.

The problem of meaning, then, is one of fitting together the partially (but never firmly) fixed semantic entities that we carry in our heads, tied to the words and forms of sentences, to approximate the way reality is fitted together as it comes to us from moment to moment. The entities are the world reduced to its parts and secured in our minds; they are a purse of coins in our pocket with values to match whatever combination of bargains, fines, and taxes is likely to come our way. The problem of meaning is how the linguistic potential is brought in line with non-linguistic reality whenever a speaker makes an utterance, or even — since we manipulate our environment almost as readily as our language — how the real is brought in line with the potential.

Exercise 1

In the following sentences, can you replace each use of the word ***meaning*** with other words which will serve to express the same thought?

a. Seven o'clock means breakfast in our household.
b. Keep out. This means you.
c. Do you mean to wait?
d. Without love, life would have no meaning.

Does any of these uses of **meaning** seem to you to be an example of the significance of this word as we use it in the study of linguistics, that is to express the relationship between the symbols constituting our system of language and the universe of perceptions to be communicated?

What about these sentences? — give brief reasons for your answers.

    e. A skull and crossbones means poison.

    f. A dove means peace.

Exercise 2

Iconic signs suggest their meanings; *symbolic* signs are arbitrary (see pages 21–23)

a. One abstract iconic sign is the crossed lines representing a railroad crossing. Can you think of others? Are some iconic traffic signs more concrete, that is pictorial?

b. Assume that green and red in traffic lights are symbolic. Would it be any easier to reverse them now than if they were iconic? Assume that they are iconic: what does red picture?

The Segmentation of Reality

The expression *outside world* does not mean what is "outside us" but what is "outside language." It may well be inside us. If I say I have a headache, or that I saw you with a red hat in my dream last night, I am relating something that no one else can observe, yet I put it into words as readily as I refer to the weather or to a major league baseball score.

This is the sense in which we must take the term *reality,* for it includes what is viewable only from within as well as what can be seen by anyone. In fact from one standpoint the inner view is the more important one, owing to the absence, in most utterances, of any correspondence with external events going on at the moment. Utterances in which we comment on what is happening, like *Now I get up, now I walk to the window, now I look out,* are exceptional; more normal are

Last night I got up because I couldn't sleep or *If you'll hand me the wire I'll attach this hook* or *Nobody's going to vote for him,* involving memory or prediction. Language would be of little use if we did no more with it than report what anyone can see just by looking. Whatever it is that represents these past and future or imagined events to our minds is a main part, if not the whole, of reality as we grasp it. Defining it is for psychologists and philosophers. In language we must assume it and go on to its links with words and sentence forms.

What conditions need to be met for the signs of language, limited in number, to designate reality, which is infinite? The first condition is that reality must be *segmented* or divided into manageable parts. Whenever we manipulate an object we separate it, in a sense, from its environment. Part of the act of separating it is the act of naming it: a cumulus cloud, a wall, a stick, a laugh. Language gives us a map of reality in which everything is covered but much detail is left out. The second condition, necessary for the first, is that the segments must be *repeatable* and that we must have some mechanism to recognize similarity between one appearance and the next so as to call the two by the same name. A wall in the dark must still be a wall in the daylight. The third condition is built-in *ambiguity;* absolute identity of segments cannot be required, for dealing with the continuum of experience would then be impossible — explicitly or implicitly we have to be able to say **X *is* Y** and mean 'X is a kind of Y,' 'X is like Y.' Otherwise we might learn to apply the name *dog* to Fido but could never extend it to other dogs (and might even fail to apply it to Fido when we saw him a second or third time). A fourth condition is simply *memory,* which is not specific to language; there must be provision for storing the linguistic units to make them available for future use.

How is the connection between unit and segment (i.e., between *dog* and Fido) made, so that when the segment presents itself the speaker will respond with the unit, or when the unit is presented the segment will be invoked? The basis for this is *permeation* (Chapter 1, page 5.) It may be that as we grow expert in the use of language, "outside world" is to be taken in a less and less material sense; but in the beginning it is concrete — the child learns his verbal responses to things in a way that makes those responses almost a part of the things themselves. For a dog to become a recognizable and repeatable segment of reality, the child needs to make enveloping contacts with it—feel the hair, see the tail wag, hear the bark—and to hear, whenever older children or adults are about, the specific pattern of sounds, /dɔg/. The attributes of a particular dog are not only a texture of hair and a certain size and shape and color of eyes; they include also the name *dog*. It is true that the name *dog* is intermittent, but the dog's bark is intermittent too and is nevertheless a characteristic. Continuity is not a requirement; all that is necessary is a predictable relationship, and just as under predictable conditions of excitement the dog will bark, so under predictable conditions of conversation he will be referred to as a dog.

Given permeation, we need one more psychological mechanism: an instinct for taking the part for the whole. This is characteristic of all human behavior. A mother is identified by a voice or the touch of a hand; a glimpse of a face is enough to identify the man behind it. If through permeation the name of something becomes a part of the complex of which it is composed, the name can then be abstracted to stand for the whole complex. Sentence patterns as well as words are names in this respect. There are only two differences between linguistic units and other identifying features: the linguistic units are assigned to things simply in order to be abstracted later, and human beings express them as sound.

Kinds of segmentation

Our words come so naturally and unconsciously that they seem rather simple tokens of reality. This is partly because on the few occasions when we do think about the relationship between words and things we almost always pick the simplest category, that of nouns, and the simplest examples from the category: *dog, toy, sun, page, house.* Yet the truth is that literally any combination of things, traits, or ideas can be segmented, or assigned a specific linguistic label. If we should ever need to talk regularly and frequently about independently operated sawmills from which striking workers are locked out on Thursday when the temperature is between 50° and 60°F., we would find a concise way to do it. Of course, it is no small accomplishment for our language to be able to perform that segmentation in the way just illustrated—by accumulating segments already named, which intersect at the desired point. Sometimes the accumulation—if it is not too long—becomes a set unit, and we forget or only dimly remember its former associations. We saw this with fusions (Chapter 6, pages 129–31), typically compounds.

But it is not necessary that a linguistic unit be morphologically complex—like a compound—in order to be semantically complex. Some of the simplest words harbor an amazingly explicit set of wayward traits, of which we are almost never aware until someone misuses them. Here are some examples:

1. The word *disease* is more formidable than its synonyms *illness* and *ailment* because it is viewed as existing apart from the person or other organism afflicted. Diseases are classified and labeled. Since it is an entity in its own right, a disease can be "caught"; we do not ordinarily say *catch an illness* or *catch an ailment*.

2. The verb *to return,* when it takes an object, refers to the source of something; its synonym *to take back* is noncommittal on this point. So **We took Junior back to the zoo** might refer to letting him visit the place again, but **We returned Junior to the zoo** identifies him as an inmate.

3. The verb *to read* includes not only the visual perception of the symbols but the ability to interpret them; it means 'to see and to understand.' But there is no companion verb meaning both 'to hear' and 'to understand.' This forces us to an awkward parallel: **If you know Spanish you will find Portuguese easier to read but Italian easier to understand by hearing it.**

There seems to be no limit to the number or kind of ingredients that may form part of the semantic recipe of a word. Yet certain of the ingredients show up in enough words that are different in other respects to tempt one to look for sets of semantic features that will allow the kind of description and analysis of meaning that sets of distinctive features allow for sounds. For example:

1. A number of verbs contain the ingredient 'success,' which their synonyms may lack. *He managed to do it* tells us that he tried and succeeded; *He was able to do it* is noncommittal. *He went home* tells us that he got there; *He headed home* leaves that question unanswered.

2. Many words either contain a 'positive' ingredient or are 'neutral.' The most typical expressions of this occur in measurement. To the question *How deep is it?* we can answer either *It's quite deep* or *It's quite shallow* — *deep* in the question is 'neutral'; in the answer it is 'positive.' Similarly with *How tall is he?* — *He is quite tall (quite short)*, *How long is it?* — *It's quite long (quite short)*, and so on. The corresponding nouns are similar, but they vary in the extent to which they lean toward 'positive' or 'neutral.' Thus, *tallness* is almost invariably 'positive' — *He couldn't be hired because of his tallness* means that he was tall; but *height* is more likely to be 'neutral' — *He couldn't be hired because of his height* does not tell us whether he was tall or short. In general, the nouns with the *-th* suffix (*width, breadth, girth, length, depth*) are likely to be 'neutral' but can be 'positive,' while those with the *-ness* suffix are 'positive.'

3. There is a wag's definition of an optimist as one who says that his glass of beer is half full, while a pessimist is one who says it is half empty. A number of words and expressions contain this ingredient of looking up or down on a scale, contrasting with others that do not look in either direction. The same concrete situation can be stated as *There were about ten or eleven eggs in the carton, There were nearly (almost) a dozen,* or *There were not quite a dozen. About* looks in neither direction while *almost* looks up and *not quite* looks down, as we see in the frequent coupling of *almost but not quite. Close to* is unstable. It tends to look up: *There were close to a dozen;* but it may be noncommittal, like *in the neighborhood of: You said fifteen but I'd say it was close* (or *closer*) *to a dozen.*

4. Probably the most pervasive ingredient of all is an attitude of "approval" or "disapproval." The adverbs **soundly** and **roundly** are synonymous, but in **He soundly berated them** the speaker indicates his approval of the action, while **He roundly berated them** is neutral. Some more obvious pairs, with the neutral term first and the loaded one second, are **big-overgrown, sweet-cloying, uninformed-ignorant, palatable-delicious, subordinate-underling, odor-fragrance, innocent-naive.**

Are some ingredients secondary, perhaps not having to do with the meaning of a word but with the circumstances of its use? Consider *at this time* and *right now* — both refer to the present moment, but *at this time* is aloof and formal while *right now* is informal and friendly: *The doctor can't see you at this time (right now).* The degree of informality, from this point of view, would be the circumstance of use. But in a broader sense any aspect of reality that restricts the use of a word is a circumstance of its use; degree of formality in *at this time* and *right now* is as much a part of reality as the time of day, and while it may be less important for some words it is more important for others — for distinguishing among **sir, mister,** and **hey, Mac** as forms of address, for example. Primary and secondary are matters of degree.

Exercise 3

In such words as **unique, perfect, unparalleled, full, empty, complete,** and **unsaturated** there is an element which we might identify as 'absolute.' The absolute element common to these words has been built into them and is not expressed separately.

a. Can you describe the usual way in which adjectives are made to indicate an absolute (superlative) quality?

b. What happens to the meanings of the adjectives listed above when intensifiers such as **very** or **most** are added?

Exercise 4

Many sets of words like *almost, nearly, close to, about,* and *not quite* contain the semantic ingredient of a position on a scale. Some words are on a scale of intensity: *to disillusion* is more intense than *to disappoint.* Place on a scale of intensity the following terms: *amaze, astound, astonish, flabbergast, surprise.*

Semantic features

Of course, it would be easy to limit ourselves to the ingredients that are obviously central to a given word, and that, in effect, is what most dictionaries do for lack of room to do more. If we adopt this restriction and in addition consciously or unconsciously select examples of just certain types of words, say those designating manmade objects or manmade institutions, our collection of words will lend itself to a comparatively neat analysis. Men make musical instruments, for example, putting various predetermined parts into them and using them in various predetermined ways, each having its name. Those names can then be listed as semantic ingredients of the words in question — we can call them, "semantic markers" or "semantic distinctive features."

The universe of meaning could then be conceived as a vast and multi-dimensional field of crisscrossing features. At the point where "keyboard instrument," "stringed instrument," and "percussion instrument" intersect we would find *piano.* Where "keyboard instrument," "reed instrument," "wind instrument," and "hand-bellows instrument" intersect we would find *accordion,* while at the neighboring intersection of the first three of these and "foot-bellows instrument" we would find *harmonium.* Whether such a treatment could ever be extended very far beyond the sphere of manmade things is debatable. But on a reduced scale it is good for showing relationships in a limited semantic field.

Exercise 5

Copy the grid, opposite, of semantic ingredients for *piano* and *harpsichord* and follow the instructions for completing it.

Musical Instruments	String	Percussion	Plucked	Keyboard	
1. piano	+	+	−	+	
2. harpsichord	+	−	+	+	

Enter *harp* and fill in the grid. Note that the features already present can do the job of defining the harp. Now add *harmonium*. You will need a new feature, for the harmonium is also a reed instrument. (Note that when a new feature is added, the previous words, as well as the new one, must be marked for that feature.) Now add *guitar:* it too will need a new feature. The pitch of a note produced on a guitar is determined by controlling the length of the strings by means of frets; you might therefore add **Fretted** as one of the distinctive features. What feature might be added for *violin?*

Built-in ambiguity:
the "something-like" principle

What makes a cut and dried treatment of meaning unsatisfactory in the long run is the fluidity of our segmentations. The inherited ones never keep their shapes, and we add to them on the spur of the moment. Reality presents itself in such a variety of faces, glimpses, perspectives, and distortions that at no time can we be absolutely certain that what we see today is the same as what we saw yesterday. We cannot expect to be presented with clear choices between either-or alternatives; human beings must work always with one or two unknowns and several maybes in their equations. This is why it is necessary to assume a mechanism for recognizing similarities as part of a child's innate equipment. This is needed not only because of nature's condition of indefiniteness but also because of its size: there would not be enough words to go around if each word were restricted to a single and exclusive meaning.

It is often said that context determines the meaning of a word. This claim can be taken in either of two senses:

1. That the "larger context"—the whole discourse or the whole experience of the speaker or the whole language—cumulatively colors each word as it occurs against one background after another. This sense will be looked at later.

2. That the immediate context, by canceling out those *known* meanings of a word that are inappropriate, leaves the one meaning that fits. This may be the context of situation—a doctor referring to an *oral passage* means something different from what a teacher about to give dictation would mean by it. Or it may be the verbal context—*evaporated water* is water vapor; *evaporated milk* is milk reduced in volume by evaporation. In this second sense, context "determines" meaning by a paring-down operation.

There is no question that the latter process does go on in the mind of the hearer every time he *de*codes a message. But what about the speaker who *en*codes it? He must bend and expand his meanings so that they will meet and cross and thereby make it possible for the hearer to get a fix with his mental sextant. Also he has to fight against time—there is not always leisure for precision even when the language supplies the means for it. When a housewife remarks *I guess it's time to turn the cereal off*, she could have said *It's time to turn the heat off under the cereal* or, still more accurately, *It's time to turn the gas off at the burner under the cereal* (or *turn the valve off*, or *turn the handle of the valve to "off"*). In this context the semantic reach of *turn off* has been expanded through a fairly long causal chain to meet that of *cereal*, which is known from the situation to be 'cooking cereal.' This process is just as important as the one that enables the hearer to understand that *turn off*, in any of the ways of expressing this operation, is not the same as *turn off* in *turn off the road*.

We can call what underlies this process the "something-like" principle. The something-like principle is essential to the segmentation of a reality that does not come in fixed forms. Since the universe never repeats itself exactly, every time we speak we create metaphors; we use one term to describe a thing that actually changes each time we name it.

When conditions are right, the something-like principle provides needed designations for new segments of reality. When straws were first used to imbibe drinks they were literally the dried stems of cereal grains. Later the same name was given to tubes made of paper or other material — attention was no longer on the material but on the function. One even hears **glass straw**. In the same way, we now drink from **glasses** made of plastic, bake waffles on **irons** made of aluminum, cool our foods in **ice boxes** that contain no ice, and so on.

Speakers share not only the same code but also the ability to see the same resemblances between what their code already designates and what they would like it to designate, and so to make the old forms reach out to new meanings. This is how a language breaks free of its rigidity.

Exercise 6

Explain what we would say if we were speaking more literally. In *d*, for example, is there actually a window?

a. Pass the milk, Hiram.
b. The flowers are about to bloom.
c. You're smoking on the left rear, I think your brake is dragging.
d. Get money orders at window number five.

Categories

Most of the time it works fairly well to speak of how a word segments reality without worrying about what kind of word it is. Yet we know that not all words deal with reality in the same way: this is the basis of syntax, which provides each category with its functions and imprints them on the words that it encompasses. In this sense the categories of syntax embody the semantic ingredients that are the most fundamental of all, for they are so important to the language that they help determine its structure. There is a "nounness" among nouns — they take a static view of the segments that they designate, even when the segments are actions (in **Murder will out,** murder, an action, is dealt with as if it were something that we could make hold still long enough to treat like a thing). There is a "verbness" among verbs—they put things in motion and pass them through time.

All the same, these ingredients are not essentially different from other kinds, and we find different languages elevating different ingredients to the status of categories of their grammar. In the Senufo languages of Africa, "size" becomes a subcategory of nouns—those designating large objects are formally distinct from those designating small ones. In Chontal, a dialect of Mayan spoken in southern Mexico, an elaborate categorization is required whenever things are counted: separate morphemes are used to classify the world of objects into people and most animals as distinct from other things; into flat objects like leaves and sleeping mats, plants and standing trees, slender objects like snakes and sticks, unharvested fruits and nuts, drops of liquids, things rolled up, objects cut lengthwise, and so on.

Sharing of the range

If instead of looking outward from the word to the segments that it carves out, we look inward from the segments of reality to the words that designate them, the picture we see is one of fierce competition. Ingredients claimed by one word are also claimed by others. Ranges of meaning are unbelievably interconnected and intricate; yet speakers do not mind these intricacies, so long as some bit of ingredient, however small, distinguishes the combined property of one word from that of the next.

Some words, such as *complex* and *complicated* or *complex* and *simple,* have ranges that are related and hence comparable. Others, such as *amorous* and *axiomatic,* have ranges that are not related. Relationships among ranges vary, but two are of special interest: overlap and opposition.

Synonyms are words with overlapping ranges. The term is not used, however, unless the overlap is so extensive as to make the ranges almost identical. We have no term for a slight overlap, and even words with extensive but not approximately complete overlap are not generally regarded as synonyms. Thus, *man* and *boy* overlap in all major respects except 'age,' but we do not think of them as synonyms. The reason is that it is precisely this difference that we want to emphasize; in a given conversation the fact that someone is 'human' and 'male' will probably be taken for granted, whereas the difference in age may well be the point at issue. There is also another reason. It is difficult to find two terms that do not overlap in some imaginable way: *toenail* and *typewriter* are both 'material objects.'

So the term *synonym* is not applied unless (1) the overlap is almost complete and/or (2) the area outside the overlap is, for a given purpose, unimportant. (Overlap applies, of course, to comparable ranges. *Flush* is a synonym of *blush* in the sense 'turn red,' where the overlap is almost but not quite complete. Other senses of *flush* have no bearing.)

The kind of synonymy of which *sauce* (for meat, poultry, or fish), *gravy* (for bread or potatoes), *topping* (for ice cream), and *dressing* (for salad) are examples is of little more than theoretical interest. For synonyms to be of practical interest there must be some expectation of their being substituted for each other, and with 'edible liquescent coverings for foods' that is not likely to happen, despite the semantic overlap.

We find this substitutability under two sets of conditions. The first is simply a matter of precision. A writer or speaker is about to say *He delivered a lengthy apology* and realizes that he may be taken to mean an excuse and not a justification, which he intended; so he uses *justification* instead. The second is a matter of contrast, of finding something that sounds different. Sometimes a speaker needs this to avoid distracting attention from his ideas to his words. Our stock of phonemes is not unlimited and now and then plays us false by serving up two words that sound so much alike — they may even be identical — that if we use them together we are liable to be misunderstood or thought to be making a pun: *That was a fine fine you had to pay!* If we replace the second *fine* with *penalty,* the problem is avoided. This is a milder form of the conflict of homonyms that we noted earlier; the difference is that instead of being driven out of the language the conflicting form is simply driven out of the immediate context.

In a more subtle form, contrast is a matter of semantic shading, of avoiding the repetition of the same word with the same sound when it is supposed to have a slightly different meaning, both meanings being well within the normal range for the word. The first sentence of the second paragraph of this chapter was originally written "The word *meaning* is used in many ways. . . ." When the line was edited it appeared that *word* might be taken in the sense that it had at the beginning of the preceding paragraph, that is, as a level in linguistics. To avoid this it was replaced with *term*, simply to warn the reader away from assuming a repetition of the same meaning.

The avoidance of repetition is keyed directly to the need in every context to define terms in such a way that if the least contrast is intended it will be physically manifested in the words we choose. It is possible to say **Put out the cat and put out the lights,** but we avoid it in favor of **Put out the cat and turn off the lights.** This is the beauty of having synonyms and the "something-like" freedom to expand them beyond their normal limits: if we cannot find a prefabricated contrast among the synonyms at our disposal, we can make one to order.

Do any two words different in form have exactly the same range of meanings? If they are words in common use, probably not. Interpretative change will differentiate them. A few technical terms with only slight differences in form may be close enough to be called the same, but, practically speaking, there is no such thing as an identical synonym. The language demands its money's worth from every word it permits to survive.

Antonyms are words with opposing ranges. It is as hard to pin down the "opposition" of antonyms as the "sameness" of synonyms, but one thing must always be understood: the opposition is not absolute but is enclosed within a sameness. **Large** and **small** are antonyms because they are at opposite ends of the same category—size. **Beautiful** and **unintentional** are not antonyms because they are unrelated.

Many antonyms leave a middle ground that itself carries a regular name or names. Between **large** and **small** is **medium.** Other examples are **right-center-left, good-fair-poor-bad,** and **open-ajar-shut.** A few have a middle ground that itself contains a pair of antonyms: with **always-often-seldom-never** we regard **often** and **seldom** as enclosed antonyms. A similar set is **hot-warm-cool-cold. Warm-cool** and **often-seldom** are themselves antonyms because they are the same distance away from the center line that already separates **hot-cold** and **always-never.**

Some pairs are more clearly antonymous than others. **Square** and **round** are antonyms in **square peg in a round** *hole*, but otherwise they are no more so than *oblong* and *rectangular*. *To rest* is more properly an antonym of *to be active* than of *to work*, since it differs equally from *to play*, itself an antonym of *to work* in terms of another ingredient. What makes the study of both synonyms and antonyms impressionistic rather than scientific is the fact that it consists in cataloguing words rather than analyzing semantic ingredients. If we could decompose the ingredients of two words assumed to be antonymous and identify the ones that are actually in opposition, we could define a pair of antonyms as two words which in a given context are opposed on the basis of those ingredients. The words *square* and *round* would then not be antonyms unless — as in *square peg in a round hole* — the ingredients of angularness versus curvedness were the essential opposition. This would dispel the false notion that words either are or are not antonyms. Degrees of antonymy would be recognized. High on the scale would be pairs of words regularly associated, such as *good-bad, high-low, full-empty.* Farther down would be pairs like *calm-upset* and *calm-frightened.* At the bottom would be pairs like *borrow-steal*, where the opposing semantic ingredients of (in this case 'legitimate' versus 'illegitimate') acquisition would seldom be invoked. Some pairs would appear clearly as antonyms in regular use; others would be antonymous if we make them so for the purposes of our discourse, exercising the same power that we noted earlier in adjusting synonyms to pick some advantage out of a slight difference wedged into a complex of similarities.

Synonyms and antonyms are not the only sets of words that are joined through shared or opposed semantic ingredients. There is probably no limit to the groupings that would make sense for one purpose or another. Examples are:

1. Reciprocals: *come-go, buy-sell, read-write, give-receive.*

2. Characteristic object: *eat-food, drink-beverage, hear-sound, spell-word, wrap-package, ask-question.*

3. Characteristic action: *heart-beat, mind-think, fire-burn, wind-blow, rain-fall.*

Exercise 7

Wet and **dry** might be thought to have no middle ground until one remembers a word such as **moist** or **damp.** A noise can be **loud, soft,** or **moderate,** and even with these three words the field is not covered. There are many such pairs of words in English. Write out some of them and add the third word or phrase that, like **moist,** breaks or limits the antonymy.

Exercise 8

"Shakespeare's *The Tempest* is his most enthralling work, in which *the great dramatist* pours an emotive force that is missing elsewhere — how well *the genius of the English stage* knew his public!"

a. Why has the writer of these lines used the terms "the great dramatist" and "the genius of the English stage"? Would the sentence be just as effective if these terms were replaced with "he" and "Shakespeare" respectively? Explain your answer.

b. The quotation above is an example of the mechanical application of the familiar injunction to avoid repetition. It can be carried to further extremes with the use of such epithets as "the prince of European letters," "the creator of *Hamlet*," or "the Bard of Avon." Despite possible misuse, can you think of contexts in which these epithets might be effectively used?

Exercise 9

Contrast the words **capital** and **lawn** in such uses as *capital crime, capital city, capital letter, lawn sprinkler, lawn tennis.* To what extent has each held a cohesive central meaning?

Ranges that a word can cover

Ordinarily the ranges of meaning that develop within the span of a single word are complementary; they may not agree, but they do not disagree, and they still resemble one another closely enough to be classed together as the meanings of a single word. However, the opposite may happen; antagonistic ranges may develop, and if they do, one whole range has to go. Except for students of etymology, there is no difference between the conflict within the meanings of *saloon* and the conflict illustrated by *queen* and *quean*—we might as well speak of two words both pronounced /səlun/ and spelled *saloon.*

Multiple senses of a single word are typical. Most words branch out into two or more semantic directions. The reason is that individual words are only a step up from morphemes and, like morphemes, exist within larger combinations rather than as entities—we do not operate with individual words in one-word sentences as a rule, but with more or less fixed combinations. The difference between morphemes and words is one of degree; the combinations of morphemes are simply tighter than those of words.

If more or less predictable combinations are the rule, then we do not depend on a word's formal individuality to identify it. The combination in which it occurs will take care of that. Take the word *cell.* In a sentence like *The cells of the human body have various forms and functions; some cells carry nutrients, oxygen, and hormones,* we know that the second *cell* is *cell of the human body* just as in *pre- and post-natal care* we know that *pre-* is *pre-natal.*

With combinations to fall back on we can tolerate a word's branching out in several directions from a central core. *Cell* can refer to protoplasmic cell, dry cell, honeycomb cell, and communist cell, among others.

If it were not possible to use individual words in this way, a language would require a vastly larger stock. The situation is much the same as with phonemes; by reusing them in different combinations we restrict their number. With words there is the advantage that the central core of meaning is an aid to storage and a jog to memory. If we had to use different words for each variety of cell, for each separate sense of *time (time to go, time enough to eat, a good time, time of day),* for each action subsumed under the verb *feel (feel pain, feel love toward someone, feel the wind, feel the surface with your hand),* our powers of association might well break down.

It appears that there are two ways in which a hearer may get a clear understanding of the meaning intended by the speaker when terms or constructions are used that have more than one meaning. One way is by recognizing stereotyped combinations; the other is by paring down.

In **He set the clock** the meaning of **set** is immediately determined by the noun **clock;** this is a stereotyped combination, one that is recognized on sight.

On the other hand, in **They set the clocks and put out the lights before going to bed,** some kind of paring-down operation may be called for. This would involve keeping two alternatives before us —**did set** or **do set? did put** or **do put?**—not committing ourselves until a decisive word comes along, but when one does, paring the meanings down accordingly. Even here, however, we may resort to prediction and not invoke the paring-down process unless something goes wrong. This means simply taking the verbs **set** and **put** one way or the other, past or present, and hoping for the best. If we miss, and take the sentence to mean that they always do these things before going to bed, and then the speaker goes on to add **but forgot to lock the doors,** we are forced to reassess the verb and pick a different meaning.

The Arbitrariness and Nonarbitrariness of Meaning

If the history of writing gives hints about the history of language, the first forms of communication must have been imitative. The use of pictograms to convey messages long before the development of syllabaries and alphabets — not to mention the universality of imitative and expressive gesture — seems so natural that we can only suppose a primitive stage in which sounds were related to sense. The imitation need not have been perfect — in fact, the very difficulty of copying the sounds of nature with the human voice would have been an advantage because speakers would have had to ignore imperfections and accept substitutions that were less and less like the originals — but mimicry there must have been.

Those colorful beginnings have faded to a uniform gray. Even in our common onomatopoetic words the imitation must give way to the system of sounds that the language imposes. The result is almost always an imperfect copy. If we listen to the note of the whippoorwill we observe an appreciable pause between *whip* and *poor: whip-poorwill, whip-poorwill.* But English has the habit of reducing interior syllables and clicking them off at a faster rate, the result is that we say something like *whipperwill.*

But if through the centuries our art has declined, our apparent sophistication has grown. We are not bothered by imperfect copies. Until someone calls them to our attention we do not even notice them. Perhaps it is not sophistication so much as conditioned reflex. If a bell is as good as a taste to the salivary glands of Pavlov's dog, *ding-dong* can be as good as the ringing of a bell to us. This is the effect of permeation.

So it would seem that language should be set down as an almost purely conventional code, with a few exceptions listed as curiosities. Certainly there is no essential relationship between the sound of any phoneme, or the combined sounds within any word, and any event beyond language, barring the frayed remnants of an occasional example of onomatopoeia.

But how is it then that language can express reality? Does not this rough denial of expressiveness do language an injustice? If we look at the stippling in a picture or the grain in a photograph, we note an equal lack of correspondence between dots or grains and the flesh of the human face, whose image is nevertheless clearly reproduced. Perhaps words are only the grain of language and the nonarbitrary picture is filled out at a higher level.

In fact language becomes expressive and far from arbitrary when it is formed into sentences to communicate about some real situation. The words *cat, bite,* and *dog* may have an arbitrary relationship with their meanings, but if a dog bites a cat we can reasonably expect that these words will appear in any explanation of the event: this of course is nonarbitrary. If when a particular event occurs we can predict with some certainty what is going to be said about it—and our daily experience proves that we can, even with events that have never occurred before—then we know that the correspondence of the parts of our sentences with parts of reality is anything but arbitrary.

Phonesthemes

Even the units turn out to be somewhat less arbitrary than they appear at first sight if we look beyond the primary association of word and thing. Given a particular word for a particular thing, if other words for similar things come to resemble that word in sound, then, no matter how arbitrary the relationship between sound and sense was to begin with, the sense is now obviously tied to the sound. The relationship between sound and sense is still arbitrary as far as the outside world is concerned (and would appear that way absolutely to a foreigner), but within the system it is no longer so.

So we find words clustering in groups with a vague resemblance in sound—too hazy to carve out as a definite morpheme—to which has been given the name *phonestheme*. Most of the words ending in *-ump* suggest heaviness and bluntness: ***rump, dump, hump, mump, lump, stump, chump, thump, bump.*** Children sense these associative possibilities and coin words with them: ***If the house is as old as that it's raggy, shaggy, and daggy,*** remarked one seven-year-old; and referring to the muck at the bottom of an excavation the same speaker said ***It's all gushy—it's like mushy dushy.*** The makers of multiple-choice tests find phonesthemes useful as distractors for their questions; if ***twisted*** is offered as an equivalent for ***knurled,*** as was done in one test, it is on the assumption that persons not fully acquainted with ***knurl*** (meaning 'a knot in wood') will assume that it is related to ***twirl, whirl, furl,*** and ***spiral.*** Shifts of meaning often go in the direction of a family of words having phonesthematic ties. The word ***bolster*** no longer suggests a padded and comparatively soft support but rather a stiff and rigid one, because of the attraction of ***brace, bolt, buttress.*** (Of seventeen persons tested on this point, thirteen voted for 'rigid.') Phonesthemes are often a principal ingredient of new words: ***hassle*** probably follows from ***tussle, bustle, wrestle.***

If words become parts of things to our minds, as they must if language is to do its job efficiently (in spite of our trying, in philosophical moments, to break the bondage), at least a partial association of sound and sense can hardly be avoided. When other aspects of things meet our eyes we do not hesitate to infer a kinship in the things if we detect a similarity in the aspects, and it is only natural for us to do the same with words: no two girls ever toss their heads in the same way, but one's doing it should mean somewhat the same as another's; two words such as *flout* and *flaunt* are not identical, but they are similar enough so that they *ought* to be related in meaning.

Exercise 10

a. How many words can you name which are phonesthematically related to **groan?**

b. Can you identify the quality conveyed by the "gr" sound?

c. Do these words have any phonetic elements in common in addition to the initial "gr"?

Exercise 11

The definitions which a seventeen-year-old offered for the list of words below are clearly inaccurate. You will be able to find the source of the confusion in each case by identifying the associations which this student made with the given word. Indicate the word or words which have been confused with each word from the original list.

> *Ossify:* this means to astonish, to frighten to death.
> *Palpable:* good to the taste, good to eat.
> *Pander:* that means run fast, panting down the track, thundering down, you know, pander, pander, pander, that's the way it sounds.
> *Platitude:* that's how high aviators get into the air.
> *Aptitude:* that is the feelings you have about something. Your father says, "I don't like your aptitude toward using the car."
> *Brandish:* that is what you have in restaurants sometimes, brandish cherries. They burn with ice cream.
> *Flagrant:* that is the way flowers smell, or a field of daisies.

How does this confusion relate to the confusion of sense known as a *malapropism?*

chapter 11

Mind in the Grip of Language

Control by Language

A little girl asks, "What does the wind do when it doesn't blow?" or "Where did I live before I was born?" — and most parents smile at her naiveté. But if she asks, "Where will I live after I die?" most people in our culture will take her seriously, though it will not be easy for them to answer.

The idea embodied in those questions has weighed on linguists and on sociologists working at the borders of linguistics for a long time: "To what extent is our thinking influenced by the language we use?" A number of thinkers have held that language can reduce as well as increase the scope and accuracy of our thought. What is meant by the following sentence from a speech by Walt Rostow, former Special Assistant to former President Johnson? — "It is the ability of a community to achieve consensus on the great issues and compromise on the lesser issues which lies at the heart of the democratic process. . . ." The critical reader must ask: Can communities as a whole have abilities? Can the difference between great and small issues be recognized? Is there ever consensus without compromise? Is democracy a process?

The Whorf hypothesis

It remained for a linguist, Benjamin Lee Whorf, to turn the question away from individual words and toward the structure of language as a whole. Whorf's perception of language as a pair of glasses with more or less warped lenses through which we view our surroundings was sharpened by his work with a language about as different from English as any language can be—that of the Hopi, a tribe of Pueblo Indians living in Arizona.

One of the chief things that English and its sister languages fasten upon the experience of all their speakers is a prior categorization of the reality outside us into nouns and verbs. The noun pictures things as detached from the processes that surround them, making it possible to say *The wind blows* or *The light flashes,* though wind cannot exist apart from blowing nor flashing apart from light. Not only does it *enable* us to say such things, it *forces* us to: by itself, *snowing,* as our English teacher said, "is not a sentence"; where no subject is handy, we must throw in a plug for one: *It is snowing.*

Besides categorizing reality into nouns and verbs, English and other languages we know best do the same with the "flowing face of nature," in Whorf's words, as with isolated objects: they segment it to accommodate their own needs and local interests. Words like *sky, wind, hill,* or *swamp,* treat some aspect of nature as a distinct thing, almost like a table or chair. The degree of arbitrariness of this kind of segmentation is illustrated by the history and present use of the word *vitamin.* It was coined in 1912 to designate a group of substances supposed at the time to be amines, and now covers such a strange agglomeration of chemicals that *Webster's Third New International Dictionary* requires fourteen lines to define it, in spite of the fact that it is given only one sense. Yet to the average user of the term it seems to name something as clear and definite as the house next door. 'A thing in nature' becomes 'a thing in commerce,' and the pill-taker is not concerned with what it "really is." Similarly, the term *complex* was applied around 1910 to a combination of psychological factors that, as the name implies, were difficult to separate and simplify; but the existence of the term, and the identification of some particular ailment as a "complex," gave all that was needed for a new entry among our realities.

Coupled with the categorization of "thingness" in nouns is the categorization of "substance" in words called "mass nouns" which are used after formalized "counting" words when we want to refer to a part of a mass or substance: *a piece of meat, a glass of water, a blade of grass, a grain (bushel) of corn, a stalk of celery.* The resulting picture is one of a universe filled with masses that can be clipped into pieces, *earth, air, stone, iron, light, shade, fire, disease,* even — and especially — abstractions like *love, honor, dismay, courage, dictatorship,* and *accuracy.*

Out of this notion which views *jewels* as "contained in" *jewelry* and *guns* as "contained in" *artillery,* our language has evolved an elaborate vocabulary having to do with an all-containing *space* — the term *space* itself is a mass noun that includes in an abstract way all other mass nouns. And here is where the world view of our language departs most radically from that of the Hopi. We are able to transfer our concepts of space almost totally to *time.* We treat time as a mass, and carve it into units and count them: *five hours.* We use the same prepositions for both concepts: *before, after, in, at;* the same adjectives: *long, short, same, different, right, wrong, hard, nice, more, less;* and many of the same nouns: *stretch* of time, *segment* of time, *amount* of time. And, of course, we capture events in our space-like nouns — the word *event* itself, plus *dance, movement, rain, stir, riot, invasion, courtship,* and countless others.

This, Whorf points out, is almost never done in Hopi. There is no counterpart to our noun *time.* While the Hopi do have a concept roughly akin to our term *duration,* it seems to be inconceivable in terms of space or motion; the Hopi conceptual scheme is so different from ours, a clear and brief account of it in English appears to be impossible — one would need to learn Hopi to understand it. Our custom of quantifying time is illustrated by the sentence **Ten days is greater than nine days,** which contrasts with the Hopi expression of the same idea in terms of duration, **The tenth day is later than the ninth.**[1] Events of brief duration cannot be captured as nouns in Hopi: "lightning, wave, flame, meteor, puff of smoke, pulsation, are verbs."[2]

So where Western philosophers — from Plato and Aristotle to Kant — have imagined that they were intuiting general laws that applied to all of nature or at least to all of mankind, what they actually were doing was exteriorizing a way of looking at things that they inherited from their language. Much that is difficult in recent physics as well as in philosophy and logic has been the struggle to climb out of this rut, all the harder to escape because we are in it, unconsciously, from the moment we begin to speak. Whorf surmised that a world view such as that of the Hopi might be more congenial to the concepts of modern physics than the languages of Western Europe.

Partial escape from the trap

Linguists now feel that Whorf's position was exaggerated. Western philosophers and physicists *did* evolve their analyses in spite of their language; Whorf *does* explain his position in English, implying that a reader of English can grasp the concepts that English presumably fails to embody in its structure. It must be, then, that languages are more flexible than a catalog of their bulkier categories seems to suggest. For example, English escapes from its hidebound subject-predicate, noun-verb formulas in the construction **There's singing at the church,** using an **-ing** form. We use the **-ing** form precisely because it blurs the line between noun and verb, and omits the subject.

Another example is inceptiveness, the "get-going" phase of an action which will continue. Some languages, like Latin, have a formalized means of investing verbs with this meaning. English expresses it with the verb **start,** as in **She started to amble down the road.**

Many languages have clearly formalized categories of animate things and inanimate things, distinguished in the form of the words, and it might seem that English speakers, lacking the form, must also lack the appreciation. But while in English a man may be *sick in the head,* a car is never *broken in the engine.* This and other examples suggest that the difference in capacity between one language and another is not so much in kind as in explicitness and degree. What one language builds into the broadest layers of its structure, another expresses informally and sporadically; but both have it.

All the same, this does not mean that some very common category in our language will not magnify certain ways of seeing things and diminish others. Better examples than those in comparisons of structure can be found in comparisons of vocabulary, for we do unquestionably "structure" our universe when we apply words to it—sometimes quite arbitrarily—especially when the phenomena themselves are flowing and continuous.

The example most frequently cited is that of colors. The visual spectrum is a continuum which English parcels out into six segments: *purple, blue, green, yellow, orange,* and *red.* Of course painters, interior decorators, and others concerned with finer shades and saturations employ a more elaborate vocabulary; but the additional words are generally defined with those six as reference points: *turquoise* is 'between blue and green'; *reseda* is 'between green and yellow'; *saffron* is 'between yellow and orange.' In Zuni, orange and yellow are combined into a single range named *łupzʔinna* (whose borders are not necessarily the red end of orange and the green end of yellow—all we can say is that *łupzʔinna* roughly coincides with our orange plus our yellow). In Navaho, the two colors *łičííʔ* and *łico* divide somewhere between red and orange-yellow. How these different habits of naming can affect our "thinking"—symptomized by the efficiency with which we communicate—can be shown through recognition tests: the monolingual Zuni, presented with a small set of different colors and then asked after a brief period to pick out the ones he saw from a much larger collection, will have trouble recognizing the ones for which his language does not have convenient names. Other continuums present the same problem across languages—temperature, for example, where the English *hot-warm-cool-cold* do not coincide with the corresponding terms in other languages.

Continuums are the limiting case. Where the experience is discrete, languages are apt to have more easily translatable terms. It would be strange if *dog* or *tooth* did not have a corresponding term in every language of the world, exactly equivalent at least in the central area of its meaning. But in between the continuums and the fragments are all the other things we experience, which are carved up in different ways. In Khacchi, a language of India, a single verb is used for 'eat, drink, smoke.' English represents 'eat, drink' with *ingest* and 'eat, drink, smoke,' and a great deal more with *take in,* but the borderlines do not coincide. We are faced everywhere with a semantic mismatch that simply reflects the areas of experience that our culture renders important for us or—and here the dead hand of the past is laid on our eyes—at one time *did* consider important and now passes on to us in its old images. There is no reason to expect, for example, that any other language than English will give itself the luxury of insisting that a chicken *molts* but a snake *sheds,* or that any other language than Malayan will focus on the same minute and specific area as *kĕloṅkah-loṅkah,* 'the sound of loose planking straining in a ship in heavy weather.' Yet each speech community maintains such distinctions carefully. The child who would rather not have to distinguish between *jar* and *bottle* is quickly driven into line.

Exercise 1

Mr. Carswell and his son Lincoln are looking at a fast sportscar. Mr. Carswell says *That's a bad car.* Lincoln, however, thinks *That's a good car!*

a. Does Mr. Carswell's comment tell us something about the car or something about his taste in cars?

b. What do you suppose a good car might be like according to Mr. Carswell? To Lincoln?

c. Does the structure of Mr. Carswell's statement suggest that it is a statement of fact or a statement of opinion? (Compare: *That's a red car, That's a good car, I like that car.*)

d. In light of your answers to the above questions, analyze the real and apparent meaning of a parent's comment, *He is a good boy.*

Exercise 2

a. The ways we learn to speak of events can influence the ways we experience those events. Imagine how a child would feel being told when he cried: *You are having a tantrum* rather than *You are angry.* Imagine a person told *You have an inferiority complex* rather than *You feel inferior.* How is the individual encouraged to look at his situation in the first sentence of each pair? In the second?

b. Do you think there is any validity to the child's response in this typical exchange? — *What were you playing? — Nothing, I was just playing.*

Control Through Language

Neutrality and the semantic differential

If the lenses of our language that stand between us and reality are slightly warped, they are also tinted. It is one thing to see a certain kind of fish narrowed down to *eel;* it is something slightly different to see eels as repulsive creatures. Yet our language — plus other associations that we *act out* in connection with eels under the influence of fellow members of our culture — decrees both things: the focus and the affect. Every term we use apparently has the power to sway us in one direction or another. Experiments on this "semantic differential" show that persons presented with pairs of antonyms such as *wise-foolish, good-bad, deep-shallow, light-heavy,* and the like will relate other terms in rather consistent ways to each of these extremes, even when there seems to be no logical connection. The technique is to draw a seven-point scale with the antonyms at either end, for example

light _____ _____ _____ _____ _____ _____ _____ *heavy*

and to give subjects a term such as **skittish** with instructions to locate it at one of the points. While it would not be surprising, in view of associations with other terms such as **light-headed**, if everyone agreed that **skittish** ought to go well over to the "light" end, what is surprising is that subjects will even agree on where to locate something as apparently outlandish as **wood** on a scale between **severe** and **lenient.**

Does this mean that, in addition to making us see reality in certain shapes and sizes, our language is also one of the most powerful factors in forcing us to take sides? If all the speakers of a given language share a prejudice, language will transmit it. Take for example the associations of insanity. Most of them are "funny": **crazy, nutty, loony, daffy, half-witted, hare-brained, loopy,** and so on. They reflect a culture in which psychopathological states are not diseases to be treated but deviations to be laughed at. It has required a vigorous reorientation of our attitudes to put mental disease on a footing other than ridicule or shame so that it *could* be treated. We can excuse language by saying that the way we behave colors the words we use; but it is just as fair to say that the words, in their daily use and with their associations, color the way we behave.

Of course, a competitive society results in competing values, and some measure of neutrality is thereby achieved. Language is used by all parties to every controversy — Republicans and Communists, atheists and religionists, militarists and pacifists; by being pulled in all directions, it is forced to remain more or less impartial.

A better term would be *potentially* impartial. If people use language to get the cooperation of their fellows, then little if anything that is ever said is entirely neutral; communication is more often to influence than to inform. Influencing in this way is known as "suasion."

From the orator or advertising man who calculatingly chooses expressions that will sway his audience to the scientist who in his enthusiasm over his discovery calls it **proof** or **an important departure,** every speaker is guilty of decorating his information. And since everyone does it, the devices for doing it go deep in the language and are hard to avoid even when we try.

If accusing language of this form of seduction seems a strange idea, we can trace our surprise once more to the false importance that our culture gives to writing. Some degree of impartiality can be achieved in print. But in speech we must contend with intonation and its running emotional commentary, insinuating whether we like what we say, whether it is said to persuade or command or to abase ourselves or overawe another, and in which some elements are always more highly colored and stand out as more important than others. Leaving this out, as writing manages to do in part, creates the illusion of uncolored fact. But the colors are still there, only paler.

In the world view distortion that we saw in English versus Hopi there was an indeterminacy of *things* with respect to *language*. In a distortion of world views the very form and substance with which reality is revealed is affected. In suasion there is an indeterminancy of *language* with respect to *things*. A given bit of reality can be *presented* in several ways within a single language. Both processes are normally unconscious, but the first is seldom otherwise while the second may be not only conscious but deliberately and often maliciously cultivated. The degree of consciousness corresponds fairly well with the grading of linguistic devices from crude to subtle, from straightforward name-calling to the hidden bias of a syntactical construction.

Exercise 3

In the last chapter, we discussed the possibility that a meaning of a word can be described with semantic features. The features were chosen by analysis: you inferred the existence of a feature by the existence of a difference in meaning between two words. The difference between **harpsichord** and **harp** led you to the feature 'keyboard.'

There are other important kinds of meaning besides analytical meaning. The meaning of **lion** is not simply the list of objective characteristics a zoologist would come up with. We must include subjective associations such as 'king of beasts' and 'Tarzan's enemy.' The meaning of **flute** includes our reactions to its tonal qualities, and our memories of flute music we have heard and flute players we have known. Often the majority of people in a community agree on a group of associations that cluster around a concept. Such is the case with many of the associations around *lion.*

a. The semantic-feature chart can be extended to present such information. This exercise shows how it might be done. The immediate subject of the exercise is the various clusters of associations that inhere in the words for some pastimes. Make a chart like the one below and fill it out according to the instructions which follow.

```
        good ____:____:____:____:____:____:____ bad
        hard ____:____:____:____:____:____:____ soft
     passive ____:____:____:____:____:____:____ active
      stable ____:____:____:____:____:____:____ changeable
   defensive ____:____:____:____:____:____:____ aggressive
  optimistic ____:____:____:____:____:____:____ pessimistic
        calm ____:____:____:____:____:____:____ excitable
     colorful ____:____:____:____:____:____:____ colorless
    negative ____:____:____:____:____:____:____ positive
   masculine ____:____:____:____:____:____:____ feminine
        cold ____:____:____:____:____:____:____ hot
        sane ____:____:____:____:____:____:____ insane
 competitive ____:____:____:____:____:____:____ cooperative
 insensitive ____:____:____:____:____:____:____ sensitive
      severe ____:____:____:____:____:____:____ lenient
        rash ____:____:____:____:____:____:____ prudent
      humble ____:____:____:____:____:____:____ proud
 interesting ____:____:____:____:____:____:____ boring
```

If you feel that the word in question, such as *reading,* is "very closely related" to a word at one end of the scale, place an X on the line next to that word. If it is "closely related," place an X on the line one step farther in. If it is "only slightly related," place the X still farther in. If you associate *reading* with each word equally, or if you have no associations, place the X in the center space. Please do not omit any decisions. The important thing is your word associations, not your sense of logic. Once you have completed a chart for the word *reading,* do charts for the words *baseball, Monopoly,* and *dancing.*

b. Complete charts like the above for the words *Democrat, Republican, conservative, radical, mother, father, sister, brother.*

c. Compare your charts with those of other students. Ask members of your family, community, and your friends to fill out similar charts using the same words. Is there a consensus of associations? Can you describe and account for any differences?

Naming

As we inherit our nouns — and the categorizations of reality that they represent — we also inherit the right to *make* nouns, which is one of the few truly inventive privileges that our language affords us: anyone can make up a name for something and many people do, while inventing a new suffix or a new syntactic pattern is practically impossible.

The act of naming, with all we have seen it to imply in the way of solidifying and objectifying experience, becomes one of our most powerful suasive tools, enabling us to create entities practically out of nothing. The speaker who says **We want no undesirables around here** projects his inner dislikes onto the outer world. Turning **undesirable** into a noun makes it possible to avoid a clearly tautological **We don't want the people we don't want.** A noun tells us "It is there; it is something that can or ought to be dealt with": as long as people were left to their own resources to find things to do, 'being without work' was generally a matter of choice or ability; when large numbers became dependent upon industry, the condition was objectified as **unemployment.** We are used to having **things** about us; naming reassures us that the elusive threat has been cornered, as the following anecdote, taken from a doctor's notes, illustrates:

> I learned a useful trick from a certain noted doctor. I wondered how he got by without the criticism I encountered when I failed in an attempt to get fluid from the pleural cavity. Occasionally, following pneumonia or pleurisy, fluid will accumulate between the lung and the chest wall, giving such discomfort that it must be drawn off. Whenever I tapped a side and failed to find what I was looking for, the patient or relatives would question my skill, but the noted doctor seemed to be able to create increased confidence, even if he failed to find the fluid.

I finally learned his secret, when I had an opportunity to call him in consultation on a case of suspected pus in the pleural cavity. He asked for a hollow needle, and pierced the chest wall several times without getting a drop. With an air of satisfaction, he turned to the patient and parents, and exclaimed, "Ah, great! I've got it!"

"What is it, Doctor?" cried the interested ones.

"A dry tap! A dry tap! Splendid! Better than I expected!" The patient and relatives said, "Isn't it wonderful? A dry tap." Everybody was happy, and the noted doctor remained noted.[3]

The importance of the name, rather than the real virtues, of a commercial product is proved by the long record of litigation over trade names like *aspirin* and *cola*.

Favorable and unfavorable naming: epithets

Over and above the mere fact of naming—which already to some extent prejudices the case—is the clearly prejudicial application of epithets, terms that are crudely and frankly favorable or unfavorable. We find them in all four of the "content" parts of speech—nouns, adjectives, verbs, and adverbs—and they operate at all levels of awareness; but in general the adjective and adverb are more aboveboard than the noun or the verb. If someone says *That wretched picture bored me to death,* the hearer can deal with the detachable adjective and, if he likes, replace it: *I didn't think it was wretched; I thought it was interesting.* Similarly with *He deliberately insulted me*—the hearer is free to substitute *But perhaps he did it unintentionally.* The adjective and adverb are a kind of simile, an overt and explicit attachment of one idea to another. The noun and verb are metaphors: the comparison is smuggled in, the person or thing or act is not *like* something good or bad but *is* that something. It is no coincidence that many epithets actually are metaphors of fairly recent memory: *He is a bum, He is a prince, She is an angel, She is a tramp, She cackled, He brayed.* The hidden temptations that the lexicon offers the average user of the language are practically irresistible. Most of the areas of our experience are mapped out epithetically, and the person who wants to steer a middle course has to keep his eye constantly on the narrow and shifting channel between good and bad. The most insidious examples are not the ordinary antonyms like *clumsy-graceful, easy-difficult,* or *democratic-fascistic* but terms that are synonyms in that they name the same objective fact, antonyms in the attitude that they solicit toward the fact. *Virtuous* and *puritanical* are examples of such pairing of terms.

A brief history of the term *hoarding* will illustrate how epithets fluctuate in popularity, how they are applied in different situations to influence action, and how the colorful import outweighs the literal one.

Hoarding is now used with the connotation of 'undesirable saving.' The primitive sense of the word had to do with the laying by and keeping of goods. As happened with so many Old English words, this one eventually leaned toward the unfavorable. In the present century it has enjoyed two periods in the limelight, the first in 1932–33 and the second in 1942. The first grew out of the Depression, when persons owning money or securities were frightened into holding them and spending as little as possible. This created a tight-money situation that aggravated the causes that had produced it. Articles appeared with titles like "Insurance Policies as Hoarding" and "How to Bring Currency from Hoarding."

A year later the reference changed. In 1933 the United States abandoned the gold standard; gold coin was called in, and when it was announced that the government was going to pursue hoarders, everyone knew that gold hoarding was implied. From 1934 to 1937 the word all but dropped from view; but the 1937 recession brought out a brief flurry of examples in 1938, with the same meaning as in 1932. The year 1939 saw it wane again, but the war fright of 1940 battened savings down once more, and the cry of *hoarding* was used again in 1940 and 1941 to pry them loose.

The second upsurge occurred in 1942 with the entry of the United States into the war and the threat of rationing. *Hoarding* now meant 'the undesirable saving of trade goods for consumers, especially food.' Six articles on this type of hoarding appeared in national magazines in April alone.

After the war, with plenty of money and no rationing, *hoarding* fell into disuse. The fallout shelter campaign of

1959–62 brought advice from the government to do — with food and other necessities — the very thing that two decades earlier would have been deemed unpatriotic. But now it was called *stocking up* or *stockpiling.*

Exercise 4

Column 1 is a list of favorable expressions or terms for which unfavorable terms are listed in column 2; match them.

Column 1	*Column 2*
a. conciliation	*1.* militarization
b. patriotism	2. showoff
c. defense	3. leer
d. right-hand man	4. old maid
e. brilliant	5. puritanical
f. liquidate	6. brainwashing
g. smile	7. shyster
h. indoctrination	8. chauvinism
i. progress	9. interfere
j. intercede	10. starry-eyed idealist
k. attorney	11. murder
l. bachelor girl	12. reaction
m. upright	13. appeasement
n. man of vision	14. lackey

Elevation and degradation

Since the epithet is language aimed at the heart of social action, it is bound to receive from the culture as well as give to it. While we are not concerned here with semantic change — that is a question of the evolution of language — but rather with the existence at any one time of linguistic forms that influence us, it is pertinent to note how the stock of terms with favorable or unfavorable connotations is maintained against the social realities that undermine it. Two processes are at work, or rather two directions of a single process, which are generally called *elevation* and *degradation*. If for reasons that have little or nothing to do with language a thing that has carried an unfavorable name begins to move up in the world, the name moves up with it. In religion, many once-opprobrious names have faded. Probably the majority of religious eponyms — names imitating the personal name of the founder — were to begin with unfavorable; but many were in time adopted by the followers of the religion (**Christian, Lutheran, Calvinist**), others have become milder (**Campbellite**), and few but the most recent might still be resented (**Russellite, Buchmanite**).

The opposite effect is observed in the negative associations of a term attached to something that moves down. Where **captives** were put to menial tasks and forced to live wretchedly, **caitiff** took on the meaning of 'wretch, villain.' As we saw earlier, where separation of the races came to be viewed as morally wrong **segregation** was debased. The most prolific source of negative connotation and of the constant replacement of terms that are downgraded is the phenomenon of social **taboo.** The taboo against strong language results in minced oaths: **darn** for **damn, gee** for **Jesus.** The taboo against referring to certain bodily functions results in a succession of replacements, each term being discarded as it comes to suggest the offensive term it had been replacing. H. L. Mencken listed two pages of synonyms for **latrine,** itself borrowed as a polite word from French (it orginally meant the same as one of its modern substitutes, **washroom**). What was a denatured term for one generation ceases to be for the next one, as the direct association with the buried taboo reasserts itself.

This denaturing process we have identified as *euphemism* (see Chapter 6). In political life, favorable reference to the enemy is taboo: in World War I **sauerkraut** became **liberty cabbage** and the **Katzenjammer Kids** were renamed the **Shenanigan Kids;** in 1940 the Nazis changed the name of **Wilson Station** in Prague to **Main Station.** Likewise in politics, it is taboo to admit the unpleasant; so we have **fair trade** for **price-fixing, training** for **conscription, depression** (and later **recession**) for **panic, casualties** for **dead and wounded.** As one writer points out, "If you hear someone say that it is time for a government to follow a realistic line, you can interpret this as meaning that it is time for principles to be abandoned." The same taboo applies doubly to the business world. One could find material for an essay on how not to say **small:** in soap brands we find series like **giant, family,** and **regular; large, medium,** and **guest; giant, large,** and **medium.**

The word *pint* has virtually disappeared from beverage sizes —it is now the *half quart*. *Imitation* becomes *costume* (jewelry) or *simulated* (pearls). Radio and television *advertisements* become *announcements*. Hair *dye* becomes *rinse*. A *salary cut* becomes an *adjustment*. And so on. Ordinary noncommercial and nonpolitical euphemisms, which cover our nakedness and other shortcomings, tend to be humorous: the plea is not to elevation but to tolerance. *Belly* becomes, besides the elevated *abdomen,* the facetious *paunch, corporation, bay window,* and *embonpoint*. A *libertine* is a *wolf.* The synonyms of *drunk* have proliferated to the point where a nonsense word inserted in the blank of *He was just a little bit* _____ will suggest it.

Exercise 5

a. With the aid of a dictionary and a thesaurus, determine a few delicate words or expressions that are often used to replace the words below. In some cases the words below are themselves euphemisms. *Bathroom* has a long history of euphemisms, among them *siege-house, bog-house, Sir John, Aunt Jones,* and *throne room.*

death	war
corpse	bathroom
pregnant	damn
an old person	poor

b. Can you name a field or activity that does not use euphemisms?

Hints and associations

True finesse is found not in the ordinary epithet or euphemism but among the less obvious loaded terms that hint rather than designate. Here the "semantic differential" comes into its own. The associated term is not obviously epithetical and therefore gets past our guard; but it is colored, darkly or brightly, and the color rubs off.

The lexicon abounds in loosely associated semantic sets having intimate ties with codes and practices in society, which for lack of a better name will be called *norm classes.* They comprise a catalog of "fors" and "againsts" to which we pay unthinking and often ritualistic respect. The norm classes — the associated word sets — are enough by themselves to invoke this respect. Merely mentioning one of the words will command it.

Since human circumstances are always particular, never general, the problem with any particular act, in order to give it a place in a well-regulated society, is to fit it to the proper symbol. The extreme case is that of interpretative law: a homicide has been committed; the jurors must determine whether it was **self-defense** or **murder.** **Self-defense** belongs to the norm class of **preservation of life, a man's house is his castle, resistance to aggression,** and so on. **Murder** belongs to that of **destruction of life, taking the law into one's own hands, disobedience to the Commandments,** and so on.

A less dramatic example is the norm class of **clothed (covered, decent, modest)** versus that of **naked (exposed, immodest, exhibitionist).** As beach attire has grown scantier and scantier, bathers can be said to be approaching a state of nakedness; yet the emphasis is on the fact that they do have something on, and this has usually been enough to prevent legal interference. And we may be sure that if ever the last vestige is cast off, it will be in the name of **nature (Praxiteles, Michelangelo, the nobility of the human figure),** not of **nakedness.**

Very early in life the child is made aware that he is expected to justify himself; in the average home, by the time he is able to talk almost every youngster faces the inquisition of "Why did you do it?" after any willful act. When we pick the right norm class to explain or ask about what was done thoughtlessly, however, we serve propriety almost as well as if we had thoughtfully picked the right behavior in the first place; and in the course of time we became quite expert at this substitution. Hitting upon the right norm class gives the emotional release of discovery, and skill at doing it is esteemed: the person accused of running up a **white flag** wins the argument by saying that he ran up a **white banner.**

A frequently used shift of norm class involves substituting a *physical* context for a *social* one — an instance of the fallacy of reduction. A man interfering with police work by erasing the chalk marks left by a traffic officer might say that he was only **rubbing off white stuff**. The classical example of the fallacy of reduction is "The table in front of you is only atoms."

Exercise 6

Words embody attitudes. Dr. S. I. Hayakawa, in *Language in Thought and Action*,[4] made use of an idea of Lord Bertrand Russell's to show clearly how words embody attitudes or *norm classes*. Consider the following "conjugations":

> I may not know much about art, but I know what I like.
> You could profit by a course in art history.
> He is an uncultured ignoramus.
> Or: My son is rambunctious and high-spirited.
> Your son is maladjusted and deprived.
> His son is a little hoodlum.

"Conjugate" the following statements in a similar way.

    a. I am slender.
    b. I am a trifle overweight.
    c. I am a police officer.
    d. I am a peace marcher.

Speech level

On the surface it appears that when a speaker shifts from one style of speech to another, he does so with the intention of influencing his hearer in other ways than directly through his message. It is not necessary for the style adopted to be one that was previously out of the speaker's normal range (as when an American imitates a British accent), though that is the kind of shift whose latent purpose is most evident since he is apt to be clumsy at it. He may shift from one level to another within his average capabilities, to keep himself in tune with his audience—a labor official addressing members of his local union in their hall does not use the same modes of expression as when he addresses a ladies' discussion group.

Viewed this way, the very existence of a number of different speech levels within a single society appears to aid suasion in some form or other. But viewed differently the observation is trivial; it is the same as saying that when I address my English-speaking friends in English rather than in German I do so with a concealed motive. The motive, if one can call it that, is simply to be understood; and if my speech level within English is the same as that of my hearers, it is to be better understood, to have nothing in my speech that will distract. Even the phenomenon of speakers adopting a dialect other than their own in order to be accepted by the members of some other group can be likened to that of learning another language in order to be accepted by its community of speakers. The desire to belong can hardly be separated from the desire to communicate.

Nevertheless, there are shifts of level whose primary intent is to influence rather than to be understood. The test is simple: instead of aiding understanding they interfere with it, and are used anyway. The typical example in our society is *authoritative language,* adopted on suitable occasions by anyone who wants to impress his reader or hearer, but most characteristic of bureaucrats and writers of official reports. It is a conglomeration of abstract vocabulary and grammatical involutions that yields such things as **It is imperative that the present directive be effectuated expeditiously** where the meaning is **Do it now.** One famous example was the order concerning blackouts during World War II, submitted to President Roosevelt for his approval:

> Such preparations shall be made as will completely obscure all Federal buildings and non-Federal buildings occupied by the Federal Government during an air raid for any period of time from visibility by reason of internal or external illumination. Such obscuration may be obtained either by blackout construction or by termination of the illumination. This will, of course, require that in building areas in which production must continue during the blackout, construction must be provided that internal illumination may continue. Other areas, whether or not occupied by personnel, may be obscured by terminating the illumination.

The President amended this to:

> Tell them that in buildings where they have to keep the work going, to put something across the window. In

buildings where they can afford to let the work stop for a while, turn out the lights.[5]

Americans have perhaps been more severely bitten by aspirations of grandeur than other speakers of English. At least, its symptoms have been with us for a long time and its condemnation likewise. James Fenimore Cooper remarked that the man of true breeding "does not say, in speaking of a dance, that 'the attire of the ladies was exceedingly elegant and peculiarly becoming at the late assembly,' but 'the women were well dressed at the last ball'; nor is he apt to remark, that 'the Rev. Mr. G___ gave us an elegant and searching discourse the past sabbath,' but, that 'the parson preached a good sermon last Sunday.'" Cooper himself was no angel of clarity. In *The Last of the Mohicans* he wrote, "Without any aid from the science of cookery, he was immediately employed, in common with his fellows, in gorging himself with this digestible sustenance." Mark Twain chided him: "This was a mere statistic; just a mere cold, colorless statistic; yet you see Cooper has made a chromo out of it. . . . Cooper spent twenty-four words here on a thing not really worth more than eight. We will reduce the statistic to its proper proportions and state it this way: 'He and the others ate the meat raw.'"[6]

Authoritative language has its stereotypes, which are designed to impress. But its success is also due to another quirk of human nature, our willingness to accept complication for profundity. Where profound thoughts make for hard words, hard words pass for profound thoughts.

Exercise 7

Translate the following sentences to ordinary English:

a. The major limitation on the exchange programs of the Department of State appears to be their chronic fiscal starvation.

b. The principal use of federal funds today is to accelerate the development of particular university resources when university priorities in on-going programs do not accord with national needs.

c. The evolution of an optimum scientific payload will require a continuing dialogue among all potential investigators and the engineers responsible for implementing their scientific goals. ("Scientific payload" refers to the cargo of instruments that a space craft would carry for an exploration of Mars.)

Constructional nonneutrality

Words are plentiful enough to supply all needs, suasive and other. It is possible, as we have seen, to have a class of epithets whose primary purpose is to influence, besides other words tinged in every imaginable way.

Structures are too few to exhibit this variety. A prepositional phrase cannot in itself be specialized for suasion since it has too many other things to do. Nevertheless, certain structures are, at least partly, better able to persuade than others. Even a proper choice between active and passive voice can be a form of suasion.

Intonation Intonation is the one part of linguistic structure whose chief function is suasion. Intonation is *intended* to influence the attitude of the hearer toward what is being said. This is clearest in solicitations — questions and commands — in which information content is generally low; and these types of utterance are the ones in which intonation is most marked. But it is also true of statements, for which intonation wins acceptance by commanding or wheedling.

Morphology Certain bound morphemes are used mainly in coining epithets. A label of the 1964 presidential campaign was *Goldwaterism,* with the suffix *-ism* nowadays found most frequently in epithets: *McCarthyism, reductionism, fascism.* The related suffix *-ite* is similarly used, as is the prefix *pro-* and the suffix *-phile* in *pro-German, pro-Hitler, Francophile, Russophile.* English is not as systematic in its favorable and unfavorable affixes as some other languages are, but their number is still large: *-phobe, -kin, -let, -ify, -itis, -ette, -ling, -ese,* and so on.

An instance of a suffix that is not in itself suasive but is heavily used in epithets is -/ər/, spelled *-er* or *-or.* Normally this suffix means a "professional, habitual agent"; a *singer* is one who sings, an *actor* one who acts, a *bookseller* one who sells books, and so on, all referring to *occupations*. The epithet adopts this for things that are not occupations, implying that the person stigmatized does them as consistently as if they were: **hymn-singer, boot-licker, trouble-maker, muckraker, Bible-banger, herring-choker, mud-slinger.** It may go even further, making the same allusion with an act that is performed just once: a person who tells a single lie is a **liar;** one who deserts just once is a **deserter** or **defector;** one who commits only one murder is a **murderer.** It is as if to say, 'These acts, like occupations, brand indelibly.' Though it is out of place here, we may note an identical use of the perfect tense, which is normally 'indefinite' as to time and whose indefiniteness is capitalized upon to suggest persistence of effects. Of a man who was in jail once, we say **He has been in jail,** no matter how long ago it was. We would not say **He is suing because he has been turned away from that hotel** if the situation is that he was turned away two years ago; but we might well say **He is suing because he has been accused of disloyalty,** when the accusation was two years in the past — this is something that puts its brand on a man.

Syntax The syntactic devices that lend themselves to suasion fall into three classes: animation, indeterminacy, and ambiguity.

Animation — the attributing of qualities of living beings to inert things — can be a device for shifting responsibility, for making ourselves out to be the victims of circumstance rather than its masters. The usual pattern consists of the verb, typically reflexive, with inactive (usually impersonal) subject and often with personal object. In describing an automobile accident, a speaker may say **I was driving down the street when all of a sudden that other car presented itself broadside to me,** or **I was driving down the street when all of a sudden that other car aimed itself directly at me;** either way, he wins — the responsibility is on the other car, which is pictured as capable of self-directed action.

The devices of animation, of course, are mixed — they rely partly on structure and partly on individual words. Our syntax facilitates animation because it permits us to fill the "actor" slot — suggesting, of course, capability of action — with anything we please. Our lexicon facilitates it by providing reflexive verbs, or by permitting a verb to be used both transitively and intransitively, or by offering semantic pairs like *fall-drop* and *escape-forget.* Examples of reflexive verbs are the *presented itself* and *aimed itself* sentences just quoted. Examples of intransitive verbs are *It broke (on me)* instead of *I broke it* and *It tripped me* instead of *I tripped over it.* Some semantic pairs might be: *It escaped me (slipped my mind)* instead of *I forgot it* and *It fell (out of my hands)* instead of *I dropped it.* Here also belong the verbs *seem* and *appear*, which pair with *infer, see*, and so on, and with which the inactive subject is often personal: *Smith seems to offer only three explanations,* a common excuse given by reviewers of books that saves the trouble of re-reading and counting up to four. The forthright equivalent is *As far as I have taken the trouble to see, Smith offers only three explanations.*

Another syntactic device for evading responsibility is *modification in noun phrases,* and the freedom with which it is allowed to shift sometimes from one element to another. When we permit a modification like *red paint* we imply something close to a logical proposition: 'There is paint that is red.' But now and then we throw in the modifier almost at random, trusting to luck that the hearer will attach it where it belongs: *She's lost her first tooth* for 'She's had her first loss of a tooth,' *Put on some warm clothing* for 'Put on some clothing that will keep you warm,' *There is a definite shortage* for 'There is definitely a shortage,' and so on. This makes it possible to refer to a *careless mistake* or an *uncertain origin* instead of 'a mistake made by a careless person' or 'an origin about which people are uncertain.' The heavy dependence of modifiers on context leaves a convenient loophole through which we can pass and shed our errors on the way or deal politely with another's errors.

Indeterminacy finds its place in those structures where some item of information is left out and the speaker is able to take advantage of its absence. In the active voice, the presence of a grammatical subject is obligatory; in the passive, the corresponding noun phrase with *by* may be omitted: *Joe Doakes accuses President of bad faith, President accused of bad faith (by Joe Doakes).* The ordinary speaker will use the passive with *got* to escape responsibility: *The dishes got*

broken; or will use the passive with **be,** omitting the **by** phrase, to suggest that the agent transcends mere individual human beings: "As a white housewife in a Birmingham supermarket told Robert Baker of the *Washington Post* (September 19), it [the retaliation against Negroes] was 'terrible' but 'that's what they get for trying to force their way where **they're not wanted.'** "[7] (The passive here does much the same thing as the noun **undesirables** in the example on page 258.) One verb is stereotyped in this way: **to be supposed to.** Newspapers use the passive with **be**—but with **be** omitted in headlines—to cover up the insignificance of the actor. It seems safe to say that one reason the passive voice has survived is that it enables the speaker to be noncommittal.

Ambiguity is the suasive device most apt to be consciously dishonest. Ambiguity in choice of words is fairly easy to detect. The word **brown,** for example, signifies 'brown in color,' but also, in the compound **brown sugar,** signifies a certain process of manufacture in which cane sugar retains some of its color. A refiner of beet sugar has taken advantage of the ambiguity to market as **brown sugar** a mixture of refined beet sugar, molasses, and coloring.

Constructional ambiguity is more elusive, but certain types have been heavily used, especially in advertising. One is the unmodified subject: **Athletes have found chewing a natural aid to high-speed effort.** The subject in this construction may mean 'some athletes' or 'all athletes.' The advertiser protects himself legally with the first meaning and hopes that the reader will infer the second. We have already seen one perversion of the perfect tense; here is another example: **John Jones has switched to X-brand chewing gum**—a literally true statement but silent on whether he has switched back.

A study of the uses of ambiguity makes us realize that probably the most important ingredient of communication is the attitude of the communicators toward each other: an intention on the part of the speaker not to misinform, and good will on the part of the hearer in trying to interpret as the speaker intends. Literal truth is not enough, if for no other reason than because there is so much about language that is always present but only in the realm of association and scarcely subject to definition. Take for example the simple matter of coordination in a sentence and the matter of sequence of the items coordinated, and what we infer from these two things. Coordination implies "These items are on the same level": we do not say *He is an embezzler and a lover of horses,* even though each part of the coordination taken separately may be true. As for sequence, if there is a possibility of inferring one item from another we normally place first the one on which the inference can be based: *The clock is accurate and dependable* is more likely than *The clock is dependable and accurate; The house is broken down and uninhabitable* is more likely than *The house is uninhabitable and broken down.* So when a certain brand of meal puts on its package the statement *Enriched and degerminated,* it is falsifying on both counts: enrichment and degermination do not belong on the same level, and nothing about degermination can be inferred from enrichment. The reader is tricked into regarding degermination, which he only vaguely grasps anyway, as a virtue. A truthful statement would read, "We are ashamed to say that in order to keep the stuff from spoiling we had to remove the germ, but we *did* add some synthetic vitamins to compensate for the loss."

A language that would enable us to report things as they are and that would be used by speakers without the infusion of their own personalities and prejudices is the ideal of every science; and every science has to some extent developed a denatured language to make this possible. But whether our human condition will permit it to be realized generally is doubtful; if Whorf was right, we do not grasp things as they are but always to some extent as our language presents them to us —or, in broader terms, as our society incorporates them in terms of all its habits of acting and talking. And as for avoiding the body heat of our likes and dislikes, the irony is that scientific language itself takes on authoritative overtones. The moment it finds its way into general use, we are plagued as much by pseudo-scientific pretentiousness as by any other form of nonneutrality. It would seem that language is bound to be suasive as long as it is human, that the effort to be neutral cannot be carried out in the language as a whole but must represent a will and a purpose in each small act of speech.

Exercise 8

Write out the intonational patterns which might be used in stating *She has a college degree* by

    a. her husband, who's proud of the fact
    b. her son to an interviewer from the Census Bureau
    c. her best friend, who objects to the menial job and low salary she has been given in spite of her degree.

Use intonational patterns like those on pages 48–50.

Exercise 9

a. A mother explains that she often cannot understand her son because *he speaks teenage-ese.* What is implied by this phrasing that would not be conveyed in the statement, *I often don't understand some of the slang words Joey uses?*

b. Suppose she said, *I can't understand Salim because he speaks Lebanese.* Explain the difference in the suasive impact of the two words, *teenage-ese* and *Lebanese,* both of which share the affix *-ese.*

c. In light of your answer to the above, comment on the difference in suasion between the following: *underling-gosling, tonsilitis-baseball-itis, bibliophile-Russophile, peacenik-sputnik.*

d. Consider the terms *leftist, rightist, moderate.* Do the suffixes *-ist* and *-ate* differ significantly in meaning? in suasion? What about the suffixes in *communism, fascism, socialism, democracy?* Why do you think the terms *capitalism* and *capitalist* have acquired unfavorable overtones?

Exercise 10

The following sentences illustrate the use of the intransitive verb form of different semantic pairs. Rewrite each sentence replacing the intransitive form with the transitive or active form, and making any other necessary changes.

    a. The coffee spilled on my dress.
    b. The roast fell on the floor.
    c. The antique mirror broke.
    d. She seems to be a nice girl.
    e. There doesn't seem to be any trouble, Sir.

Exercise 11

Identify the syntactic devices illustrated by the following sentences and rewrite the sentences, explaining what really happened (in some sentences there may be more than one device used).

    a. My memory played a trick on me.
    b. Smith gives the impression that he doesn't care.
    c. You have drawn a foolish conclusion.
    d. He is rumored to be in love with his neighbor's wife.
    e. Appetite improves one hundred percent with Polyvims.
    f. He can't vote because he has been convicted of a felony.
    g. Have some mouth-watering pork and beans.

chapter *12*

Language and Authority

Authority in Language

Hell is for those who are offered the light but ignore it. The heathen is blameless if he ignores a gospel that he has never heard, but damnation awaits our neighbor who has been shown the way and refuses to take it. Speakers of a foreign language are like the heathen; they are forgivable because their only fault has been the lack of opportunity to learn to talk as we do. But we resent the speaker of some unfamiliar dialect of our own language because he has had the opportunity—he proves this by the fact that we can usually understand him—but has obviously misapplied it. The foreigner is so unlike us that we can make no invidious comparisons; he challenges our magnanimity.

The universal dislike of variation is a reflection of the conventional nature of language. The slightest deviation poses the threat of a greater one and must be stamped out. A community can be educated to disregard this threat to a certain extent, but our primitive social desire for uniformity continuously asserts itself. The pressure to abolish differences in behavior—above all in linguistic behavior—is unrelenting.

Fortunately we are not single-minded in demanding recognition for our particular mode of speech, but are willing to acquiesce in a larger standard. This comes from long practice. A language community is not closed to the inexperienced; there are always learners—outsiders moving in, young generations moving up. As children we all accept authority; the habit of learning and willingness to take others as guides is implanted early and never lost.

So authority in language imposes itself through the need to keep variations at a minimum and through our willingness to make certain adjustments in our own speech to keep it in line with the speech of others. But uniformity is never achieved without some discomfort, and we are particularly resentful when authority is arrogantly enforced.

Two kinds of authority

A language or dialect can impose its authority formally or informally. Informal authority is the pressure exerted by the speakers with whom an individual identifies. It has no formulated rules but provides a model to follow and acts immediately—through the surprise, incomprehension, or amusement of its users—to drive offenders back into line. The mistakes are not identified; they are simply fumbles.

Informal authority is inseparable from the speech level or geographical or occupational dialect that enforces it. It may be oriented in any direction: a literary speaker may be ridiculed into being colloquial or a colloquial speaker into being literary. Until he learns the jargon every newcomer feels out of place, and whether it is high or low, nautical or rural, Northeastern or Midwestern, makes no difference.

Formal authority, on the other hand, is self-conscious. Rules of correctness are its stock in trade. It comes into existence where informal authority cannot be exercised in the normal way. Informal authority depends on the overpowering effect of the many on the few. One newcomer in a community does not need a school to teach him how to speak; but where large groups of speakers are isolated from their models, the latter must assume artificial forms — codified rules and schools to transmit them. In America this happens chiefly among tight groups of migrants in new communities, who cannot hope to enter the larger society until they are familiar with its forms of speech. At the same time, their very isolation prevents them from acquiring the familiarity. Formal authority attempts to answer the need.

Formal authority in language creates the same problems as formal authority anywhere else. It is dedicated to the preservation of laws and conventions which may not be applicable or useful to all the individuals who must yield to it. Thus, when it comes to the study of English, instead of an affirmative day-to-day practice in what the community does or approves on various levels of usage from literary to colloquial, the student is given a list of the forms he is not permitted to use.

Concentration on errors is like the concentration on sin in an old-time religion. The list of thou-shalt-nots is somewhat longer than the Ten Commandments but still brief enough so that one can substitute learning it by heart for the more arduous task of acquiring a second dialect of English. (The first has already been learned at home.)

Authority on the grand scale

Formal attempts to impose one dialect as standard on all the speakers of a language are usually superfluous, because the conditions that make standardization desirable — closer communication and greater economic and political interdependence — are already at work in informal ways to bring about a kind of standardization. As speakers of different dialects are thrown together, they absorb more and more from one another where doing so enriches their communication, and discard more and more of the idiosyncrasies which would be detrimental to it.

Yet for various reasons and in numerous places people have felt that attaining a standard by natural accommodation would be too slow a process, and reformers and would-be reformers, official and unofficial, have stepped in. The impulse may come from a burgeoning nationalism that seeks identity in a common language, or from a centralization of government with the need to communicate with all citizens quickly and efficiently, or from a technological or commercial interdependence that must no longer be hobbled by a division of tongues.

During the nineteenth and early part of the twentieth centuries the spread of literacy was promoted as a consequence of the democratization that followed the American and French revolutions. Its mechanical genius was the printing press, which demands standardization: a single dialect and a uniform spelling. Its scope was usually confined to the limits of a single language; the speakers all more or less understood one another already and reforms were relatively painless — making them so was one of the aims of the reformers.

Take the standardization undertaken in Norway by Ivar Aasen a century ago. Norway was emerging from domination by Denmark, and the Norwegian peasantry had become a political force. Aasen sought an authentic Norwegian language with which to replace the Danish that was still used by the ruling classes, and he found it by synthesizing Norwegian dialects into a language that all patriotic Norwegians would feel was natural and right. The result was the New Norse, or *Landsmål,* which is still extensively used.

More typical of the problems faced by language planners now is the rise not of submerged classes but of submerged peoples. It is no longer dialect against dialect but language against language, and easy adjustments are impossible. This is the situation that confronts most of the new nations that have emerged and consolidated themselves since World War II — about forty in Africa alone, besides Indonesia, Israel, Pakistan, Malaysia, the Philippines, and many more. It also confronts some political entities of long standing, such as India and China, whose loosely federated parts the new nationalism has pulled more closely together. In all these countries important segments of the population speak mutually unintelligible languages, so that it is difficult to make any one of them official. At the same time, nationalistic fervor demands that the language of the colonial power — which paradoxically had fed nationalism during the colonial period by supplying a unity that had not existed before — be thrown off.

The upshot is that these nations have had to decide what language to adopt and then seek ways to have it accepted by persons who do not speak it natively. There is a parallel to the consolidation and mergers that one observes on the American business scene, where small enterprises, like languages with but a few speakers, cannot survive in a world of competitive giants. How well this new variety of politico-linguistic authority will succeed against internal rivalries, old colonial attitudes, and simple inertia remains to be seen.

Exercise 1

The following instructions are among those most often issued to students in English classes as blanket injunctions seeking to regulate their use of the language. Explain why the original forms are not necessarily incorrect: you may want to use a dictionary, but you will need to rely chiefly on your own sense of the differences in meaning or emphasis which many such regulations disregard.

> **Faze:** *"You could not faze her by your criticism.* Say *daunt."*
> **Claim:** *"He claims that he was cheated.* Use *says, declares, maintains."*
> **Plan on:** *"We planned on an early departure, We planned on leaving early.* Say instead *We planned an early departure, We planned to leave early."*
> **Blame on:** *"Don't blame the accident on me.* Say *Don't blame me for the accident."*
> **Lose out:** *"Omit out except in referring to sports."*

Exercise 2

Match the following sentences and phrases with the "rule" of usage they have violated and rewrite according to the rule.

SENTENCES

a. I want to just sit down.
b. The most perfect specimen.
c. The man I was talking about.
d. Everybody has their preferences.

RULES

1. Restrict *they* and *their* to plural contexts.
2. Never end sentences with a preposition.
3. Never split infinitives.
4. Avoid the comparative or superlative with absolutes.

The dictionary

Ideas about authority in language have not been restricted to the classroom. For years the fondest hope of the commercial dictionary publisher was that his book would not only be comprehensive but would be considered—as the *New International* once dubbed itself—the "supreme authority." With the appearance of *Webster's Third New International Dictionary* in 1961, a new criterion was adopted forthrightly for the first time in a large unabridged dictionary. But the controversy that raged for several years after the appearance of the *Third*—including what amounted to a vote of censure by the editorial board of one magazine—testified to the deep-seated attitudes of the public toward what a dictionary is supposed to represent.

It is not hard to see the profound effect a dictionary calling itself the "supreme authority" might have on the speakers of language. That underlying assumption directs the way the dictionary user will think about language.

The standard dictionary gives four items of information: spelling, pronunciation, derivation, and meaning, usually in that order. (Labeling by part of speech is usually a fifth item, but it is an inheritance from Greco-Roman grammar that falls far short of showing the subtler classes and subclasses of modern grammar.) If the user needs to write a word but has forgotten how to spell it, or sees a word and is unsure of its pronunciation, the dictionary meets his needs. If he is curious about the word as a word, he will probably look for its origin; etymology is the branch of linguistics that has been with us long enough to arouse some popular interest. And if the word is new to him, he will want it defined or illustrated.

The order in which the four items are given has had certain consequences. Putting the spelling first has reinforced the tendency of the average person to take the written word as primary and basic and the spoken form as an unstable sort of nuance attached to it.

A second effect of the spelling-first order is that it fastens a left-right letter sequence on every word so that groupings are easy by beginnings but impossible by endings; if one wants to know all the words beginning with a particular prefix they can be spotted immediately, but suffixes are another matter, and English is a language in which suffixes are more important than prefixes.

The limitations that are reflected in the four-way order can be summarized in this way: they emphasize externals. Spelling is the written trace of a word. Pronunciation is its linguistic form, like the shape that a die puts on a coin, but has little or nothing to do with value. Derivation is a snatch of history. The value system, or meaning, comes last, and in reality includes so much that what the dictionary offers is hardly more than a sample, a small reminder that generally suffices only because the average user already knows the language and can guess at what is left out.

The break with authority

Webster's Third does not escape these shortcomings, but it does break with the authoritarian tradition and follow undeviatingly a trail dear to the heart of linguists that was blazed in 1947 by the *American College Dictionary* — still one of the best of the desk-size volumes — with the announcement that "no dictionary founded on the methods of modern scholarship can prescribe as to usage; it can only inform on the basis of the facts of usage." In pronunciations and definitions, and above all in the words it includes, the *Third* has abandoned the pretense of instructing the speaker. If a term is pronounced in a certain way by a substantial portion of the population, the *Third* records it, and it does the same with meaning.

However, in the area of spelling, the *Third* is almost as authoritarian as ever. And for all its reforms, the *Third* is as far behind the times as any of its predecessors when they first appeared, for just as it was moving toward a better rapport with linguistics, linguistics moved further ahead and widened the gap again.

Exercise 3

Webster's Third New International Dictionary of 1961 covers both the actual practice of English speakers and the rules of prescriptive grammarians that suggest how people ought to speak. Answer the following questions by using a copy of this dictionary (you will find it in your school library or in a public library).

a. Write the acceptable pronunciations of the following words: **foreign, barn, with, aunt, fog, new.** Underline the form you use.

b. Some words having common pronunciations that many people dislike are marked with ÷, which is called an *obelus*. Write first your own pronunciations of the following words, and then the pronunciations the dictionary has marked with the obelus: **eczema, baptist, February, licorice.** Is there a pronunciation of **licorice** accepted everywhere? Can a pronunciation marked with an obelus still be an accepted pronunciation?

Exercise 4

The dictionary gives information about the appropriateness of various inflected forms. What labels does *Webster's Third* give to the following italicized words in the use illustrated?

a. **brung** (preterite)
b. have **wore**
c. you **was** (plural)
d. you **is** (plural)
e. **ain't** (meaning 'have not')
f. John and **her** are here.
g. between you and **he**

Often the labels are not definite; usage is somewhat divided. Summarize the dictionary's entry for each italicized word as it functions in these sentences:

> *h.* He talked to my sister and *I.*
> *i.* Our people and *us* are here.

Exercise 5

The dictionary often makes distinctions between speech and writing in its discussions of usage, especially usage of inflections. Write summaries of what *Webster's Third* has to say about the following forms in both speech and writing. Note also the differences between the facts of actual usage and the positions taken by some grammarians.

> *a.* *ain't* (meaning 'am not')
> *b.* *me* (as in *It's me.*)
> *c.* *me* (as in *Me and John went yesterday.*)
> *d.* *us* (as in *It was us.*)
> *e.* *which* (as in *It was raining there yesterday, which kept us from going.*)
> *f.* *whom* (as in *the man whom you took to dinner*)

Exercise 6

If you look up *whim* in *Webster's Third New International Dictionary* you will find it marked as a noun and grouped with the synonyms *caprice* and *fancy,* and also, under *folly,* grouped with *indulgence, vanity,* and *foolery;* but there is nothing to tell you that *a little whim* refers to something small, while *a little indulgence* or *vanity* or *foolery* probably refers to an amount. In short, the dictionary fails to label the subcategories of *mass noun* and *count noun*.

Examples of count nouns are *threat* and *notion*—these nouns can be preceded simply by the indefinite article. Examples of mass nouns are *laughter* and *faithfulness*—these words may be preceded by *some.* Such nouns as *thought* and *fear* may be used as mass nouns or as count nouns. Indicate which of the following are mass nouns and which are count nouns, or whether they can be used as either: *lie, truce, peace, truth, music, heat, song, space, falsehood, fidelity, infidelity, hope.*

Ordinary Language Is Best

Language, like money, is a medium of exchange and like money was created by and for society. Yet for some reason we seldom define it for ourselves in the ordinary terms of power and prestige or of good conduct and bad. We feel that we have a right to regulate the use of money in ways that will spread its benefits, for it is the invention of society and must respond to society's needs; but we rarely think of seeing to it that the abuses of language are regulated.

The exchange of language is the sharing of experience. If we regard as the highest mark of civilization an ability to project ourselves into the mental and physical world of others, to share their thoughts, feelings, and visions, we must ask how language is to be used if we are to be civilized.

Though laws forbid the undue concentration of economic power, the only laws against the misuse of language have to do with the content of messages: obscenity, perjury, sedition, and defamation in its various forms of libel and slander. There are no laws against the unfair exploitation of language as language, in its essence. The individual may carry as many concealed verbal weapons as he likes and strike with them as he pleases — far from being censured for it, he will be admired and applauded as a clever fellow. Perhaps because we feel that language is everyone's birthright and that being born with it means that all have equal access to its storehouse, we have never seen fit to limit even by custom the ways it is used. Custom frowns on the liar, sometimes, but lies again are content, not essence. The only part of the essence that suffers from the slightest disfavor is that small segment of the vocabulary that is affected by taboo, and even that is partly content.

In a small, unstratified society all members have equal access, both to its verbal and to its material goods. No one is excessively rich in either speech or property. In more complex societies language, like wealth and color, is a weapon of *de facto* segregation. With the disappearance of the less visible tokens of birth and breeding, language has in some areas taken over their function of opening or closing the doors to membership in a ruling caste. There is no question that the Received Pronunciation of Southern British has been just such a badge of admission — this was the theme of Bernard Shaw's *Pygmalion* and its musical version, *My Fair Lady*. The lines are not so clearly drawn in America, but a rustic accent is enough to preclude employment in certain jobs, and even a person with a markedly foreign accent may have an easier time renting an apartment by telephone than someone who exhibits a particular variety of Southern speech.

Society has done much too little to erase its social and economic prejudices, and our efforts now must be toward the elimination of every sort of verbal snobbery. There is nothing intrinsically bad about words as such, and by excluding another man's forms of speech we exclude him. The task of democratizing a society includes far more than speech forms, of course, but headway will be that much more difficult if we overlook the intricate ties of speech with everything else that spells privilege.

Public cures may be long in coming, but meanwhile some of the ills of unequal access can be avoided if we recognize our personal responsibility toward the sharing of experience through language. We can discharge it by trying as hard to meet our neighbor on his dialectal terms as we would try to meet a foreigner on the terms of his language. This means never using our superior verbal skill, if we have it, or our inheritance of a prestige dialect for which we never worked a day, to browbeat or establish a difference in status between our neighbor and us. It means remembering that language is the most public of all public domains, to be kept free at all costs of claims that would turn any part of it into the property of some exclusive club, whether of scientists, artisans, or the socially elect. The virtue of language is in being ordinary.

Footnotes

Chapter 2

[1] Lambert Anderson, "Ticuna Vowels with Special Regard to the System of Five Tonemes," *Serie Lingüistica Especial*, No. 1 (Rio de Janeiro: Museu Nacional, 1959), pp. 76–127.

[2] George M. Cowan, "Mazateco Whistle Speech," *Language* 24.280-86 (1948).

Chapter 3

[1] The material that follows is paraphrased from the article by Robert E. Longacre, "Prolegomena to Lexical Structure," *Linguistics* 5.5–24 (1964). See also Kenneth L. Pike, "Language as Particle, Wave, and Field," *Texas Quarterly* 2.37–54 (1959).

Chapter 4

[1] More examples of accidental source morphemes are given in the section on Fusion, Chapter 6, pp. 129–31.

[2] John Algeo and Thomas Pyles, *Problems in the Origin and Development of the English Language* (New York: Harcourt Brace Jovanovich, Inc., 1966), p. 244.

[3] American Civil Liberties Union, Forty-third Annual Report, June 30, 1963.

Chapter 5

[1] Ralph R. Laplan, "Life in These United States," *Reader's Digest*, April, 1947, p. 90.

Chapter 6

[1] Arthur E. Hutson in *American Speech*, February, 1947, p. 20.

[2] Giulio P. Lepschy in *Linguistics* 15.48 (1965), commenting on Professor Stephen Ullmann's use of the **Fingerhut** example.

Chapter 7

[1] Shiro Hattori, "A Special Language of the Older Generation Among the Ainu," *General Linguistics* 6.43–58 (1964).

[2] John de Francis in *Georgetown University Monograph Series on Languages and Linguistics*, September, 1951, p. 50.

[3] Martin Joos, *The Five Clocks* (Bloomington, Ind.: Indiana University Research Center in Anthropology, Folklore, and Linguistics, 1962).

[4] Charles C. Fries, *The Structure of English* (New York: Harcourt Brace Jovanovich, Inc., 1952), pp. 50–51.

[5] *Ibid.*, pp. 24–25.

[6] William A. Stewart, "Sociolinguistic Factors in the History of American Negro Dialects," *The Florida FL Reporter*, Spring, 1967, pp. 1–4.

[7] Raven I. McDavid, Jr., "American Social Dialects," *College English*, January, 1965, pp. 254–60.

[8] Raven I. McDavid, Jr., "Sense and Nonsense about American Dialects," *Publications of the Modern Language Association* 81:2.7–17 (1966), p. 9.

[9] This is being attempted in Washington, D.C. by the Urban Language Study. See J. L. Dillard in *The Linguistic Reporter*, October, 1966, pp. 1–2.

[10] Hans Kurath and Raven I. McDavid, Jr., The Pronunciation of English in the Atlantic States (Ann Arbor: University of Michigan Press, 1961), p. 135.

[11] Hans Kurath, "Some Aspects of Atlantic Seaboard English Considered in Their Connections with British English," in *Communications et Rapports du Premier Congrès International de Dialectologie Générale* (Louvain, Belgium, 1965), pp. 239–40.

[12] Robert Louis Stevenson, *The Amateur Emigrant*, South Seas Edition (New York: Charles Scribner's Sons, Inc., 1925), p. 9.

Chapter 8

[1] Axel Wijk, Regularized English (Stockholm: Almqvist & Wiksell, 1959), pp. 324–25.

Chapter 9

[1] George W. Feinstein, "Letter from a Triple-threat Grammarian," *College English*, Vol. 21, No. 7 (April, 1970), p. 408.

2 Holger Pedersen, *Linguistic Science in the 19th Century*, translated by John Webster Spargo (Bloomington, Ind.: Indiana University Press, 1962), p. 155. Copyrighted by Harvard University Press.

3 Ferdinand de Saussure, *Course in General Linguistics*, translated by Wade Baskin (New York: McGraw-Hill, Inc., 1959), pp. 82–83.

4 Harry Hoijer et al., *Papers from the Symposium on American Indian Linguistics* (Berkeley: University of California Press, 1954), p. 3.

5 For the generativist, a "sentence" is any construction manifested as a noun-phrase subject with its verb-phrase predicate. This includes not only the usual declarative *He eats the candy,* interrogative *Does he eat the candy?*, negative *He doesn't eat the candy,* and passive *The candy is eaten by him,* but also other transformations: *For him to eat the candy, His eating the candy, The candy having been eaten by him,* and so on.

6 Jerrold J. Katz, "Mentalism in Linguistics," *Language* 40.134 (1964).

Chapter 11

1 Benjamin Lee Whorf, "The Relation of Habitual Thought and Behavior to Language," in *Four Articles on Metalinguistics* (Washington, D.C.: Foreign Service Institute, U.S. Department of State, 1949), pp. 37 and 24.

2 Benjamin Lee Whorf, "Science and Linguistics," in *Language, Thought, and Reality,* John B. Carroll, ed. (Cambridge, Mass.: The Technological Press of M.I.T., 1957), p. 215.

3 J. A. Jerger, M.D., "City Doctor," *American Magazine,* February, 1939.

4 S. I. Hayakawa, *Language in Thought and Action,* 2nd ed. (New York: Harcourt Brace Jovanovich, Inc., 1964), pp. 95–96. Items *a* and *b* are from page 96.

5 *The New York Times,* March 11, 1942.

6 Mark Twain, "Cooper's Prose Style" in *Letters from the Earth,* Bernard DeVoto, ed. (New York: Harper & Row, 1962), p. 140.

7 *I. F. Stone's Bi-Weekly,* September 30, 1963, p. 8.

The Phonemes of English

Full vowels

/i/ as in machine
/ɪ/ as in sit
/e/ as in rate
/ɛ/ as in bed
/æ/ as in lap
/ʌ/ as in mud
/a/ as in rod
/ɔ/ as in taught
/o/ as in rope
/ʊ/ as in stood
/u/ as in rude

Reduced vowels

/ɨ/ as in buried
/ə/ as in salad
/ɵ/ as in willow

Semiconsonants (glides)

/y/ as in yellow, Boyd
/w/ as in quick, loud
(/r/ may also be
    regarded as a
    semiconsonant or
    semivowel.)

CONSONANTS

/p/ as in pill, spill, rip
/t/ as in team, steam, Pete
/k/ as in cat, scat, take
/b/ as in boy, tab
/d/ as in dog, rid
/g/ as in get, rug
/f/ as in fife
/θ/ as in thick
/s/ as in rice
/š/ as in push
/h/ as in hot

/v/ as in shove
/ð/ as in rather
/z/ as in rose
/ž/ as in pleasure
/č/ as in rich
/j/ as in ridge
/l/ as in lip, pole
/r/ as in ride
/m/ as in mine
/n/ as in grin
/ŋ/ as in string

This set of phonemes represents one fairly widespread dialect of English. There are other dialects, some with one or two more phonemes, others with one or two less. There are also other ways of representing the same sounds as the ones here (for example, is the last consonant sound in *rich* a simple consonant, to be labeled /č/, or is it a combination of /t/ and /š/?; not all phoneticians agree).

Index

Boldface numbers refer to illustrations.